"And where two raging fires meet together, they do consume the thing that feeds their fury."

The Taming of the Shrew
Act 2, Scene 1

**"I can no other answer make but thanks,
And thanks."**

First and foremost, Anthony Del Col for being my partner in building this amazing universe. Thanks for letting me play in the sandbox unsupervised.

Andy Belanger, we miss you buddy. I hope you love Corin's work as much as I do. I think she did your legacy proud.

Crystal Luxmore, Peregrine Luxmore, Lochlan McCreery, Owen and Elizabeth McCreery, Brian McCreery.

Everyone at IDW Publishing and Diamond Comics — they continue to amaze us with their dedication to making great books.

Lisa Newal, Keith Morris, Sam Zimmerman, Dr. Toby Malone, Martha Cornog, Paola Paulino, Jason Loo, Meghan Carter, Shari Chankahamma, Ryan North, Neil Gibson, Fred Kennedy, Steve Paugh, Andrew Miller, Michael Ball, Kevin Cox, Tony Kramreither, Jethro Bushenbaum, Dawn Douglas, Chris Smith, Sharon Fleming, Ted Fleming, Al Bugeja, Rob Chiasson, Steve Lawlor, Andrew Apangu (R.I.P.), Kody Peters, Chris Walton, and Katie Musgrave.

And finally, the original slick Willy—William Shakespeare.

For international rights, contact **licensing@idwpublishing.com**

ISBN: 978-1-68405-056-7

20 19 18 17   1 2 3 4

www.IDWPUBLISHING.com

Ted Adams, CEO & Publisher • **Greg Goldstein**, President & COO • **Robbie Robbins**, EVP/Sr. Graphic Artist • **Chris Ryall,** Chief Creative Officer • **David Hedgecock**, Editor-in-Chief • **Laurie Windrow**, Senior Vice President of Sales & Marketing • **Matthew Ruzicka**, CPA, Chief Financial Officer • **Lorelei Bunjes**, VP of Digital Services • **Jerry Bennington**, VP of New Product Development

Facebook: **facebook.com/idwpublishing** • Twitter: **@idwpublishing** • YouTube: **youtube.com/idwpublishing**
Tumblr: **tumblr.idwpublishing.com** • Instagram: **instagram.com/idwpublishing**

Originally published as KILL SHAKESPEARE: PAST IS PROLOGUE: JULIET issues #1–4.

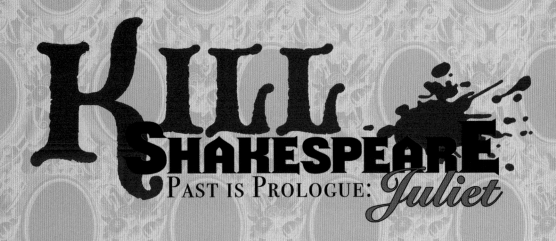

KILL SHAKESPEARE
PAST IS PROLOGUE: *Juliet*

CREATED BY
Conor McCreery
and
Anthony Del Col

WRITTEN BY
Conor McCreery

ART BY
Corin Howell

STORY EDITOR
Toby Malone

COLORS BY
Shari Chankhamma
and Alex Lillie

LETTERING BY
Chris Mowry
and Shawn Lee

ORIGINAL SERIES EDITS BY
Tom Waltz

COLLECTION COVER BY
Simon Davis

PRODUCTION ASSISTANCE BY
Shawn Lee

COLLECTION EDITS BY
Justin Eisinger
& Alonzo Simon

PUBLISHER
Ted Adams

The Story So Far...

Juliet is set six years before the events of Kill Shakespeare Volume 1: A Sea of Troubles.

It is mere months after the end of the First Richard War, and a new King sits on Illyria's throne. A rebel movement known as The Prodigals has sprung up to combat Richard's tyranny, but, few in number, they hide in the shadows waiting for their chance to strike.

In Verona, a heart-broken Juliet is still mourning the death of her love Romeo. With her Father missing in the war, the tempestuous Juliet has been left in the care of her mother, Lady Capulet and the Lady's new husband, Shylock – a one time Merchant of Venice.

But despite the turmoil, house Capulet is still a wealthy one, and with Richard as monarch, there are no shortage of villains who would like to claim that wealth...

JULIET:
A young woman haunted by the recent passing of her lover Romeo. Juliet wants nothing but to atone for her role in Romeo's death, but does that mean forgiveness, or something darker?

"CASSIO":
Cassio once served as a general in King Lear's army, but after their defeat to Richard he's become a sword for hire... and a drunkard. When he can find his way out of a bottle, Cassio is still one of Illyria's great warriors, but unless he can escape the ghosts of his past he may never recover his former glory.

CORNWALL:
Originally one of Lear's trusted allies, Cornwall betrayed the former King in order to win Richard's favour. Cornwall lacks the noble lineage of many of Richard's new 'Lords', and, ambitious and treacherous, he has come up with a plan to buy the respect his birth didn't provide him.

IMOGEN:
One of the leaders of the Prodigal movement, Imogen has dedicated her life to overthrowing Richard. The honourable rebel will be torn between her desire to help Juliet gain vengeance and Imogen's need to keep her fellow Prodigals focused on killing a King.

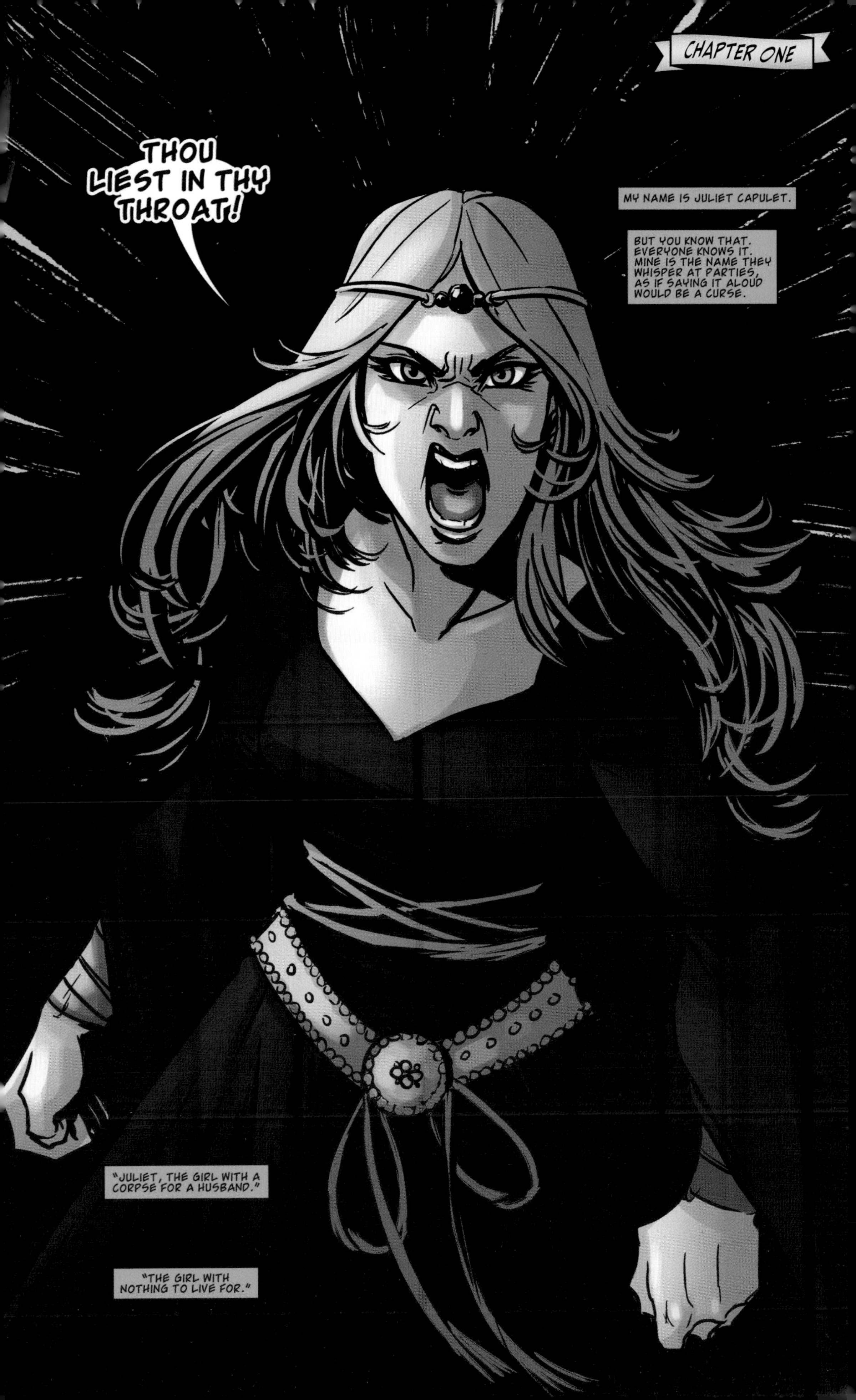
CHAPTER ONE
THOU LIEST IN THY THROAT!
MY NAME IS JULIET CAPULET.
BUT YOU KNOW THAT. EVERYONE KNOWS IT. MINE IS THE NAME THEY WHISPER AT PARTIES, AS IF SAYING IT ALOUD WOULD BE A CURSE.
"JULIET, THE GIRL WITH A CORPSE FOR A HUSBAND."
"THE GIRL WITH NOTHING TO LIVE FOR."

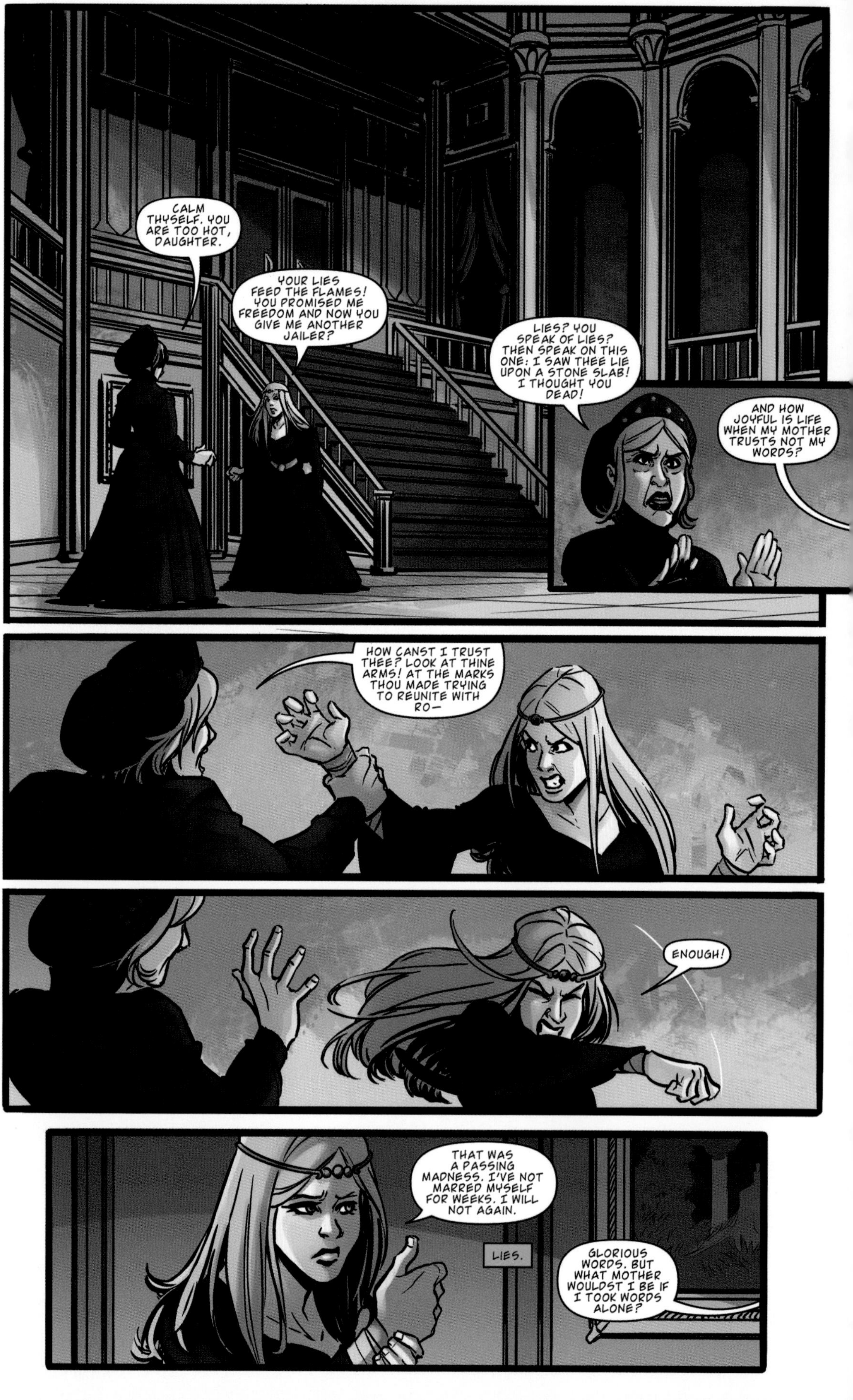
CALM THYSELF. YOU ARE TOO HOT, DAUGHTER.
YOUR LIES FEED THE FLAMES! YOU PROMISED ME FREEDOM AND NOW YOU GIVE ME ANOTHER JAILER?
LIES? YOU SPEAK OF LIES? THEN SPEAK ON THIS ONE: I SAW THEE LIE UPON A STONE SLAB! I THOUGHT YOU DEAD!
AND HOW JOYFUL IS LIFE WHEN MY MOTHER TRUSTS NOT MY WORDS?
HOW CANST I TRUST THEE? LOOK AT THINE ARMS! AT THE MARKS THOU MADE TRYING TO REUNITE WITH RO—
ENOUGH!
THAT WAS A PASSING MADNESS. I'VE NOT MARRED MYSELF FOR WEEKS. I WILL NOT AGAIN.
LIES.
GLORIOUS WORDS. BUT WHAT MOTHER WOULDST I BE IF I TOOK WORDS ALONE?

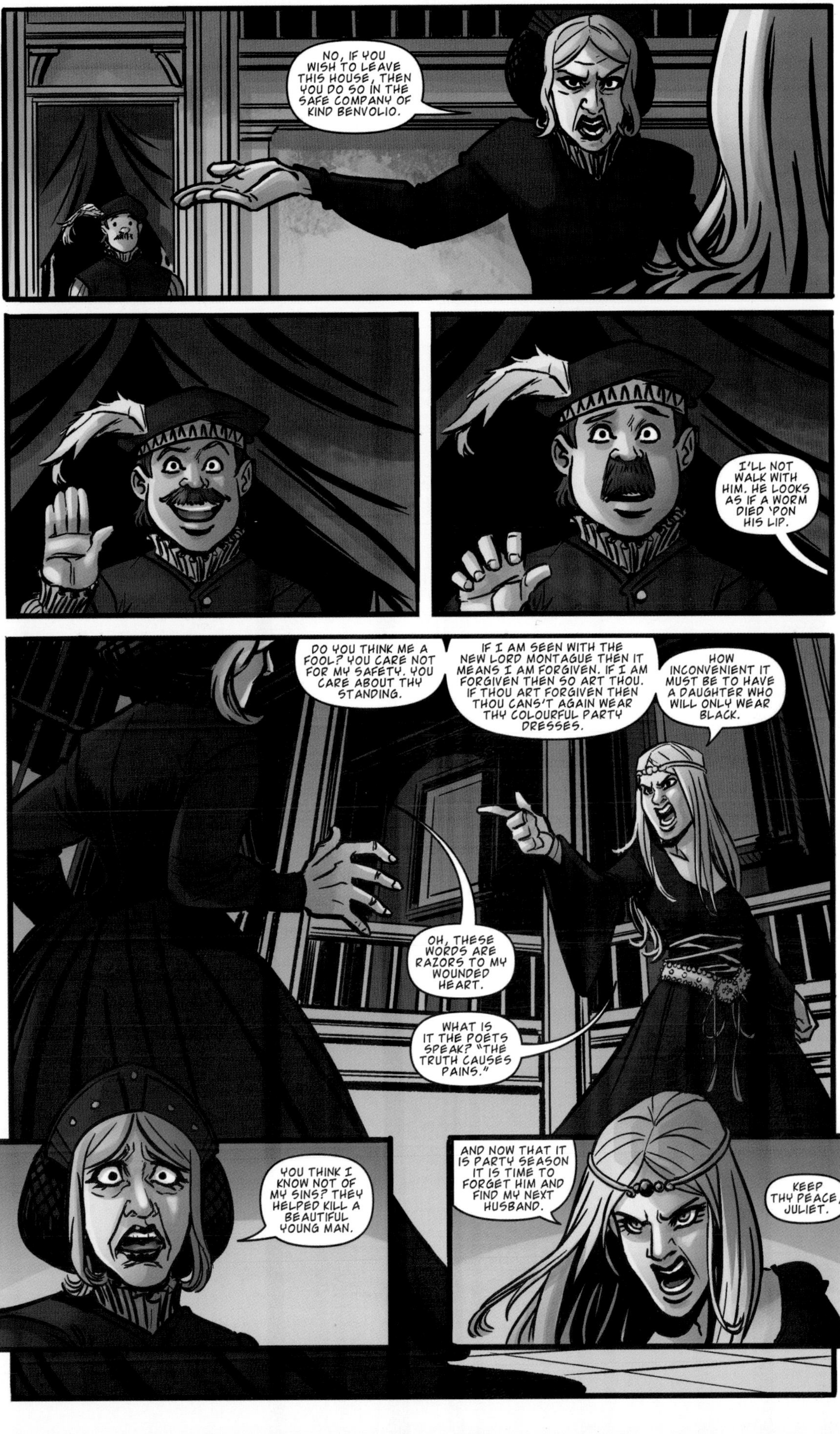
NO, IF YOU WISH TO LEAVE THIS HOUSE, THEN YOU DO SO IN THE SAFE COMPANY OF KIND BENVOLIO.
I'LL NOT WALK WITH HIM. HE LOOKS AS IF A WORM DIED 'PON HIS LIP.
DO YOU THINK ME A FOOL? YOU CARE NOT FOR MY SAFETY. YOU CARE ABOUT THY STANDING.
IF I AM SEEN WITH THE NEW LORD MONTAGUE THEN IT MEANS I AM FORGIVEN. IF I AM FORGIVEN THEN SO ART THOU. IF THOU ART FORGIVEN THEN THOU CANS'T AGAIN WEAR THY COLOURFUL PARTY DRESSES.
HOW INCONVENIENT IT MUST BE TO HAVE A DAUGHTER WHO WILL ONLY WEAR BLACK.
OH, THESE WORDS ARE RAZORS TO MY WOUNDED HEART.
WHAT IS IT THE POETS SPEAK? "THE TRUTH CAUSES PAINS."
YOU THINK I KNOW NOT OF MY SINS? THEY HELPED KILL A BEAUTIFUL YOUNG MAN.
AND NOW THAT IT IS PARTY SEASON IT IS TIME TO FORGET HIM AND FIND MY NEXT HUSBAND.
KEEP THY PEACE, JULIET.

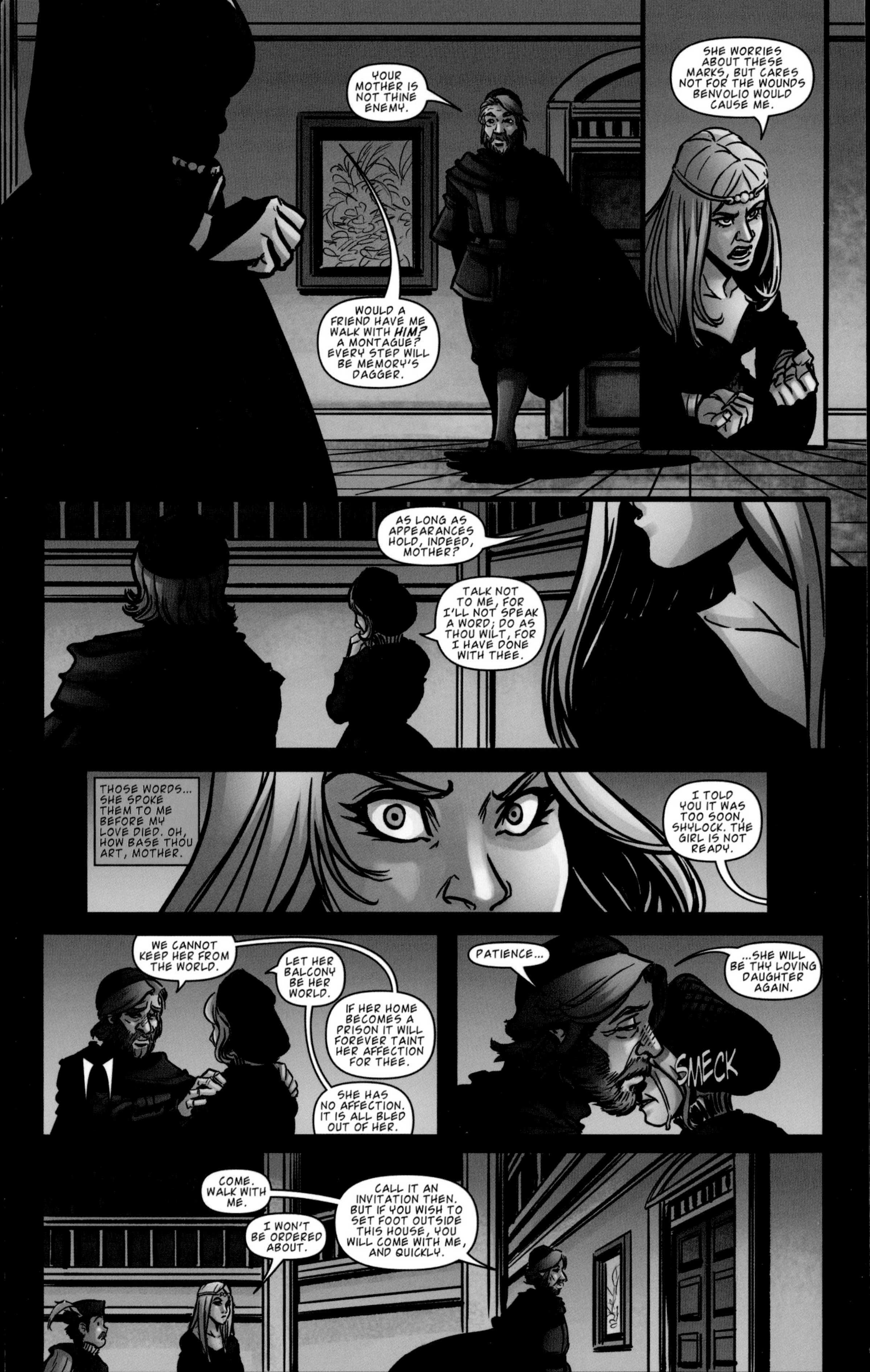
YOUR MOTHER IS NOT THINE ENEMY.
SHE WORRIES ABOUT THESE MARKS, BUT CARES NOT FOR THE WOUNDS BENVOLIO WOULD CAUSE ME.
WOULD A FRIEND HAVE ME WALK WITH HIM? A MONTAGUE? EVERY STEP WILL BE MEMORY'S DAGGER.
AS LONG AS APPEARANCES HOLD, INDEED, MOTHER?
TALK NOT TO ME, FOR I'LL NOT SPEAK A WORD; DO AS THOU WILT, FOR I HAVE DONE WITH THEE.
THOSE WORDS... SHE SPOKE THEM TO ME BEFORE MY LOVE DIED. OH, HOW BASE THOU ART, MOTHER.
I TOLD YOU IT WAS TOO SOON, SHYLOCK. THE GIRL IS NOT READY.
WE CANNOT KEEP HER FROM THE WORLD.
LET HER BALCONY BE HER WORLD.
IF HER HOME BECOMES A PRISON IT WILL FOREVER TAINT HER AFFECTION FOR THEE.
SHE HAS NO AFFECTION. IT IS ALL BLED OUT OF HER.
PATIENCE...
...SHE WILL BE THY LOVING DAUGHTER AGAIN.
SMECK
COME. WALK WITH ME.
I WON'T BE ORDERED ABOUT.
CALL IT AN INVITATION THEN. BUT IF YOU WISH TO SET FOOT OUTSIDE THIS HOUSE, YOU WILL COME WITH ME, AND QUICKLY.

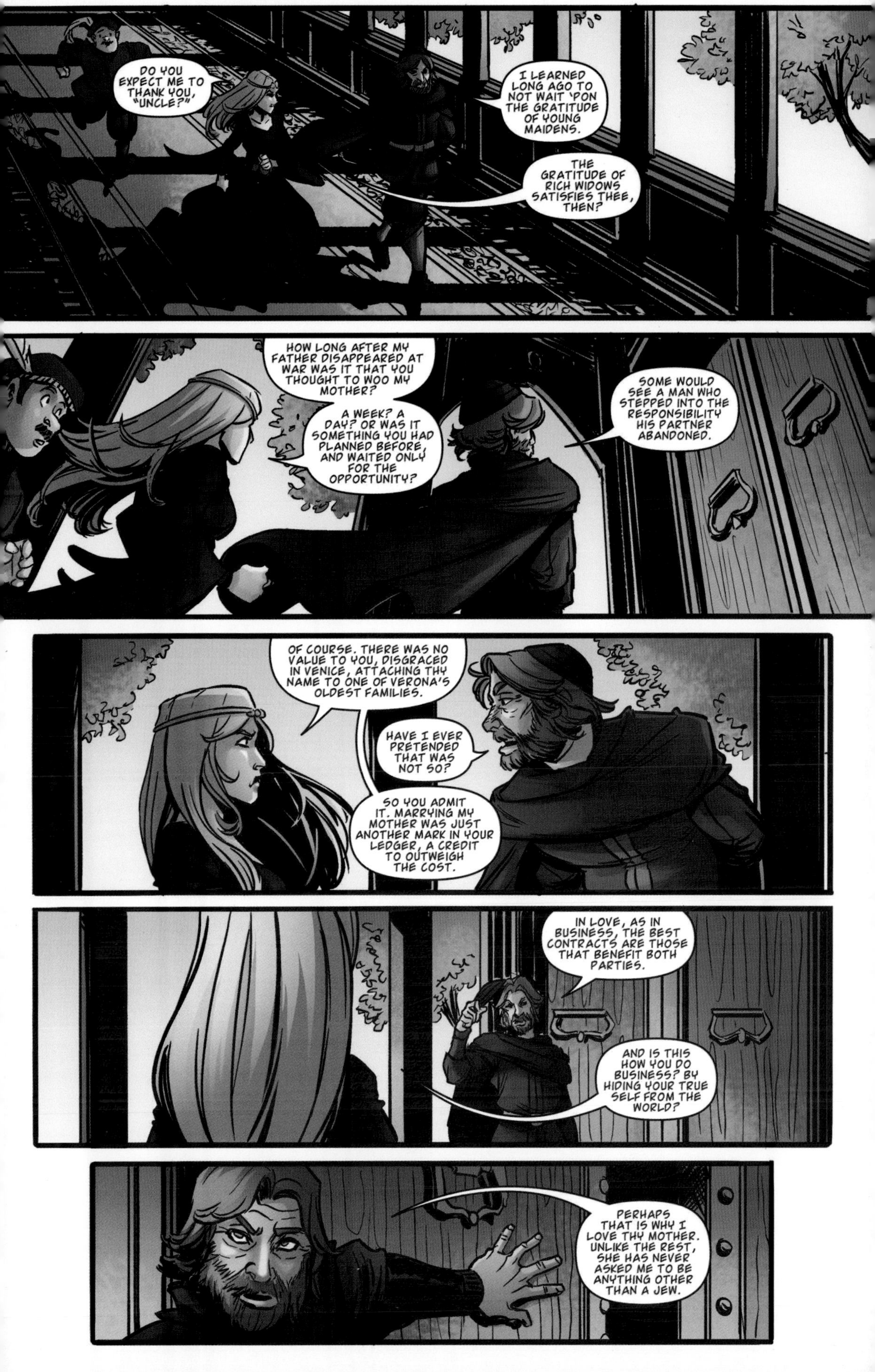
DO YOU EXPECT ME TO THANK YOU, "UNCLE?"
I LEARNED LONG AGO TO NOT WAIT 'PON THE GRATITUDE OF YOUNG MAIDENS.
THE GRATITUDE OF RICH WIDOWS SATISFIES THEE, THEN?
HOW LONG AFTER MY FATHER DISAPPEARED AT WAR WAS IT THAT YOU THOUGHT TO WOO MY MOTHER?
A WEEK? A DAY? OR WAS IT SOMETHING YOU HAD PLANNED BEFORE, AND WAITED ONLY FOR THE OPPORTUNITY?
SOME WOULD SEE A MAN WHO STEPPED INTO THE RESPONSIBILITY HIS PARTNER ABANDONED.
OF COURSE. THERE WAS NO VALUE TO YOU, DISGRACED IN VENICE, ATTACHING THY NAME TO ONE OF VERONA'S OLDEST FAMILIES.
HAVE I EVER PRETENDED THAT WAS NOT SO?
SO YOU ADMIT IT. MARRYING MY MOTHER WAS JUST ANOTHER MARK IN YOUR LEDGER, A CREDIT TO OUTWEIGH THE COST.
IN LOVE, AS IN BUSINESS, THE BEST CONTRACTS ARE THOSE THAT BENEFIT BOTH PARTIES.
AND IS THIS HOW YOU DO BUSINESS? BY HIDING YOUR TRUE SELF FROM THE WORLD?
PERHAPS THAT IS WHY I LOVE THY MOTHER. UNLIKE THE REST, SHE HAS NEVER ASKED ME TO BE ANYTHING OTHER THAN A JEW.

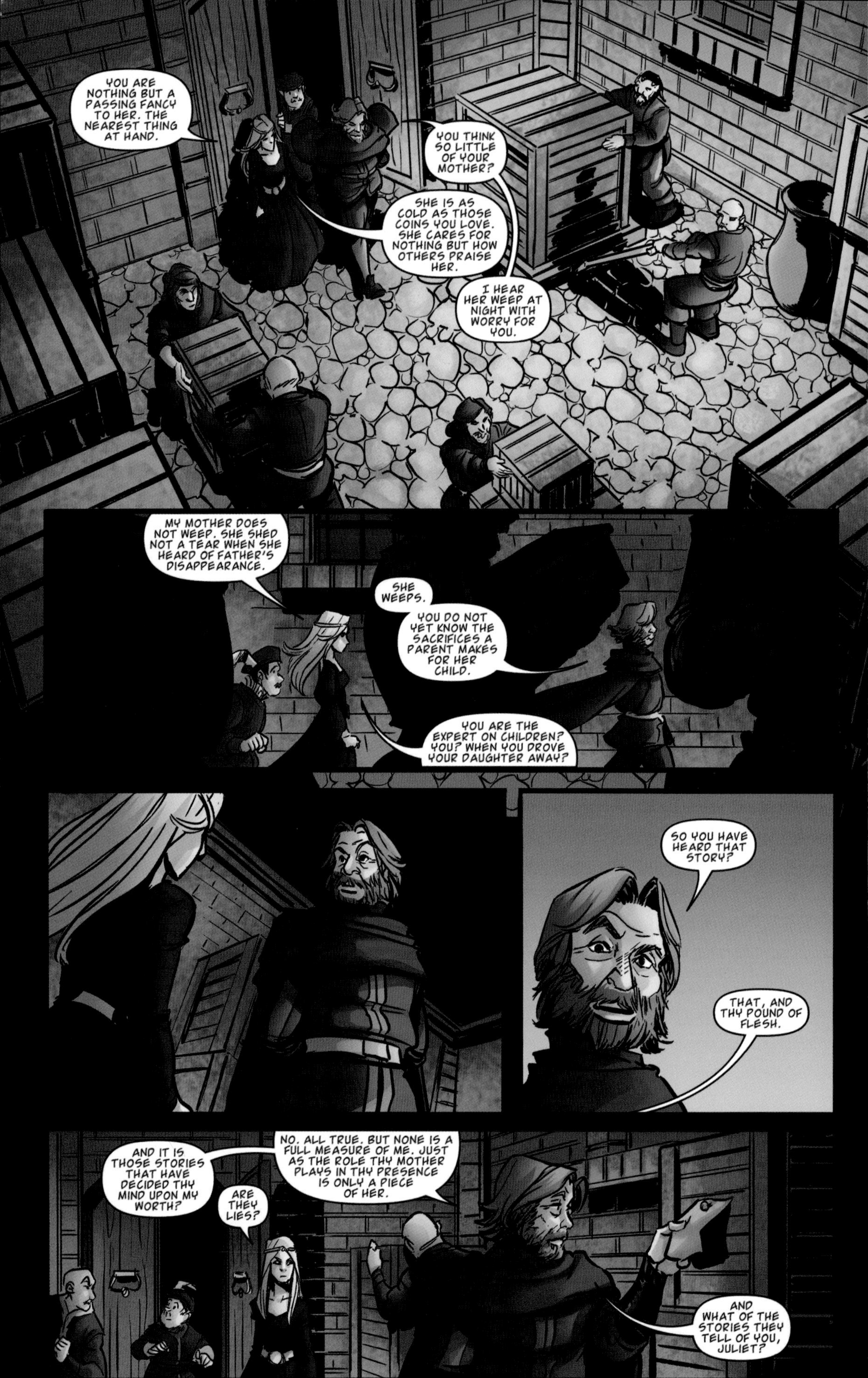
YOU ARE NOTHING BUT A PASSING FANCY TO HER. THE NEAREST THING AT HAND.
YOU THINK SO LITTLE OF YOUR MOTHER?
SHE IS AS COLD AS THOSE COINS YOU LOVE. SHE CARES FOR NOTHING BUT HOW OTHERS PRAISE HER.
I HEAR HER WEEP AT NIGHT WITH WORRY FOR YOU.
MY MOTHER DOES NOT WEEP. SHE SHED NOT A TEAR WHEN SHE HEARD OF FATHER'S DISAPPEARANCE.
SHE WEEPS.
YOU DO NOT YET KNOW THE SACRIFICES A PARENT MAKES FOR HER CHILD.
YOU ARE THE EXPERT ON CHILDREN? YOU? WHEN YOU DROVE YOUR DAUGHTER AWAY?
SO YOU HAVE HEARD THAT STORY?
THAT, AND THY POUND OF FLESH.
AND IT IS THOSE STORIES THAT HAVE DECIDED THY MIND UPON MY WORTH?
ARE THEY LIES?
NO. ALL TRUE. BUT NONE IS A FULL MEASURE OF ME. JUST AS THE ROLE THY MOTHER PLAYS IN THY PRESENCE IS ONLY A PIECE OF HER.
AND WHAT OF THE STORIES THEY TELL OF YOU, JULIET?

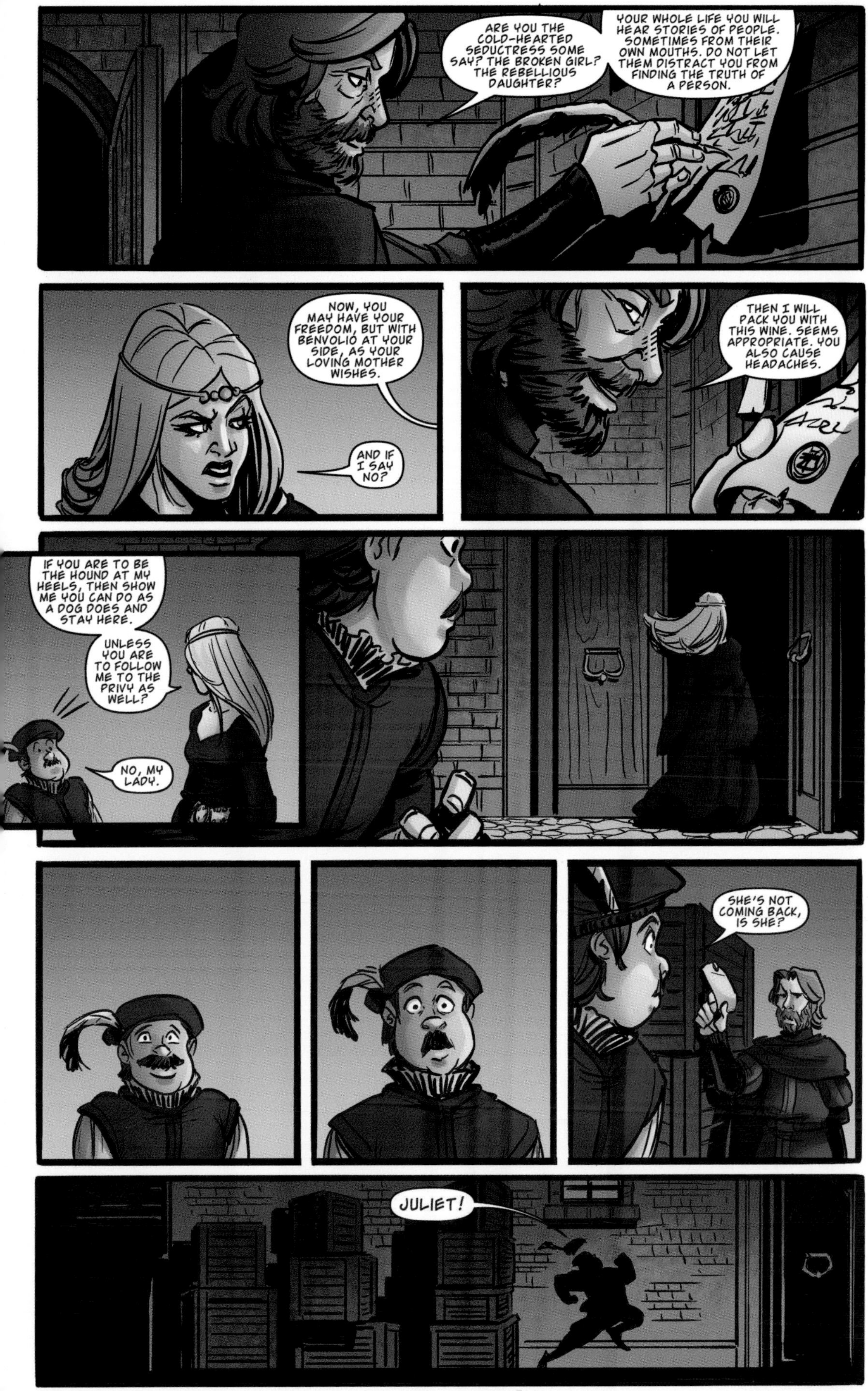
ARE YOU THE COLD-HEARTED SEDUCTRESS SOME SAY? THE BROKEN GIRL? THE REBELLIOUS DAUGHTER?
YOUR WHOLE LIFE YOU WILL HEAR STORIES OF PEOPLE. SOMETIMES FROM THEIR OWN MOUTHS. DO NOT LET THEM DISTRACT YOU FROM FINDING THE TRUTH OF A PERSON.
NOW, YOU MAY HAVE YOUR FREEDOM, BUT WITH BENVOLIO AT YOUR SIDE, AS YOUR LOVING MOTHER WISHES.
AND IF I SAY NO?
THEN I WILL PACK YOU WITH THIS WINE. SEEMS APPROPRIATE. YOU ALSO CAUSE HEADACHES.
IF YOU ARE TO BE THE HOUND AT MY HEELS, THEN SHOW ME YOU CAN DO AS A DOG DOES AND STAY HERE.
UNLESS YOU ARE TO FOLLOW ME TO THE PRIVY AS WELL?
NO, MY LADY.
SHE'S NOT COMING BACK, IS SHE?
JULIET!

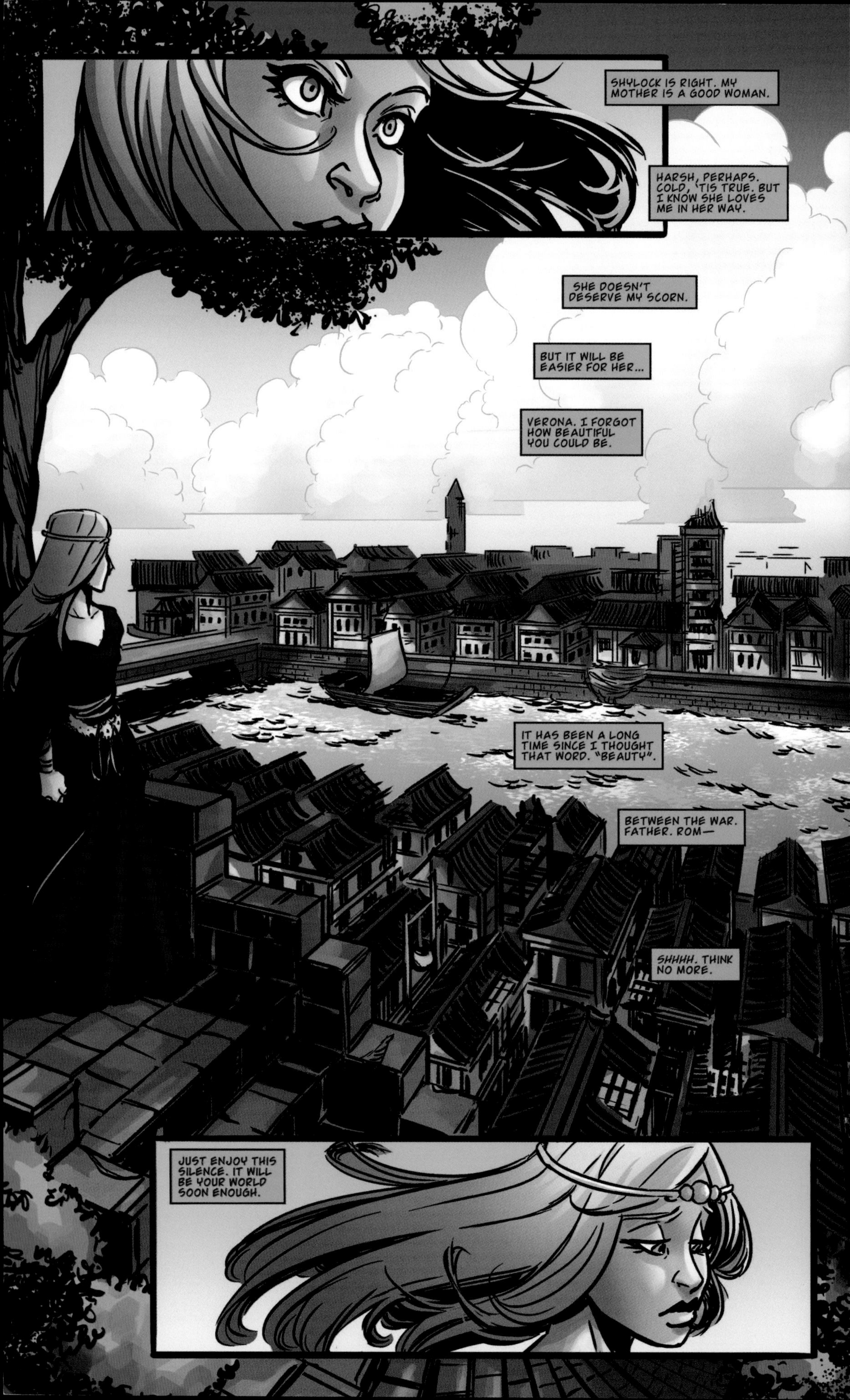

SHYLOCK IS RIGHT. MY MOTHER IS A GOOD WOMAN.
HARSH, PERHAPS. COLD, 'TIS TRUE. BUT I KNOW SHE LOVES ME IN HER WAY.
SHE DOESN'T DESERVE MY SCORN.
BUT IT WILL BE EASIER FOR HER...
VERONA. I FORGOT HOW BEAUTIFUL YOU COULD BE.
IT HAS BEEN A LONG TIME SINCE I THOUGHT THAT WORD. "BEAUTY".
BETWEEN THE WAR. FATHER. ROM—
SHHHH. THINK NO MORE.
JUST ENJOY THIS SILENCE. IT WILL BE YOUR WORLD SOON ENOUGH.

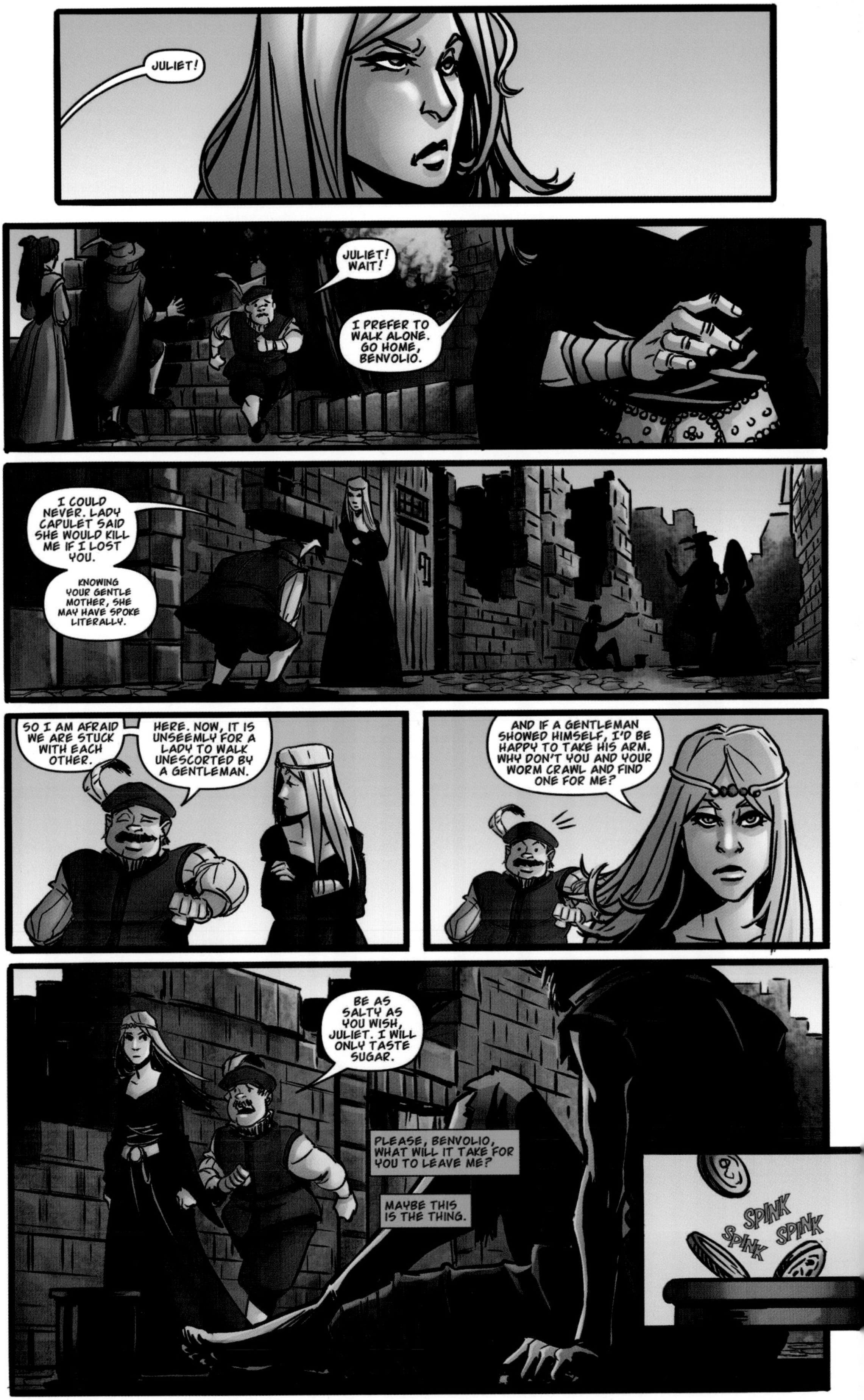

JULIET!
JULIET! WAIT!
I PREFER TO WALK ALONE. GO HOME, BENVOLIO.
I COULD NEVER. LADY CAPULET SAID SHE WOULD KILL ME IF I LOST YOU.
KNOWING YOUR GENTLE MOTHER, SHE MAY HAVE SPOKE LITERALLY.
SO I AM AFRAID WE ARE STUCK WITH EACH OTHER.
HERE. NOW, IT IS UNSEEMLY FOR A LADY TO WALK UNESCORTED BY A GENTLEMAN.
AND IF A GENTLEMAN SHOWED HIMSELF, I'D BE HAPPY TO TAKE HIS ARM. WHY DON'T YOU AND YOUR WORM CRAWL AND FIND ONE FOR ME?
BE AS SALTY AS YOU WISH, JULIET. I WILL ONLY TASTE SUGAR.
PLEASE, BENVOLIO, WHAT WILL IT TAKE FOR YOU TO LEAVE ME?
MAYBE THIS IS THE THING.
SPINK
SPINK
SPINK

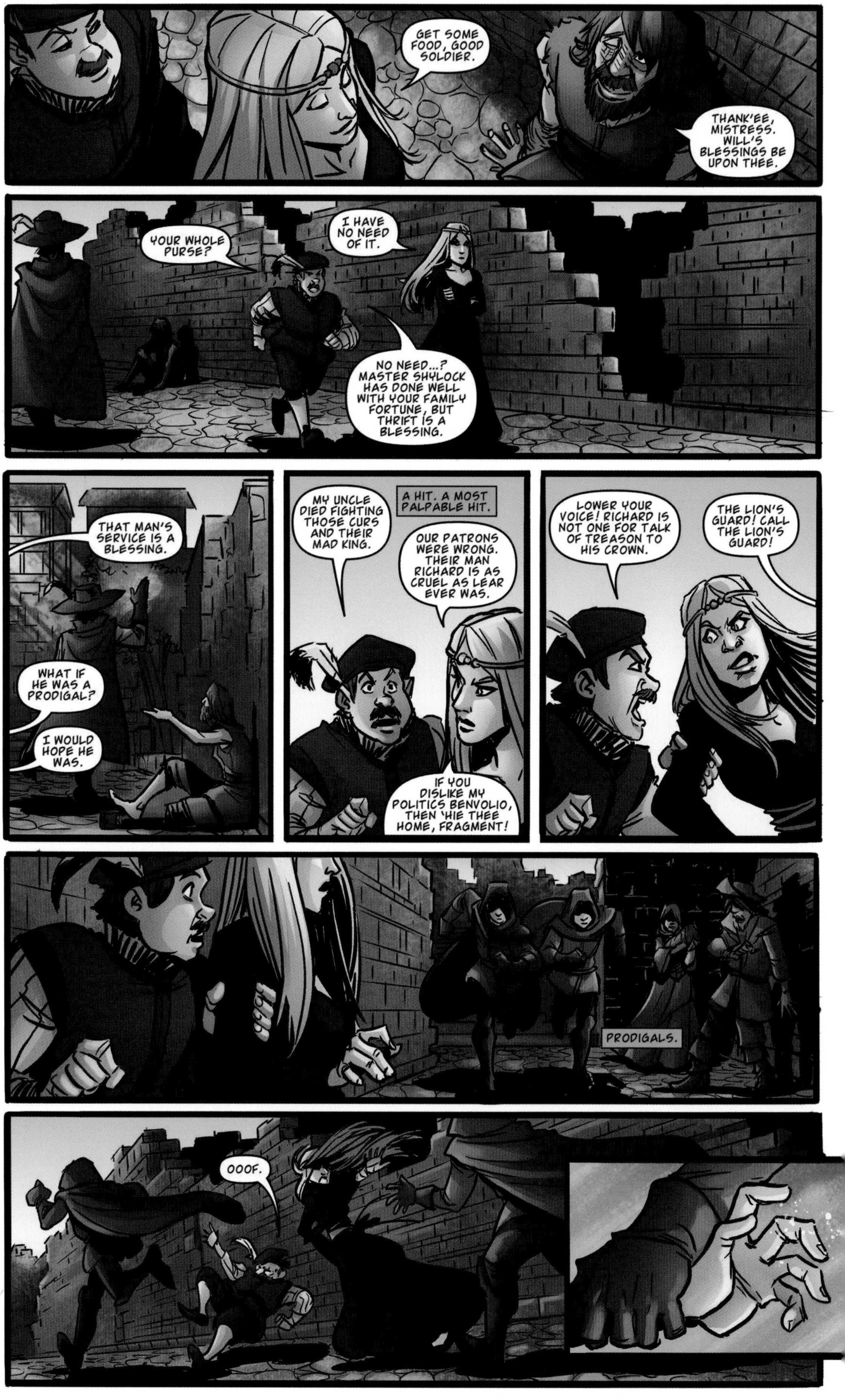
GET SOME FOOD, GOOD SOLDIER.
THANK'EE, MISTRESS. WILL'S BLESSINGS BE UPON THEE.
YOUR WHOLE PURSE?
I HAVE NO NEED OF IT.
NO NEED...? MASTER SHYLOCK HAS DONE WELL WITH YOUR FAMILY FORTUNE, BUT THRIFT IS A BLESSING.
THAT MAN'S SERVICE IS A BLESSING.
WHAT IF HE WAS A PRODIGAL?
I WOULD HOPE HE WAS.
MY UNCLE DIED FIGHTING THOSE CURS AND THEIR MAD KING.
A HIT. A MOST PALPABLE HIT.
OUR PATRONS WERE WRONG. THEIR MAN RICHARD IS AS CRUEL AS LEAR EVER WAS.
IF YOU DISLIKE MY POLITICS BENVOLIO, THEN 'HIE THEE HOME, FRAGMENT!
LOWER YOUR VOICE! RICHARD IS NOT ONE FOR TALK OF TREASON TO HIS CROWN.
THE LION'S GUARD! CALL THE LION'S GUARD!
PRODIGALS.
OOOF.

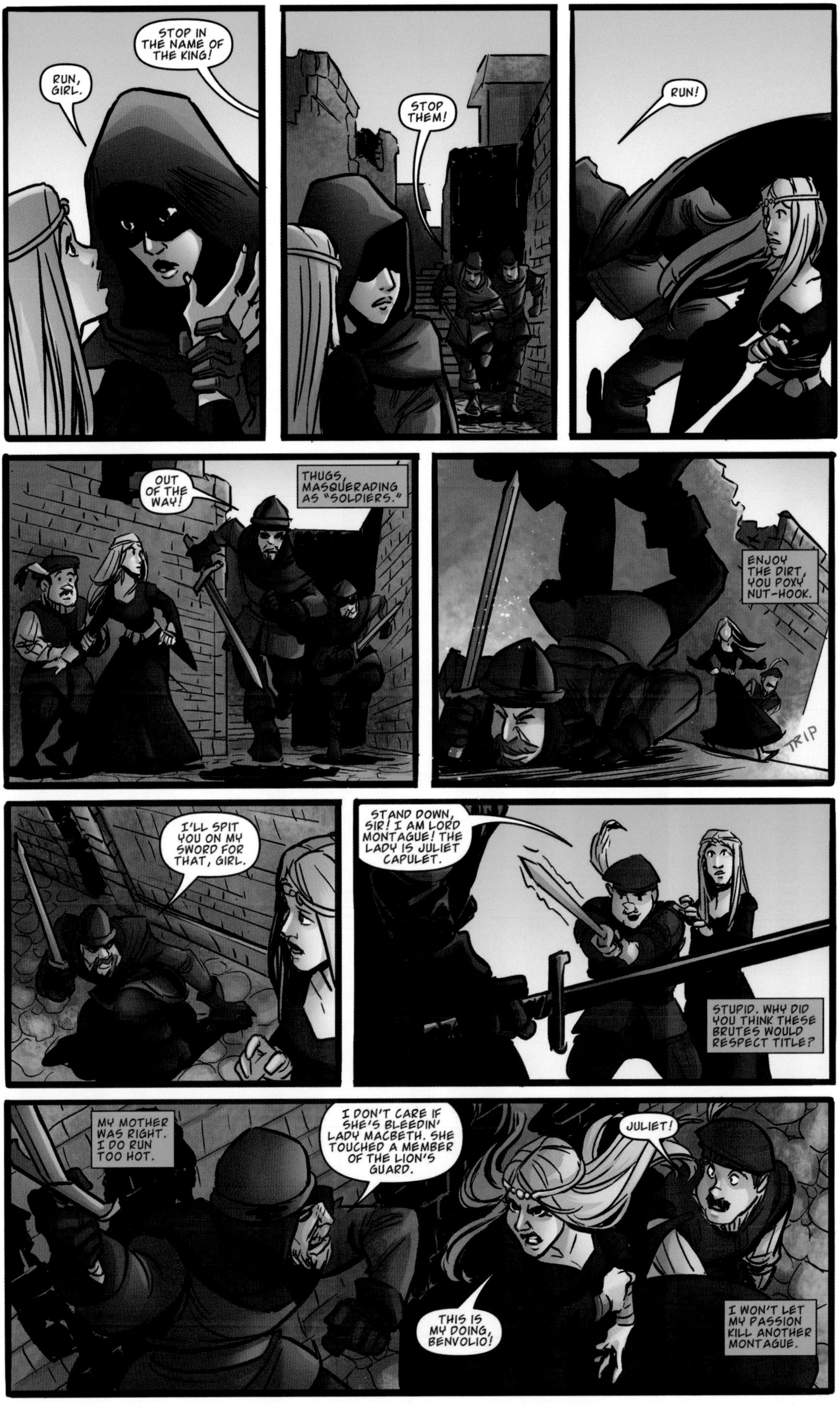
RUN, GIRL.
STOP IN THE NAME OF THE KING!
STOP THEM!
RUN!
OUT OF THE WAY!
THUGS, MASQUERADING AS "SOLDIERS."
ENJOY THE DIRT, YOU POXY NUT-HOOK.
TRIP
I'LL SPIT YOU ON MY SWORD FOR THAT, GIRL.
STAND DOWN, SIR! I AM LORD MONTAGUE! THE LADY IS JULIET CAPULET.
STUPID. WHY DID YOU THINK THESE BRUTES WOULD RESPECT TITLE?
MY MOTHER WAS RIGHT. I DO RUN TOO HOT.
I DON'T CARE IF SHE'S BLEEDIN' LADY MACBETH. SHE TOUCHED A MEMBER OF THE LION'S GUARD.
JULIET!
THIS IS MY DOING, BENVOLIO!
I WON'T LET MY PASSION KILL ANOTHER MONTAGUE.

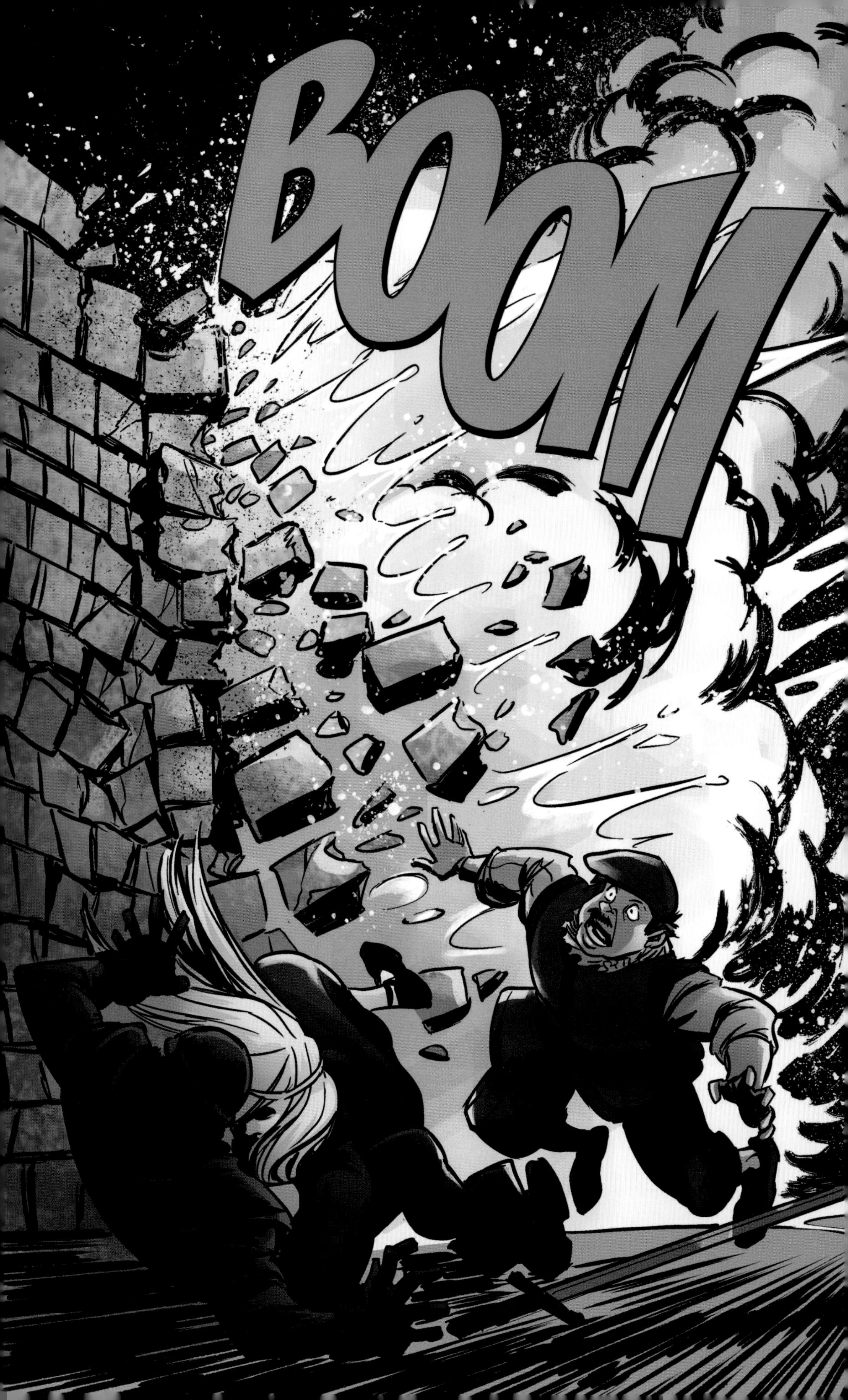
BOOM

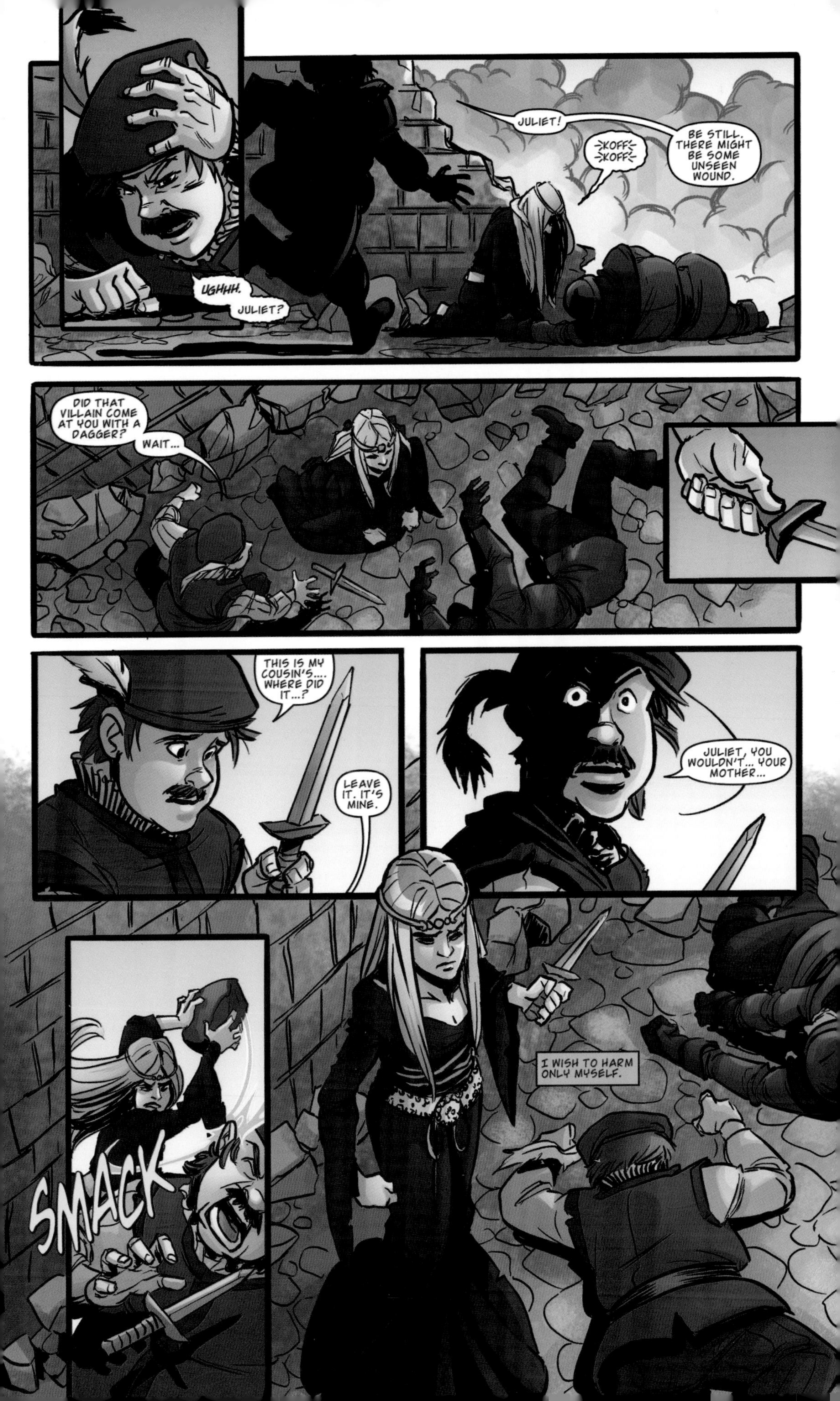
UGHHH.
JULIET?
JULIET!
KOFF KOFF
BE STILL. THERE MIGHT BE SOME UNSEEN WOUND.
DID THAT VILLAIN COME AT YOU WITH A DAGGER?
WAIT...
THIS IS MY COUSIN'S.... WHERE DID IT...?
LEAVE IT. IT'S MINE.
JULIET, YOU WOULDN'T... YOUR MOTHER...
I WISH TO HARM ONLY MYSELF.
SMACK

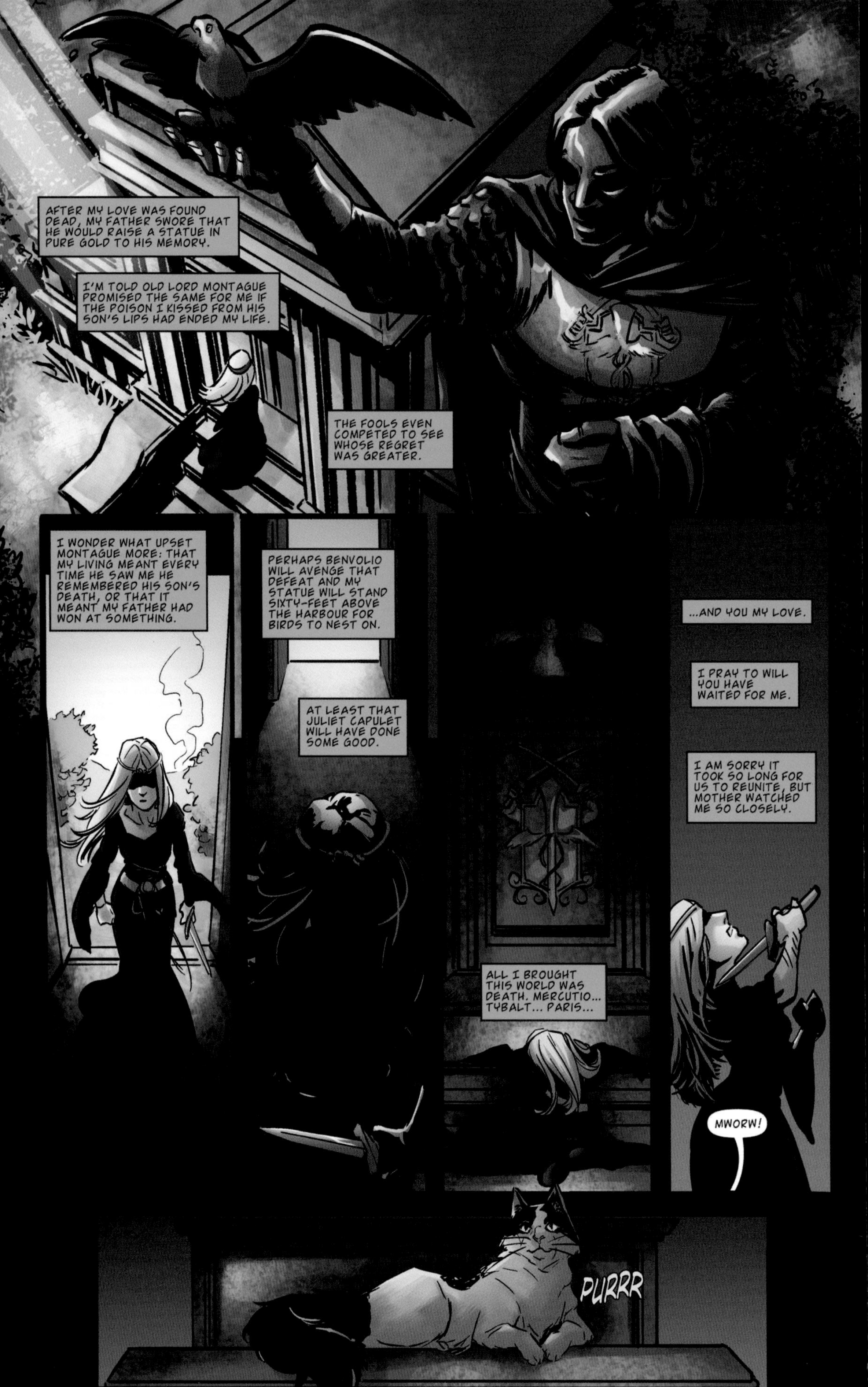
AFTER MY LOVE WAS FOUND DEAD, MY FATHER SWORE THAT HE WOULD RAISE A STATUE IN PURE GOLD TO HIS MEMORY.
I'M TOLD OLD LORD MONTAGUE PROMISED THE SAME FOR ME IF THE POISON I KISSED FROM HIS SON'S LIPS HAD ENDED MY LIFE.
THE FOOLS EVEN COMPETED TO SEE WHOSE REGRET WAS GREATER.
I WONDER WHAT UPSET MONTAGUE MORE: THAT MY LIVING MEANT EVERY TIME HE SAW ME HE REMEMBERED HIS SON'S DEATH, OR THAT IT MEANT MY FATHER HAD WON AT SOMETHING.
PERHAPS BENVOLIO WILL AVENGE THAT DEFEAT AND MY STATUE WILL STAND SIXTY-FEET ABOVE THE HARBOUR FOR BIRDS TO NEST ON.
AT LEAST THAT JULIET CAPULET WILL HAVE DONE SOME GOOD.
ALL I BROUGHT THIS WORLD WAS DEATH. MERCUTIO... TYBALT... PARIS...
...AND YOU MY LOVE.
I PRAY TO WILL YOU HAVE WAITED FOR ME.
I AM SORRY IT TOOK SO LONG FOR US TO REUNITE, BUT MOTHER WATCHED ME SO CLOSELY.
MWORW!
PURRR

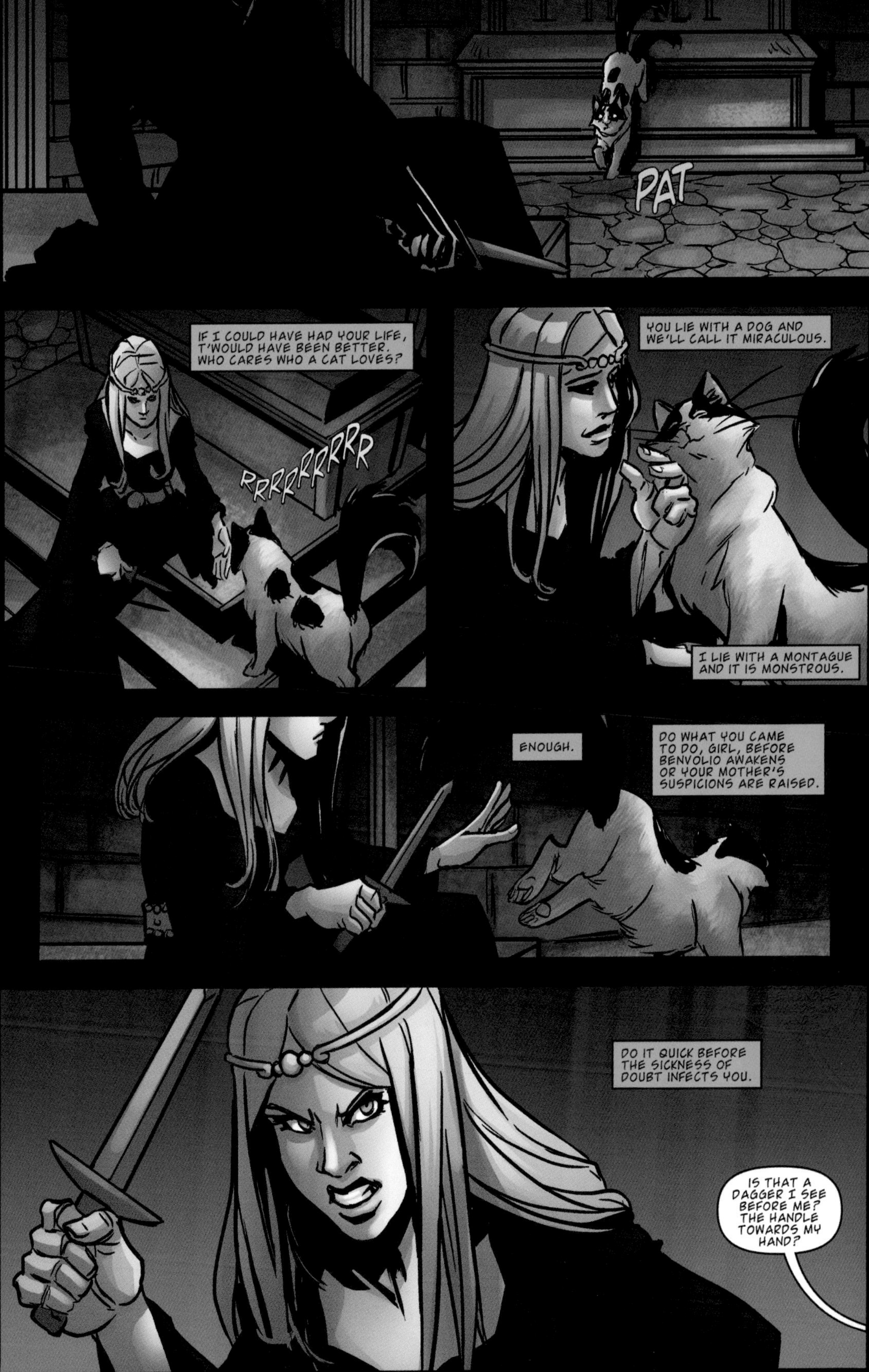
PAT
IF I COULD HAVE HAD YOUR LIFE, T'WOULD HAVE BEEN BETTER. WHO CARES WHO A CAT LOVES?
RRRRRRRRR
YOU LIE WITH A DOG AND WE'LL CALL IT MIRACULOUS.
I LIE WITH A MONTAGUE AND IT IS MONSTROUS.
ENOUGH.
DO WHAT YOU CAME TO DO, GIRL, BEFORE BENVOLIO AWAKENS OR YOUR MOTHER'S SUSPICIONS ARE RAISED.
DO IT QUICK BEFORE THE SICKNESS OF DOUBT INFECTS YOU.
IS THAT A DAGGER I SEE BEFORE ME? THE HANDLE TOWARDS MY HAND?

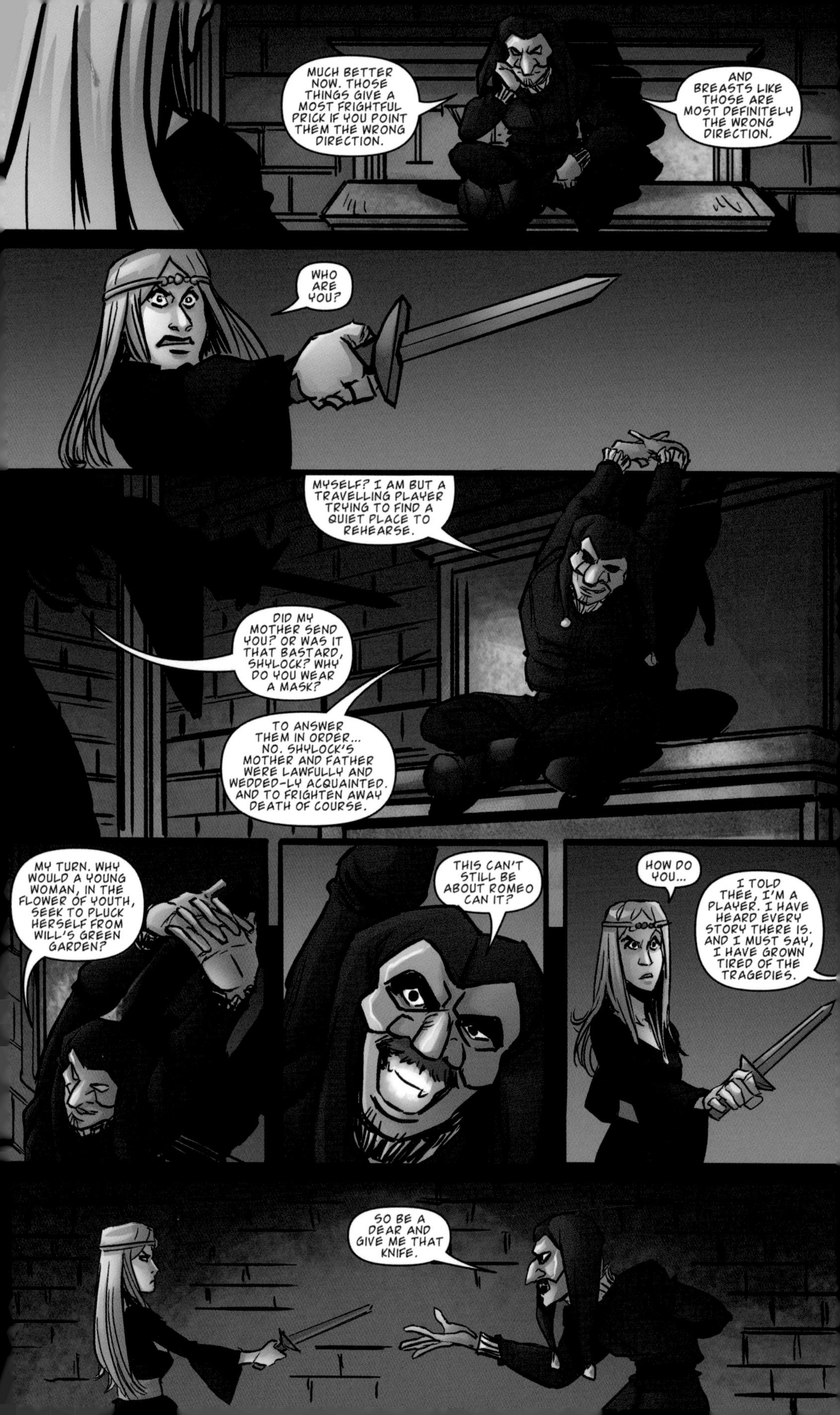
MUCH BETTER NOW. THOSE THINGS GIVE A MOST FRIGHTFUL PRICK IF YOU POINT THEM THE WRONG DIRECTION.
AND BREASTS LIKE THOSE ARE MOST DEFINITELY THE WRONG DIRECTION.
WHO ARE YOU?
MYSELF? I AM BUT A TRAVELLING PLAYER TRYING TO FIND A QUIET PLACE TO REHEARSE.
DID MY MOTHER SEND YOU? OR WAS IT THAT BASTARD, SHYLOCK? WHY DO YOU WEAR A MASK?
TO ANSWER THEM IN ORDER... NO. SHYLOCK'S MOTHER AND FATHER WERE LAWFULLY AND WEDDED-LY ACQUAINTED. AND TO FRIGHTEN AWAY DEATH OF COURSE.
MY TURN. WHY WOULD A YOUNG WOMAN, IN THE FLOWER OF YOUTH, SEEK TO PLUCK HERSELF FROM WILL'S GREEN GARDEN?
THIS CAN'T STILL BE ABOUT ROMEO CAN IT?
HOW DO YOU...
I TOLD THEE, I'M A PLAYER. I HAVE HEARD EVERY STORY THERE IS. AND I MUST SAY, I HAVE GROWN TIRED OF THE TRAGEDIES.
SO BE A DEAR AND GIVE ME THAT KNIFE.

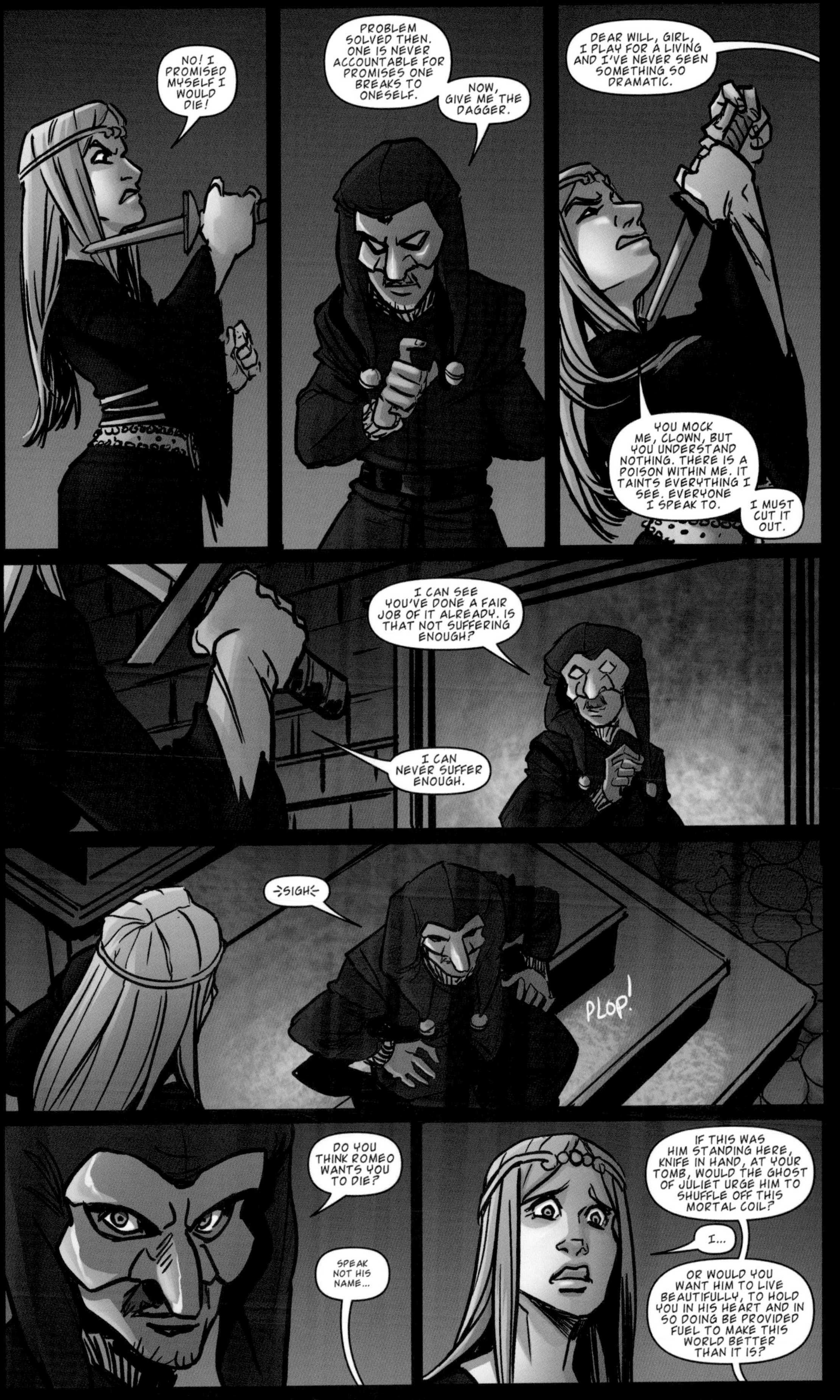
NO! I PROMISED MYSELF I WOULD DIE!
PROBLEM SOLVED THEN. ONE IS NEVER ACCOUNTABLE FOR PROMISES ONE BREAKS TO ONESELF.
NOW, GIVE ME THE DAGGER.
DEAR WILL, GIRL, I PLAY FOR A LIVING AND I'VE NEVER SEEN SOMETHING SO DRAMATIC.
YOU MOCK ME, CLOWN, BUT YOU UNDERSTAND NOTHING. THERE IS A POISON WITHIN ME. IT TAINTS EVERYTHING I SEE. EVERYONE I SPEAK TO.
I MUST CUT IT OUT.
I CAN SEE YOU'VE DONE A FAIR JOB OF IT ALREADY. IS THAT NOT SUFFERING ENOUGH?
I CAN NEVER SUFFER ENOUGH.
SIGH
PLOP!
DO YOU THINK ROMEO WANTS YOU TO DIE?
SPEAK NOT HIS NAME...
IF THIS WAS HIM STANDING HERE, KNIFE IN HAND, AT YOUR TOMB, WOULD THE GHOST OF JULIET URGE HIM TO SHUFFLE OFF THIS MORTAL COIL?
I...
OR WOULD YOU WANT HIM TO LIVE BEAUTIFULLY, TO HOLD YOU IN HIS HEART AND IN SO DOING BE PROVIDED FUEL TO MAKE THIS WORLD BETTER THAN IT IS?

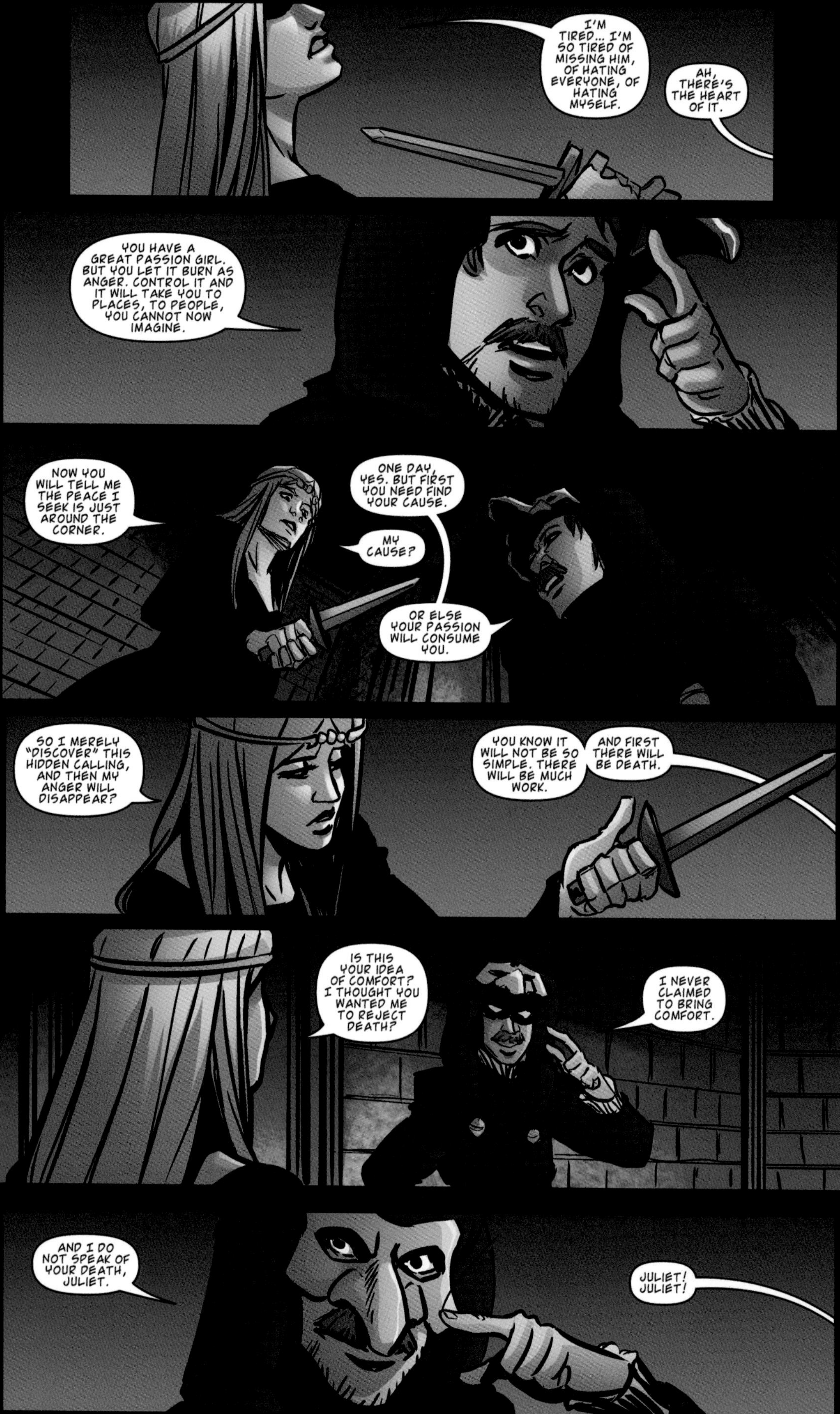
I'M TIRED... I'M SO TIRED OF MISSING HIM, OF HATING EVERYONE, OF HATING MYSELF.
AH, THERE'S THE HEART OF IT.
YOU HAVE A GREAT PASSION GIRL. BUT YOU LET IT BURN AS ANGER. CONTROL IT AND IT WILL TAKE YOU TO PLACES, TO PEOPLE, YOU CANNOT NOW IMAGINE.
NOW YOU WILL TELL ME THE PEACE I SEEK IS JUST AROUND THE CORNER.
ONE DAY, YES. BUT FIRST YOU NEED FIND YOUR CAUSE.
MY CAUSE?
OR ELSE YOUR PASSION WILL CONSUME YOU.
SO I MERELY "DISCOVER" THIS HIDDEN CALLING, AND THEN MY ANGER WILL DISAPPEAR?
YOU KNOW IT WILL NOT BE SO SIMPLE. THERE WILL BE MUCH WORK.
AND FIRST THERE WILL BE DEATH.
IS THIS YOUR IDEA OF COMFORT? I THOUGHT YOU WANTED ME TO REJECT DEATH?
I NEVER CLAIMED TO BRING COMFORT.
AND I DO NOT SPEAK OF YOUR DEATH, JULIET.
JULIET! JULIET!

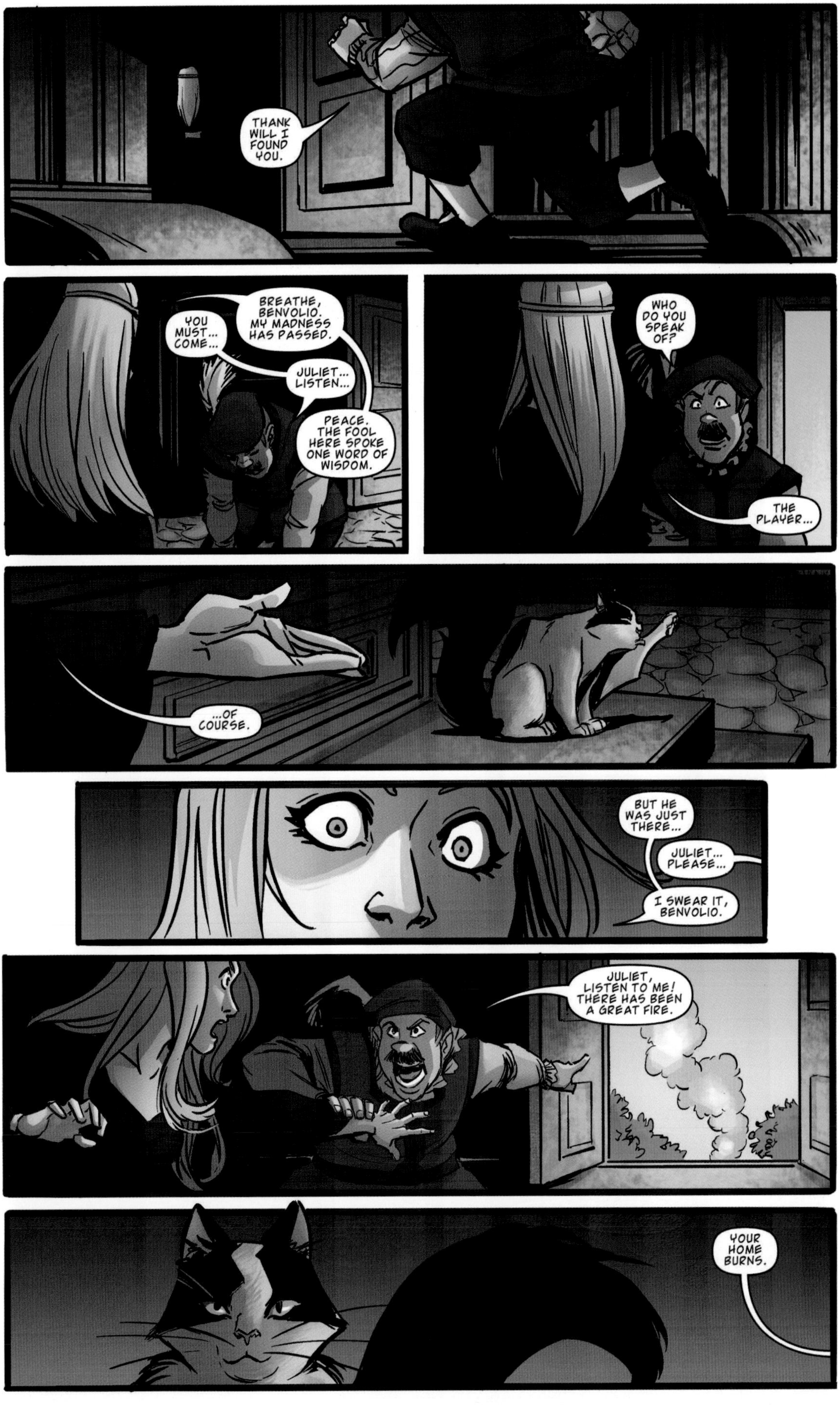
THANK WILL I FOUND YOU.
YOU MUST... COME...
BREATHE, BENVOLIO. MY MADNESS HAS PASSED.
JULIET... LISTEN...
PEACE. THE FOOL HERE SPOKE ONE WORD OF WISDOM.
WHO DO YOU SPEAK OF?
THE PLAYER...
...OF COURSE.
BUT HE WAS JUST THERE...
JULIET... PLEASE...
I SWEAR IT, BENVOLIO.
JULIET, LISTEN TO ME! THERE HAS BEEN A GREAT FIRE.
YOUR HOME BURNS.

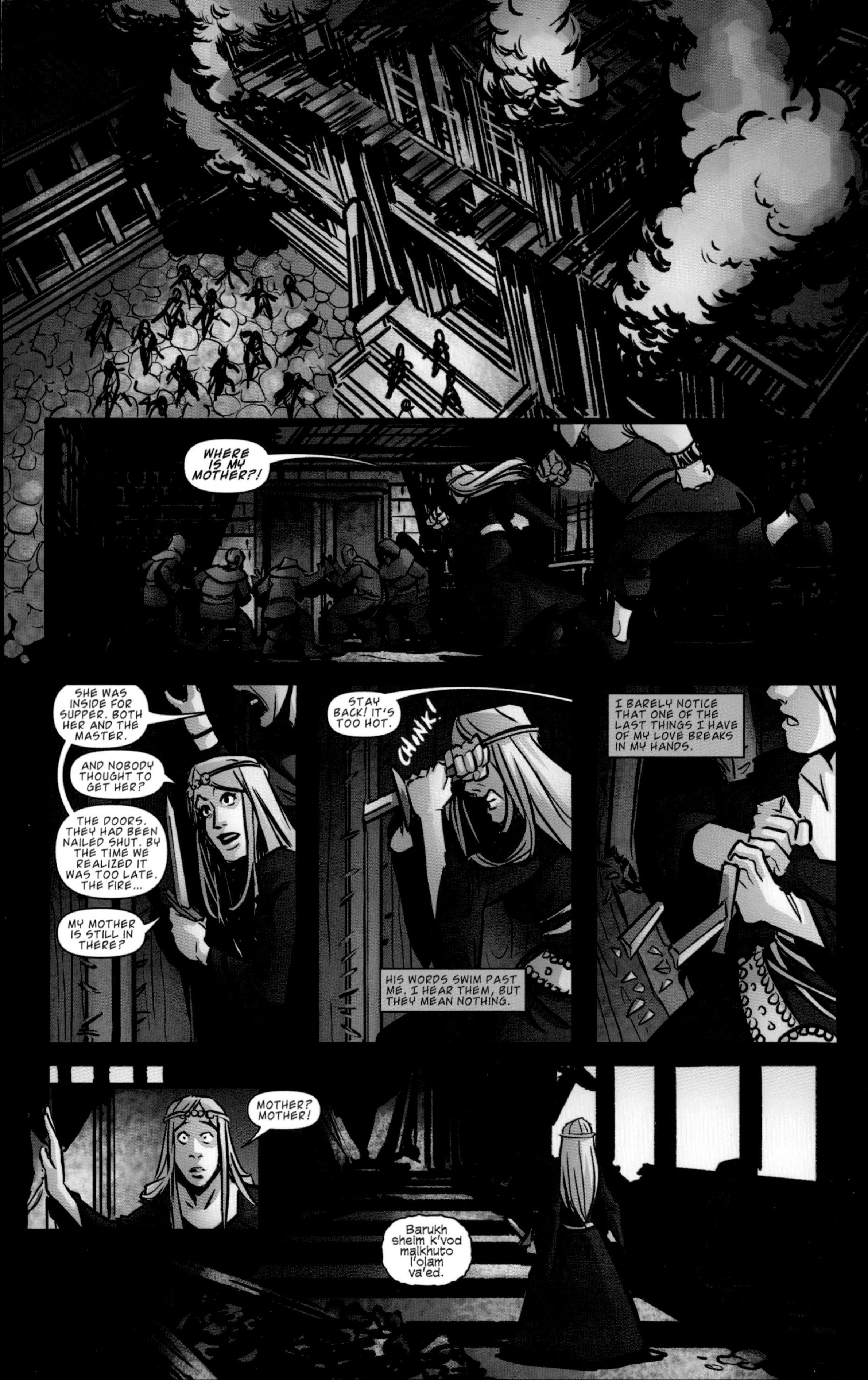
WHERE IS MY MOTHER?!
SHE WAS INSIDE FOR SUPPER. BOTH HER AND THE MASTER.
AND NOBODY THOUGHT TO GET HER?
THE DOORS. THEY HAD BEEN NAILED SHUT. BY THE TIME WE REALIZED IT WAS TOO LATE. THE FIRE...
MY MOTHER IS STILL IN THERE?
STAY BACK! IT'S TOO HOT.
CHUNK!
HIS WORDS SWIM PAST ME. I HEAR THEM, BUT THEY MEAN NOTHING.
I BARELY NOTICE THAT ONE OF THE LAST THINGS I HAVE OF MY LOVE BREAKS IN MY HANDS.
MOTHER? MOTHER!
Barukh sheim k'vod malkhuto l'olam va'ed.

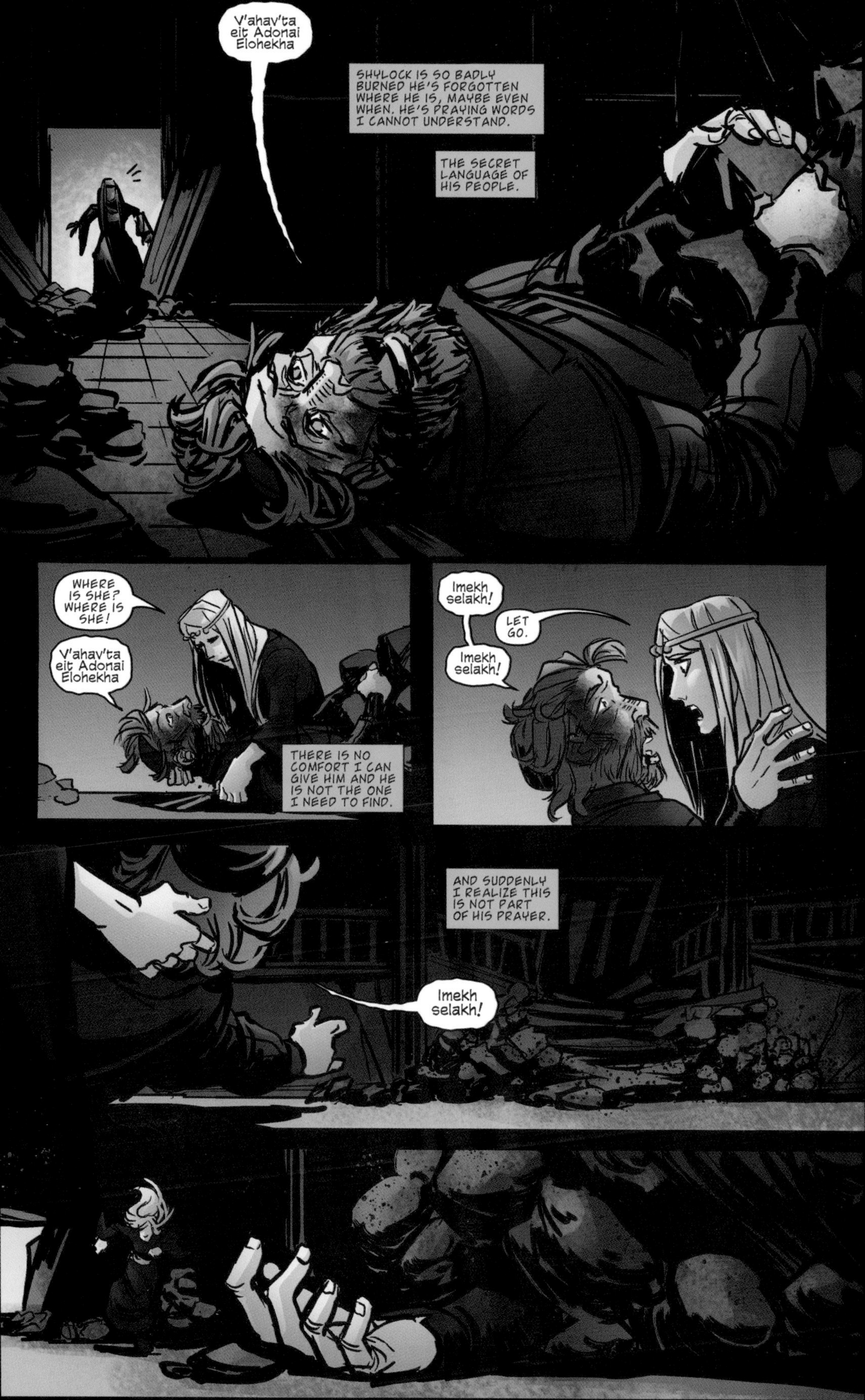
V'ahav'ta eit Adonai Elohekha
SHYLOCK IS SO BADLY BURNED HE'S FORGOTTEN WHERE HE IS, MAYBE EVEN WHEN. HE'S PRAYING WORDS I CANNOT UNDERSTAND.
THE SECRET LANGUAGE OF HIS PEOPLE.
WHERE IS SHE? WHERE IS SHE!
V'ahav'ta eit Adonai Elohekha
THERE IS NO COMFORT I CAN GIVE HIM AND HE IS NOT THE ONE I NEED TO FIND.
Imekh selakh!
LET GO.
Imekh selakh!
AND SUDDENLY I REALIZE THIS IS NOT PART OF HIS PRAYER.
Imekh selakh!

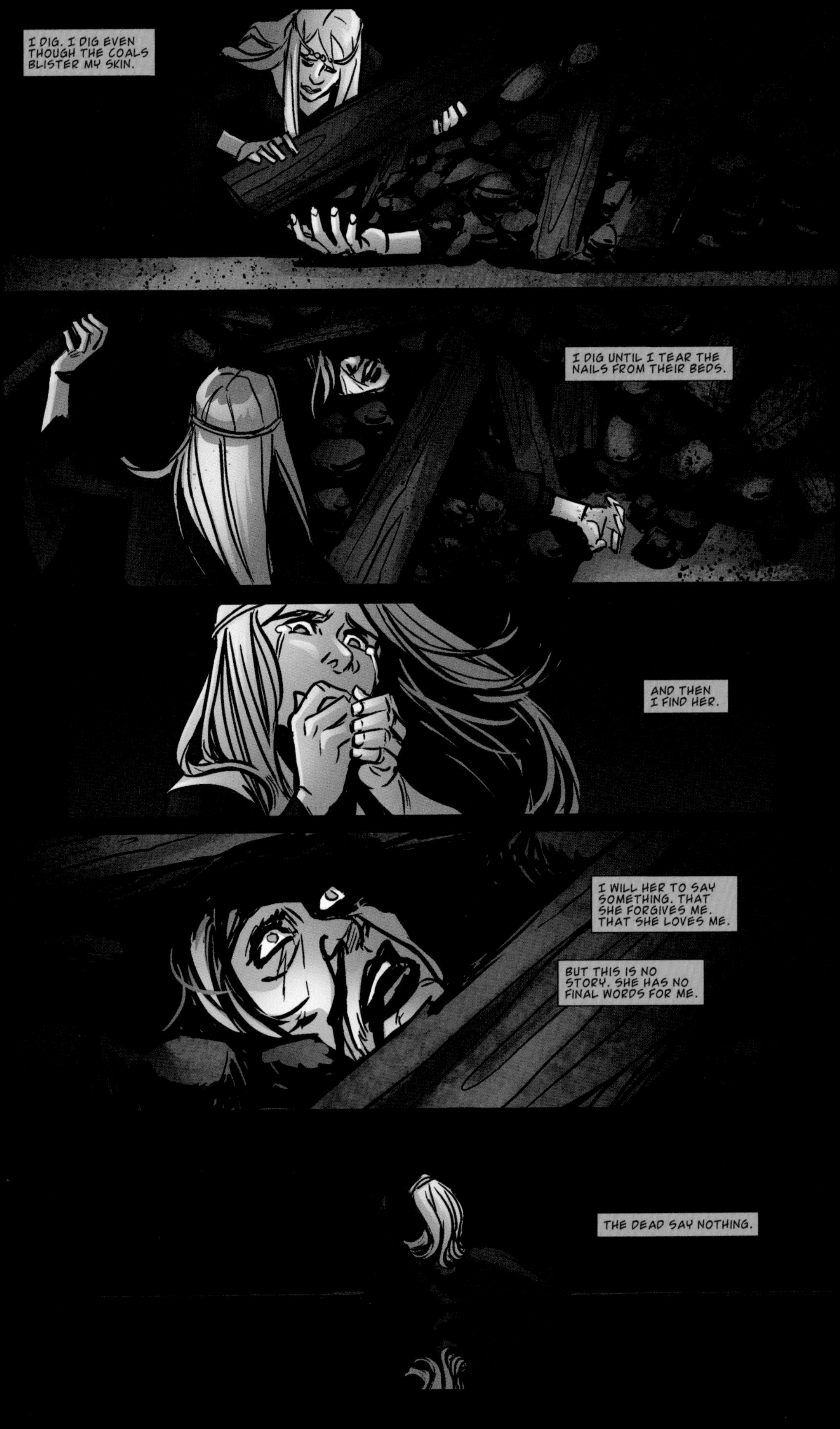
I DIG. I DIG EVEN THOUGH THE COALS BLISTER MY SKIN.
I DIG UNTIL I TEAR THE NAILS FROM THEIR BEDS.
AND THEN I FIND HER.
I WILL HER TO SAY SOMETHING. THAT SHE FORGIVES ME. THAT SHE LOVES ME.
BUT THIS IS NO STORY. SHE HAS NO FINAL WORDS FOR ME.
THE DEAD SAY NOTHING.

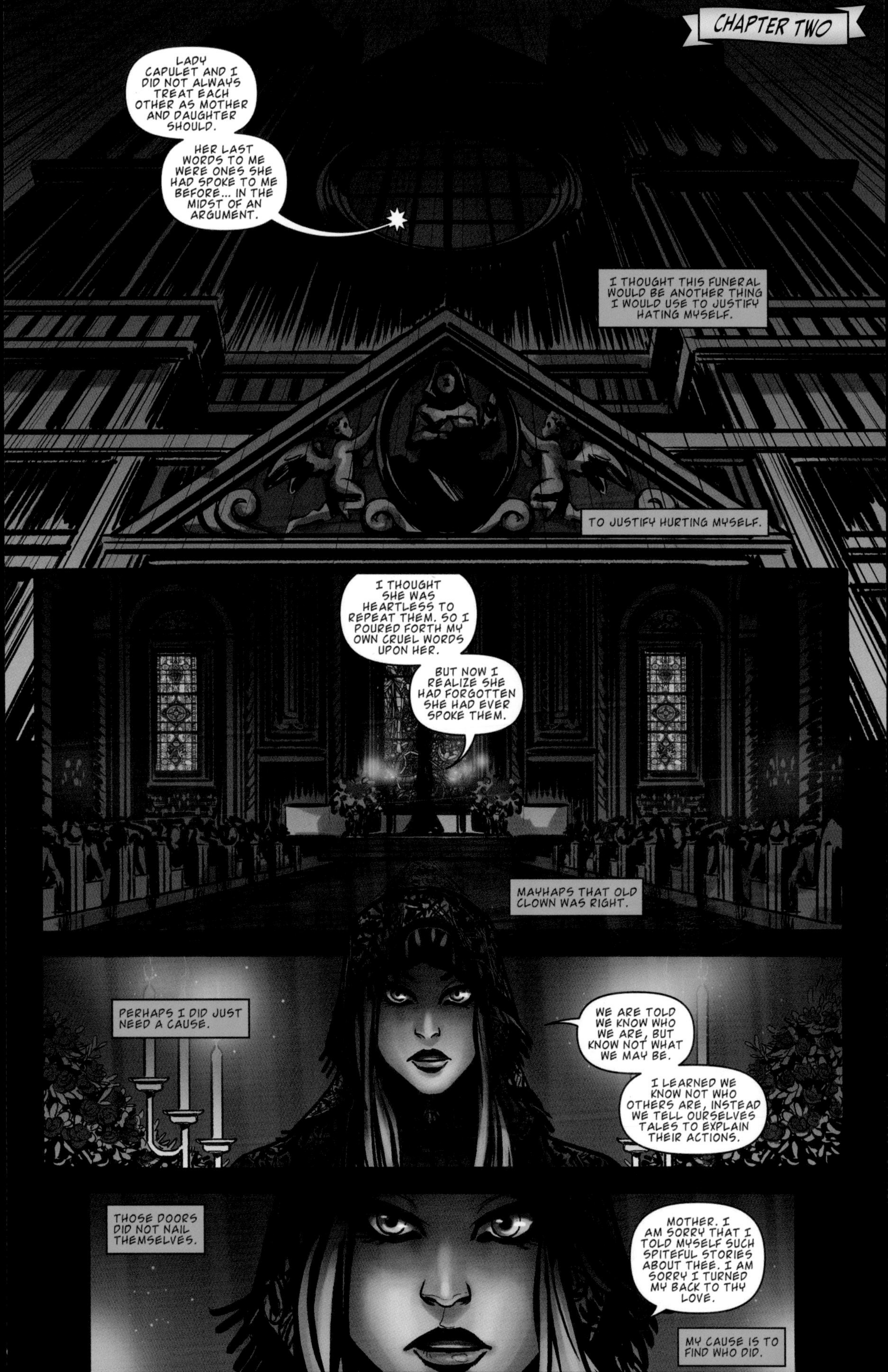
CHAPTER TWO
LADY CAPULET AND I DID NOT ALWAYS TREAT EACH OTHER AS MOTHER AND DAUGHTER SHOULD.
HER LAST WORDS TO ME WERE ONES SHE HAD SPOKE TO ME BEFORE... IN THE MIDST OF AN ARGUMENT.
I THOUGHT THIS FUNERAL WOULD BE ANOTHER THING I WOULD USE TO JUSTIFY HATING MYSELF.
TO JUSTIFY HURTING MYSELF.
I THOUGHT SHE WAS HEARTLESS TO REPEAT THEM. SO I POURED FORTH MY OWN CRUEL WORDS UPON HER.
BUT NOW I REALIZE SHE HAD FORGOTTEN SHE HAD EVER SPOKE THEM.
MAYHAPS THAT OLD CLOWN WAS RIGHT.
PERHAPS I DID JUST NEED A CAUSE.
WE ARE TOLD WE KNOW WHO WE ARE, BUT KNOW NOT WHAT WE MAY BE.
I LEARNED WE KNOW NOT WHO OTHERS ARE, INSTEAD WE TELL OURSELVES TALES TO EXPLAIN THEIR ACTIONS.
THOSE DOORS DID NOT NAIL THEMSELVES.
MOTHER. I AM SORRY THAT I TOLD MYSELF SUCH SPITEFUL STORIES ABOUT THEE. I AM SORRY I TURNED MY BACK TO THY LOVE.
MY CAUSE IS TO FIND WHO DID.

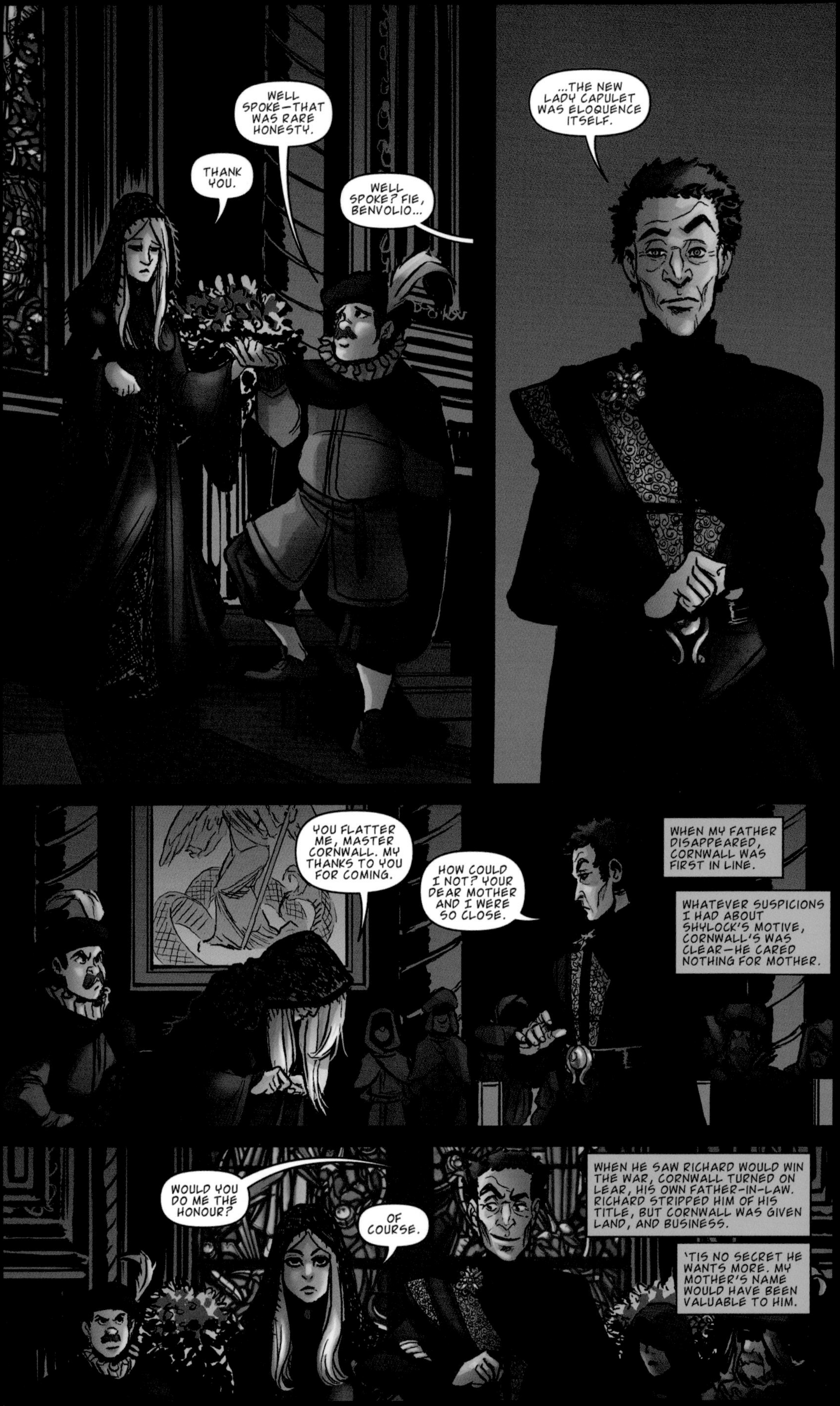
THANK YOU.
WELL SPOKE—THAT WAS RARE HONESTY.
WELL SPOKE? FIE, BENVOLIO...
...THE NEW LADY CAPULET WAS ELOQUENCE ITSELF.
YOU FLATTER ME, MASTER CORNWALL. MY THANKS TO YOU FOR COMING.
HOW COULD I NOT? YOUR DEAR MOTHER AND I WERE SO CLOSE.
WHEN MY FATHER DISAPPEARED, CORNWALL WAS FIRST IN LINE.
WHATEVER SUSPICIONS I HAD ABOUT SHYLOCK'S MOTIVE, CORNWALL'S WAS CLEAR—HE CARED NOTHING FOR MOTHER.
WOULD YOU DO ME THE HONOUR?
OF COURSE.
WHEN HE SAW RICHARD WOULD WIN THE WAR, CORNWALL TURNED ON LEAR, HIS OWN FATHER-IN-LAW. RICHARD STRIPPED HIM OF HIS TITLE, BUT CORNWALL WAS GIVEN LAND, AND BUSINESS.
'TIS NO SECRET HE WANTS MORE. MY MOTHER'S NAME WOULD HAVE BEEN VALUABLE TO HIM.

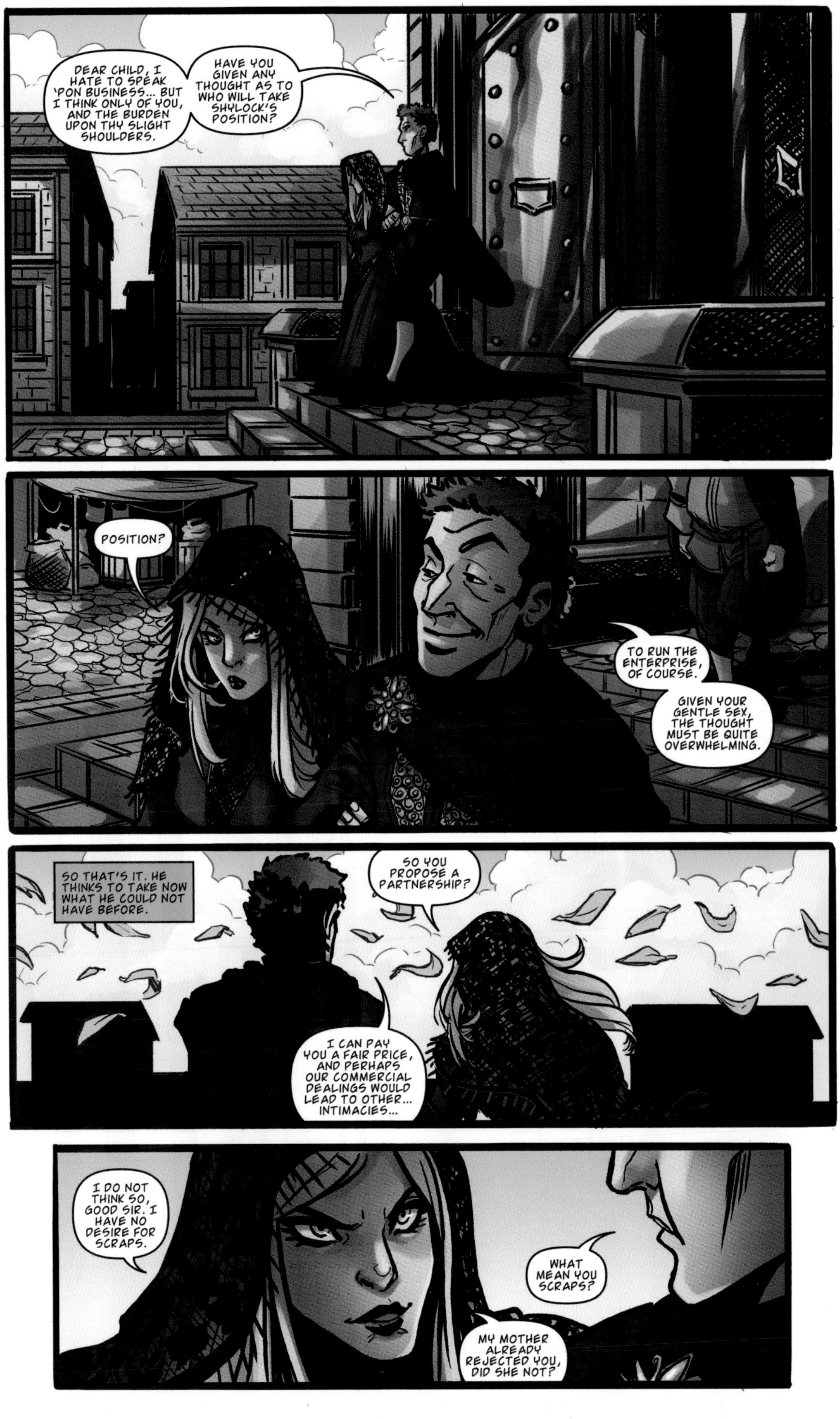

DEAR CHILD, I HATE TO SPEAK 'PON BUSINESS... BUT I THINK ONLY OF YOU, AND THE BURDEN UPON THY SLIGHT SHOULDERS.
HAVE YOU GIVEN ANY THOUGHT AS TO WHO WILL TAKE SHYLOCK'S POSITION?
POSITION?
TO RUN THE ENTERPRISE, OF COURSE.
GIVEN YOUR GENTLE SEX, THE THOUGHT MUST BE QUITE OVERWHELMING.
SO THAT'S IT. HE THINKS TO TAKE NOW WHAT HE COULD NOT HAVE BEFORE.
SO YOU PROPOSE A PARTNERSHIP?
I CAN PAY YOU A FAIR PRICE, AND PERHAPS OUR COMMERCIAL DEALINGS WOULD LEAD TO OTHER... INTIMACIES...
I DO NOT THINK SO, GOOD SIR. I HAVE NO DESIRE FOR SCRAPS.
WHAT MEAN YOU SCRAPS?
MY MOTHER ALREADY REJECTED YOU, DID SHE NOT?

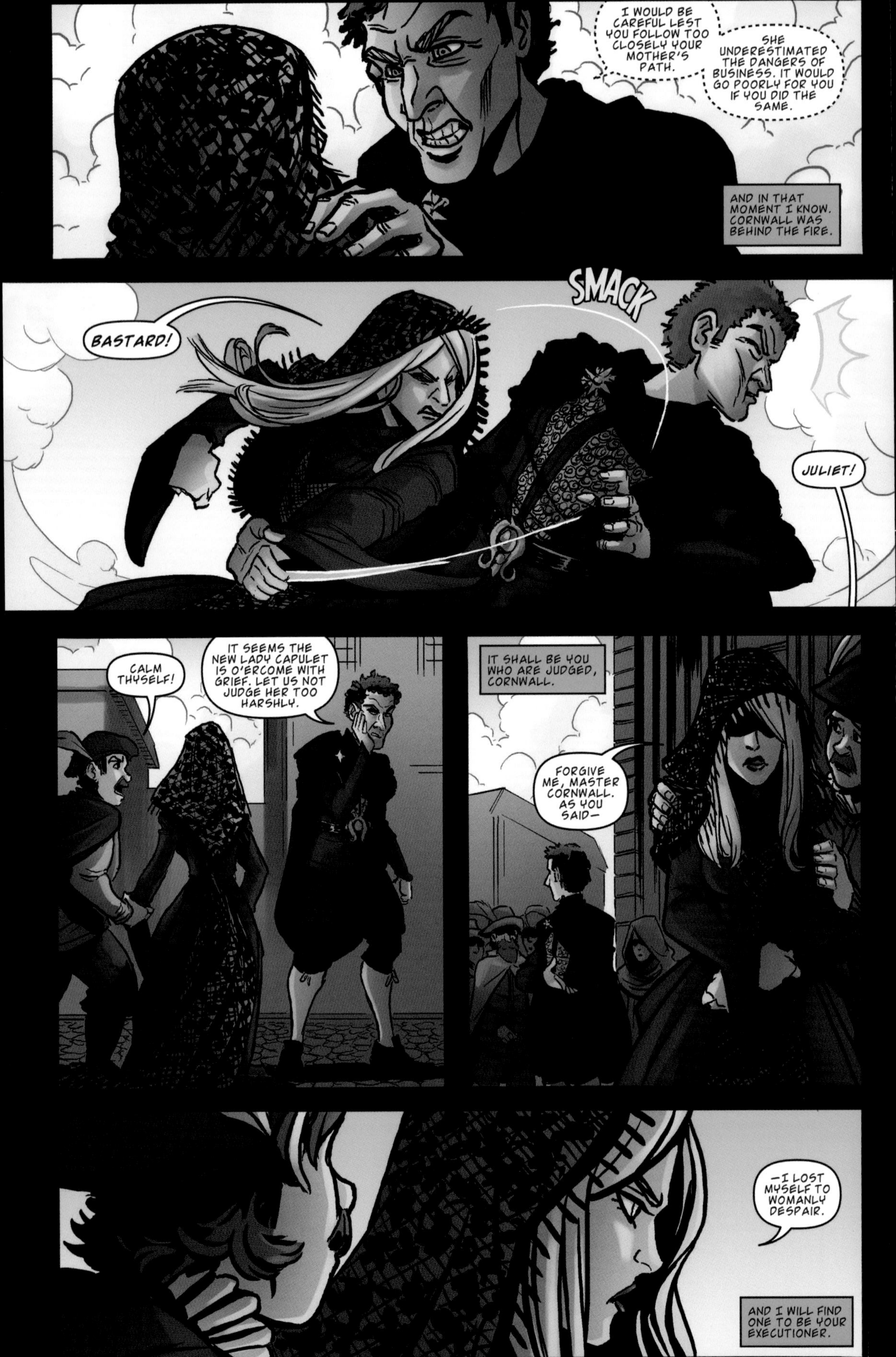

I WOULD BE CAREFUL LEST YOU FOLLOW TOO CLOSELY YOUR MOTHER'S PATH.
SHE UNDERESTIMATED THE DANGERS OF BUSINESS. IT WOULD GO POORLY FOR YOU IF YOU DID THE SAME.
AND IN THAT MOMENT I KNOW. CORNWALL WAS BEHIND THE FIRE.
SMACK
BASTARD!
JULIET!
CALM THYSELF!
IT SEEMS THE NEW LADY CAPULET IS O'ERCOME WITH GRIEF. LET US NOT JUDGE HER TOO HARSHLY.
IT SHALL BE YOU WHO ARE JUDGED, CORNWALL.
FORGIVE ME, MASTER CORNWALL. AS YOU SAID—
—I LOST MYSELF TO WOMANLY DESPAIR.
AND I WILL FIND ONE TO BE YOUR EXECUTIONER.

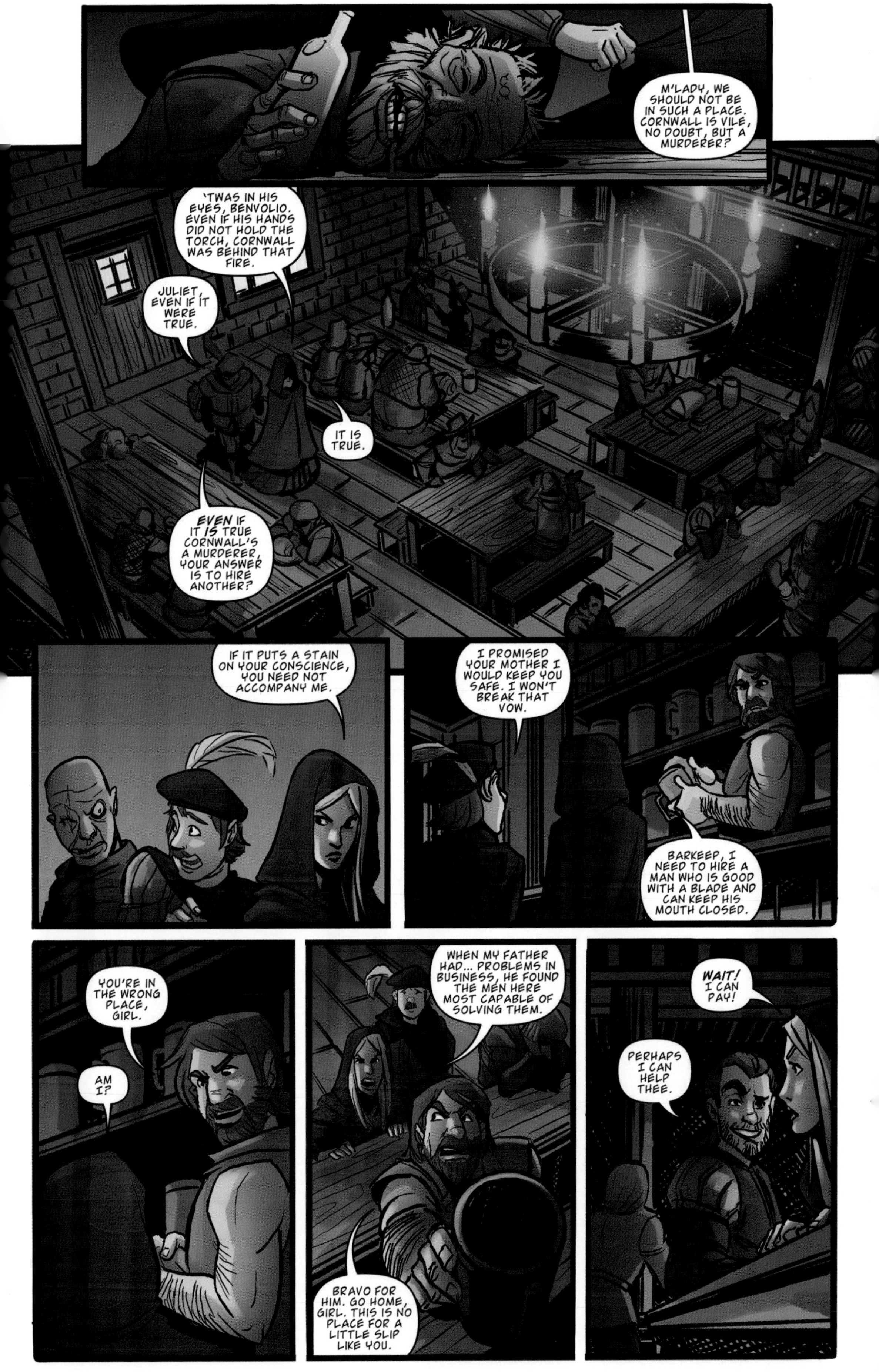
M'LADY, WE SHOULD NOT BE IN SUCH A PLACE. CORNWALL IS VILE, NO DOUBT, BUT A MURDERER?
'TWAS IN HIS EYES, BENVOLIO. EVEN IF HIS HANDS DID NOT HOLD THE TORCH, CORNWALL WAS BEHIND THAT FIRE.
JULIET, EVEN IF IT WERE TRUE.
IT IS TRUE.
EVEN IF IT IS TRUE CORNWALL'S A MURDERER, YOUR ANSWER IS TO HIRE ANOTHER?
IF IT PUTS A STAIN ON YOUR CONSCIENCE, YOU NEED NOT ACCOMPANY ME.
I PROMISED YOUR MOTHER I WOULD KEEP YOU SAFE. I WON'T BREAK THAT VOW.
BARKEEP, I NEED TO HIRE A MAN WHO IS GOOD WITH A BLADE AND CAN KEEP HIS MOUTH CLOSED.
YOU'RE IN THE WRONG PLACE, GIRL.
AM I?
WHEN MY FATHER HAD... PROBLEMS IN BUSINESS, HE FOUND THE MEN HERE MOST CAPABLE OF SOLVING THEM.
BRAVO FOR HIM. GO HOME, GIRL. THIS IS NO PLACE FOR A LITTLE SLIP LIKE YOU.
WAIT! I CAN PAY!
PERHAPS I CAN HELP THEE.

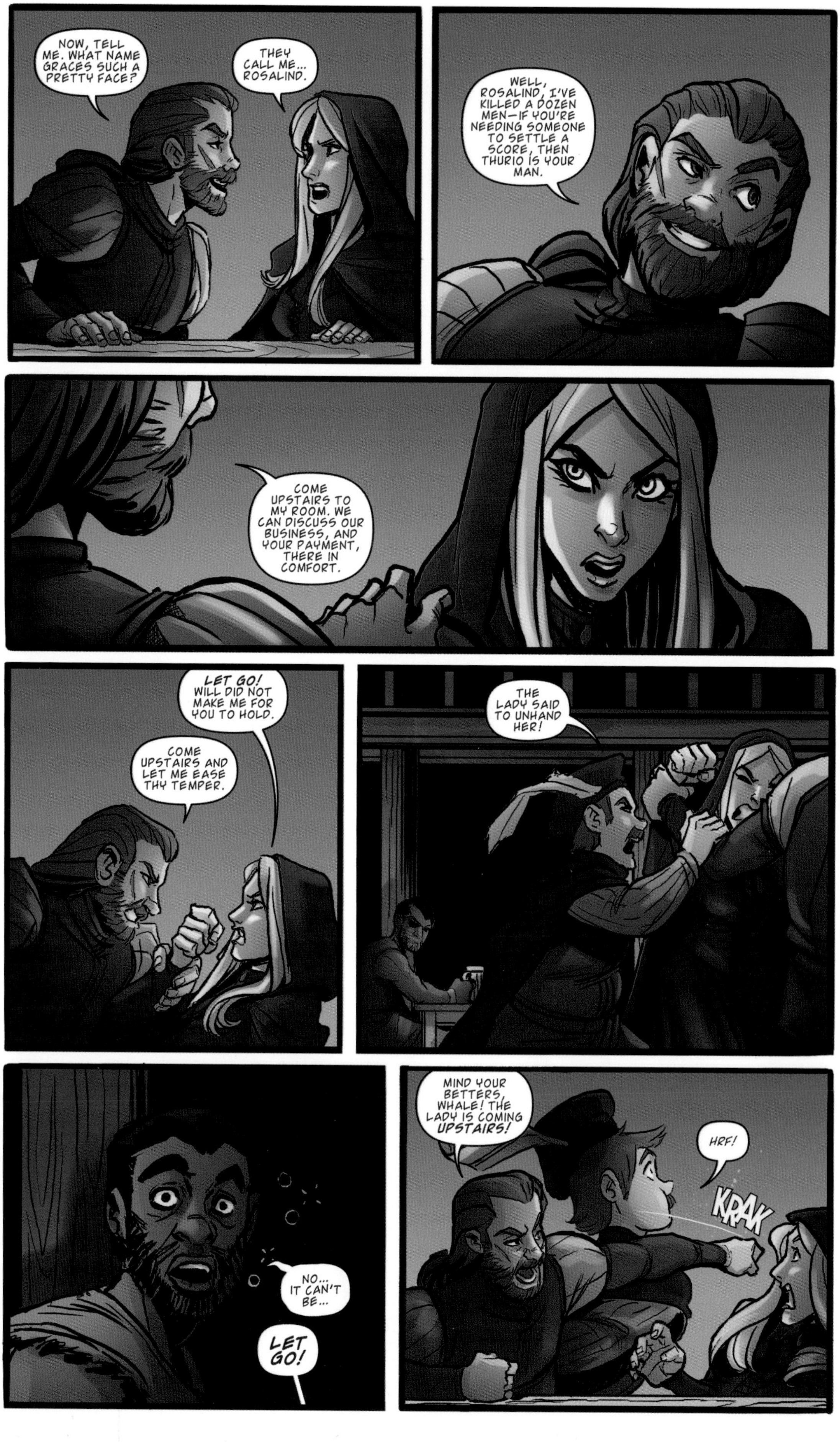
NOW, TELL ME. WHAT NAME GRACES SUCH A PRETTY FACE?
THEY CALL ME... ROSALIND.
WELL, ROSALIND, I'VE KILLED A DOZEN MEN—IF YOU'RE NEEDING SOMEONE TO SETTLE A SCORE, THEN THURIO IS YOUR MAN.
COME UPSTAIRS TO MY ROOM. WE CAN DISCUSS OUR BUSINESS, AND YOUR PAYMENT, THERE IN COMFORT.
LET GO! WILL DID NOT MAKE ME FOR YOU TO HOLD.
COME UPSTAIRS AND LET ME EASE THY TEMPER.
THE LADY SAID TO UNHAND HER!
NO... IT CAN'T BE...
LET GO!
MIND YOUR BETTERS, WHALE! THE LADY IS COMING UPSTAIRS!
HRF!
KRAK

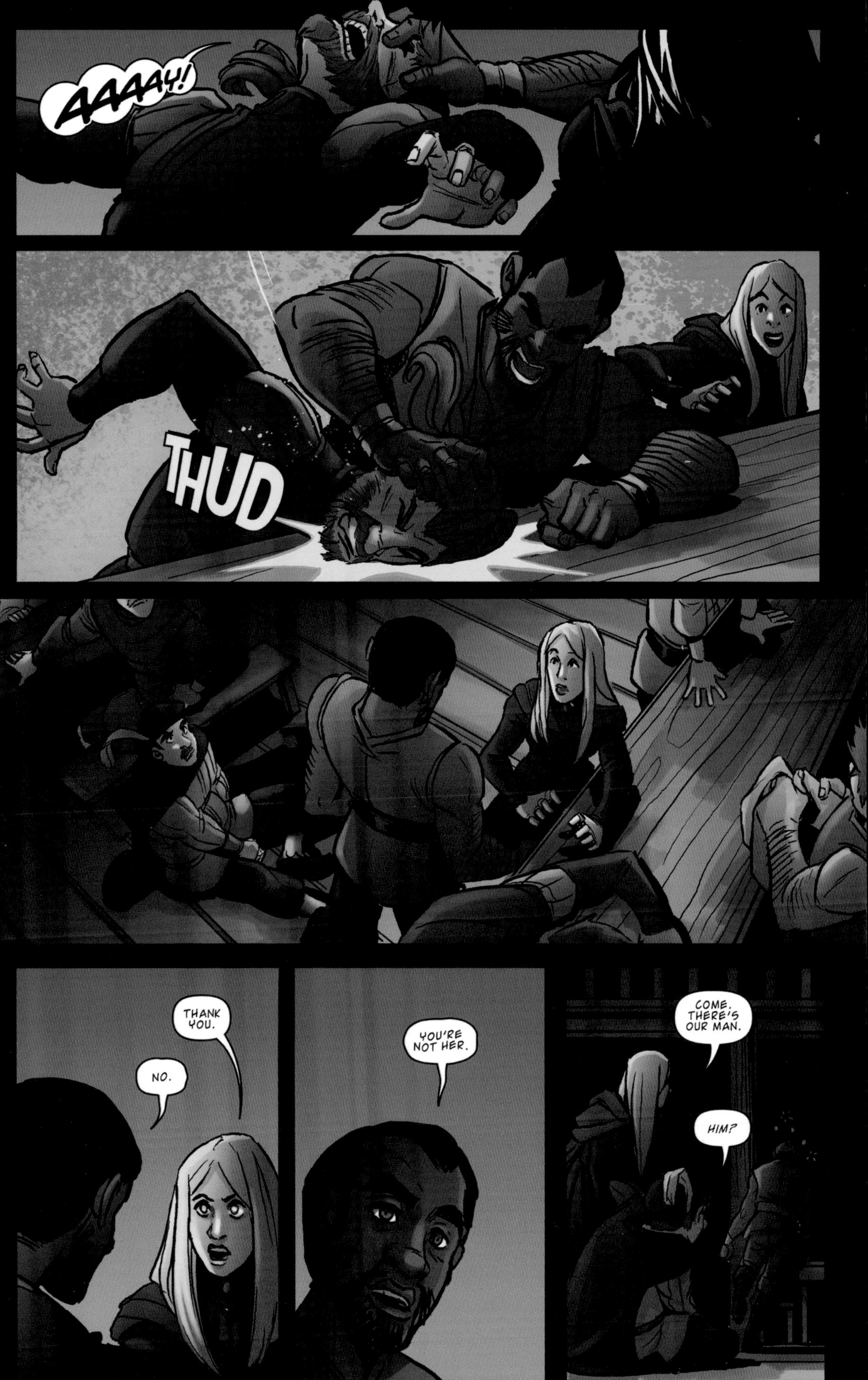
AAAAY!
THUD
THANK YOU.
NO.
YOU'RE NOT HER.
COME. THERE'S OUR MAN.
HIM?

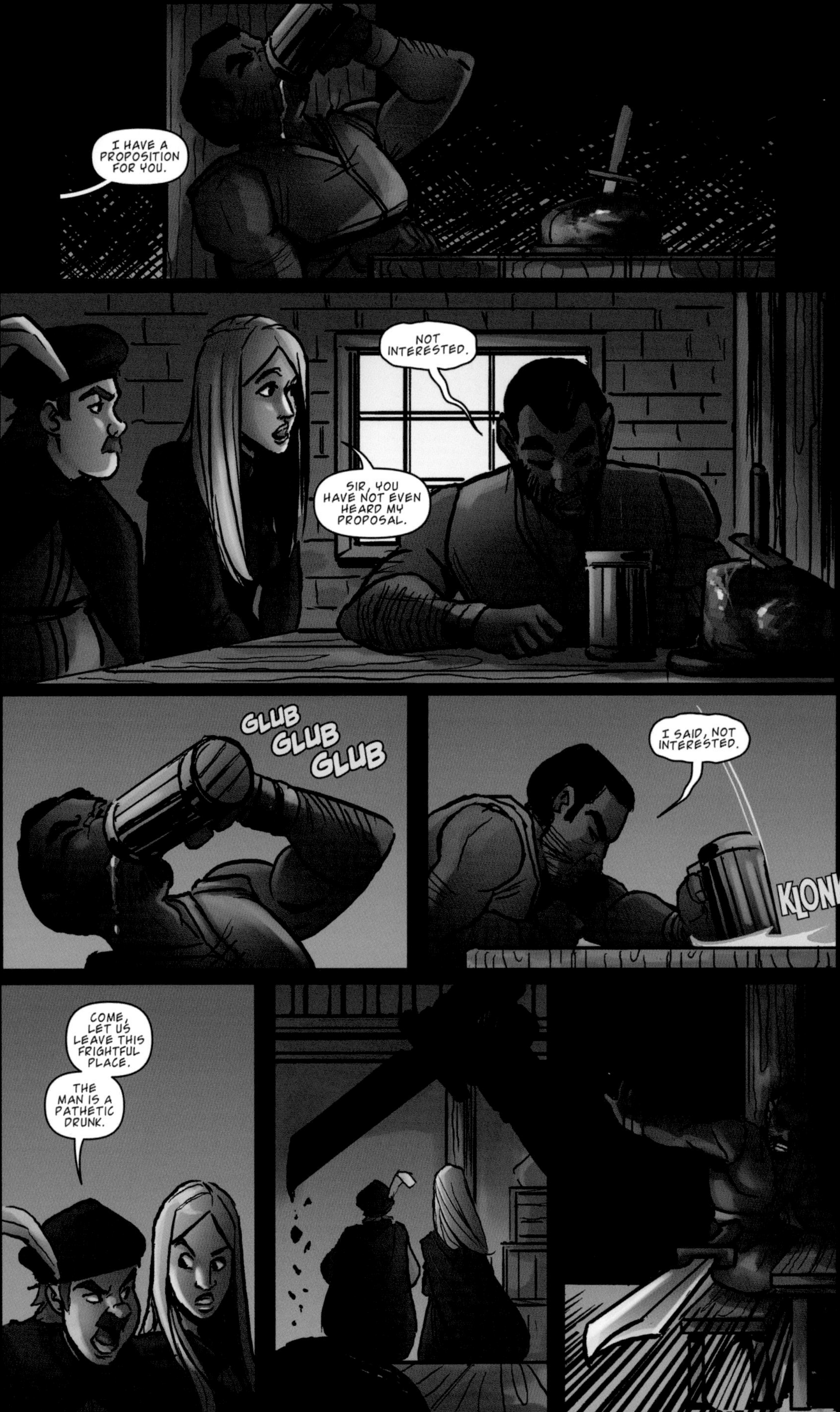
I HAVE A PROPOSITION FOR YOU.
NOT INTERESTED.
SIR, YOU HAVE NOT EVEN HEARD MY PROPOSAL.
GLUB GLUB GLUB
I SAID, NOT INTERESTED.
KLONK
COME, LET US LEAVE THIS FRIGHTFUL PLACE.
THE MAN IS A PATHETIC DRUNK.

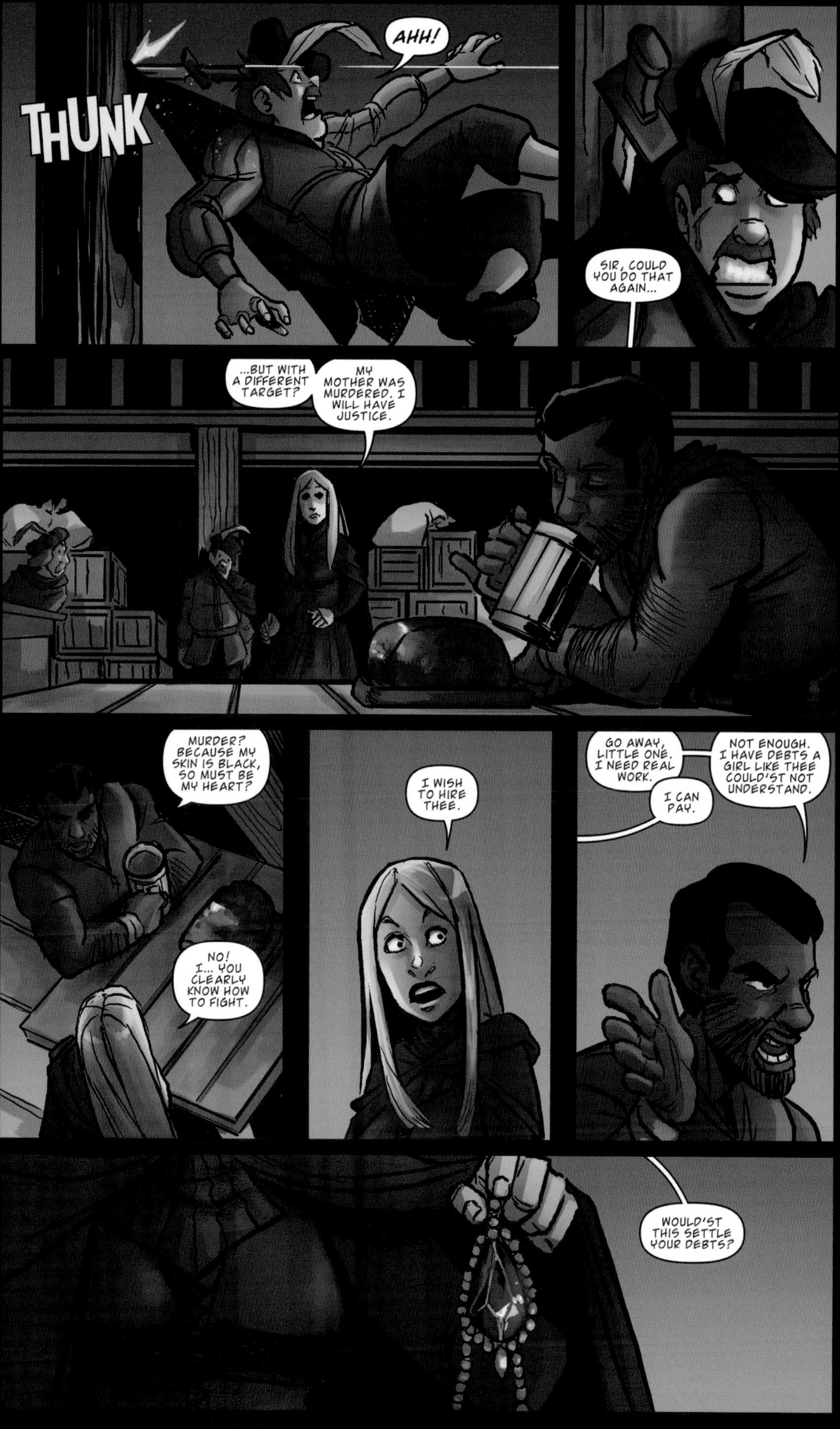
THUNK
AHH!
SIR, COULD YOU DO THAT AGAIN...
...BUT WITH A DIFFERENT TARGET?
MY MOTHER WAS MURDERED. I WILL HAVE JUSTICE.
MURDER? BECAUSE MY SKIN IS BLACK, SO MUST BE MY HEART?
NO! I... YOU CLEARLY KNOW HOW TO FIGHT.
I WISH TO HIRE THEE.
GO AWAY, LITTLE ONE. I NEED REAL WORK.
I CAN PAY.
NOT ENOUGH. I HAVE DEBTS A GIRL LIKE THEE COULD'ST NOT UNDERSTAND.
WOULD'ST THIS SETTLE YOUR DEBTS?

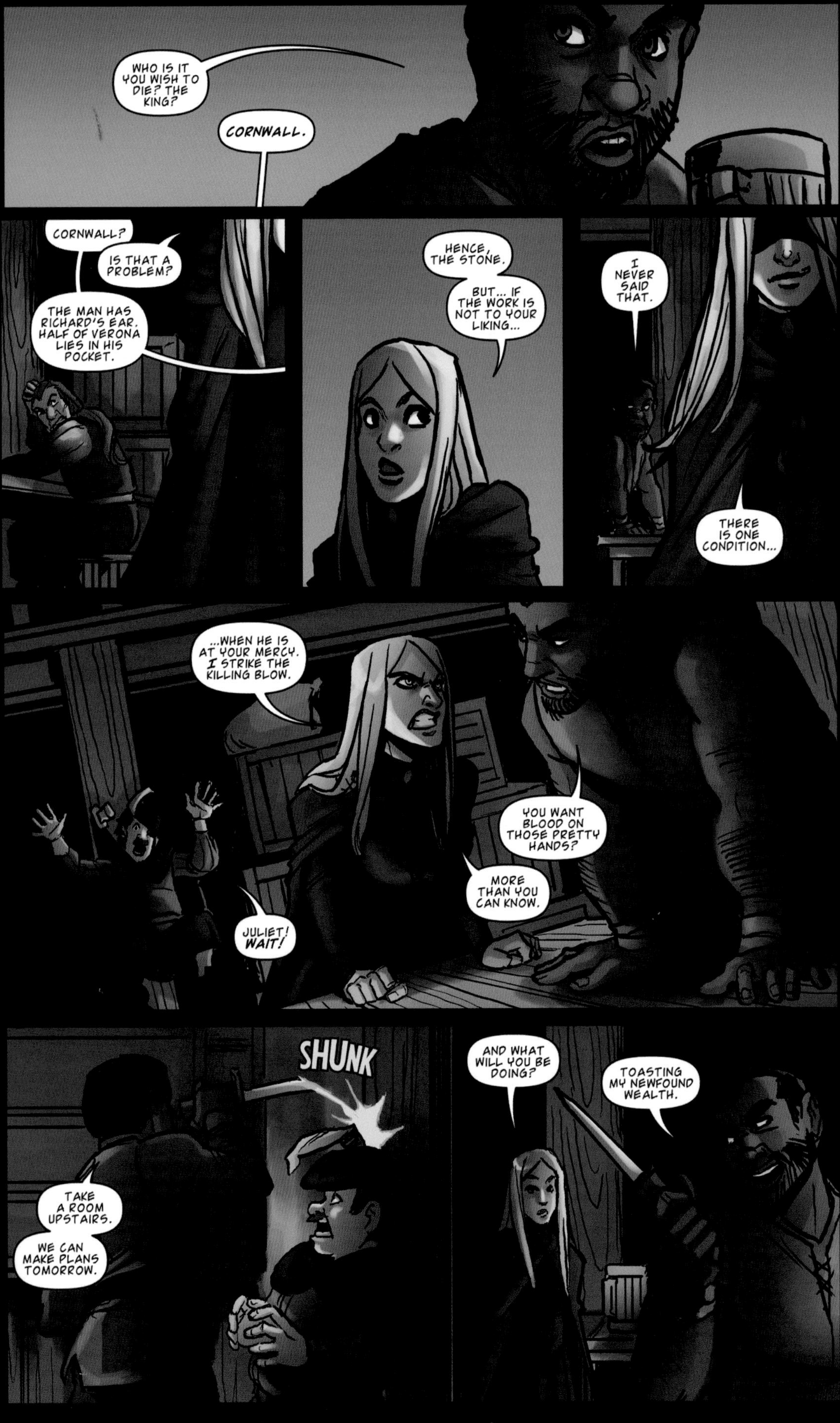
WHO IS IT YOU WISH TO DIE? THE KING?
CORNWALL.
CORNWALL?
IS THAT A PROBLEM?
THE MAN HAS RICHARD'S EAR. HALF OF VERONA LIES IN HIS POCKET.
HENCE, THE STONE.
BUT... IF THE WORK IS NOT TO YOUR LIKING...
I NEVER SAID THAT.
THERE IS ONE CONDITION...
...WHEN HE IS AT YOUR MERCY. I STRIKE THE KILLING BLOW.
YOU WANT BLOOD ON THOSE PRETTY HANDS?
MORE THAN YOU CAN KNOW.
JULIET! WAIT!
SHUNK
TAKE A ROOM UPSTAIRS.
WE CAN MAKE PLANS TOMORROW.
AND WHAT WILL YOU BE DOING?
TOASTING MY NEWFOUND WEALTH.

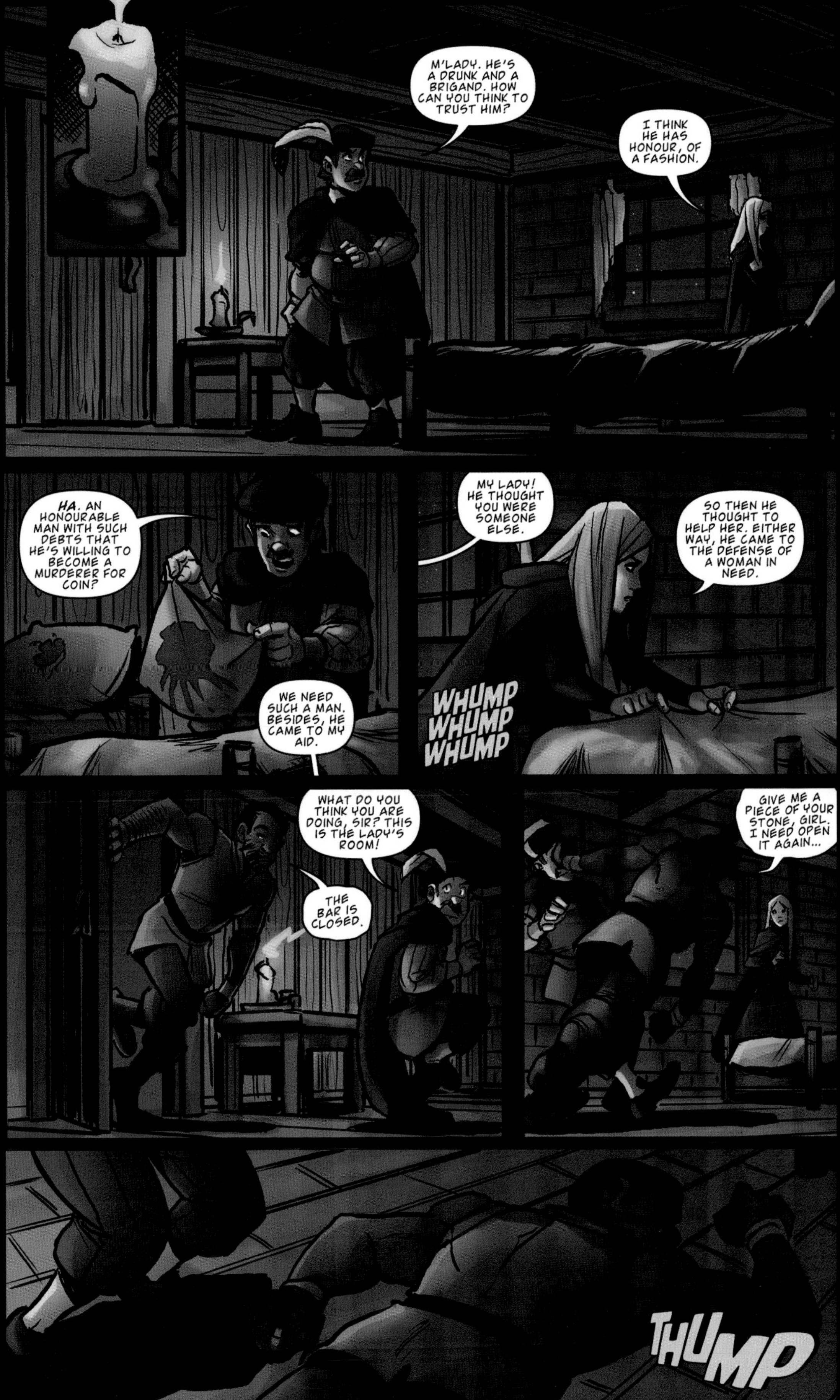
M'LADY. HE'S A DRUNK AND A BRIGAND. HOW CAN YOU THINK TO TRUST HIM?
I THINK HE HAS HONOUR, OF A FASHION.
HA. AN HONOURABLE MAN WITH SUCH DEBTS THAT HE'S WILLING TO BECOME A MURDERER FOR COIN?
WE NEED SUCH A MAN. BESIDES, HE CAME TO MY AID.
MY LADY! HE THOUGHT YOU WERE SOMEONE ELSE.
SO THEN HE THOUGHT TO HELP HER. EITHER WAY, HE CAME TO THE DEFENSE OF A WOMAN IN NEED.
WHUMP WHUMP WHUMP
WHAT DO YOU THINK YOU ARE DOING, SIR? THIS IS THE LADY'S ROOM!
THE BAR IS CLOSED.
GIVE ME A PIECE OF YOUR STONE, GIRL. I NEED OPEN IT AGAIN...
THUMP

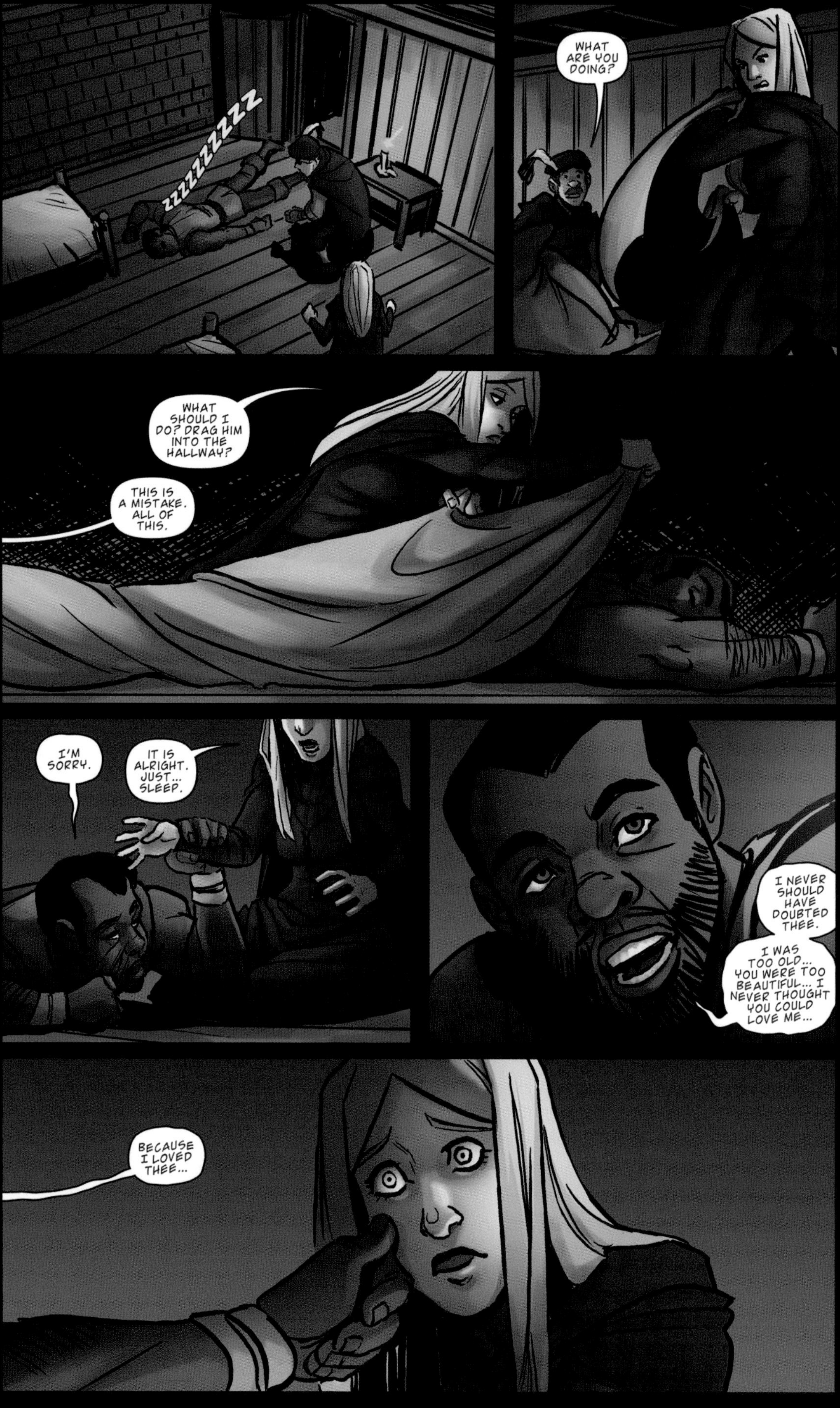
ZZZZZZZZZ
WHAT ARE YOU DOING?
WHAT SHOULD I DO? DRAG HIM INTO THE HALLWAY?
THIS IS A MISTAKE. ALL OF THIS.
I'M SORRY.
IT IS ALRIGHT. JUST... SLEEP.
I NEVER SHOULD HAVE DOUBTED THEE.
I WAS TOO OLD... YOU WERE TOO BEAUTIFUL... I NEVER THOUGHT YOU COULD LOVE ME...
BECAUSE I LOVED THEE...

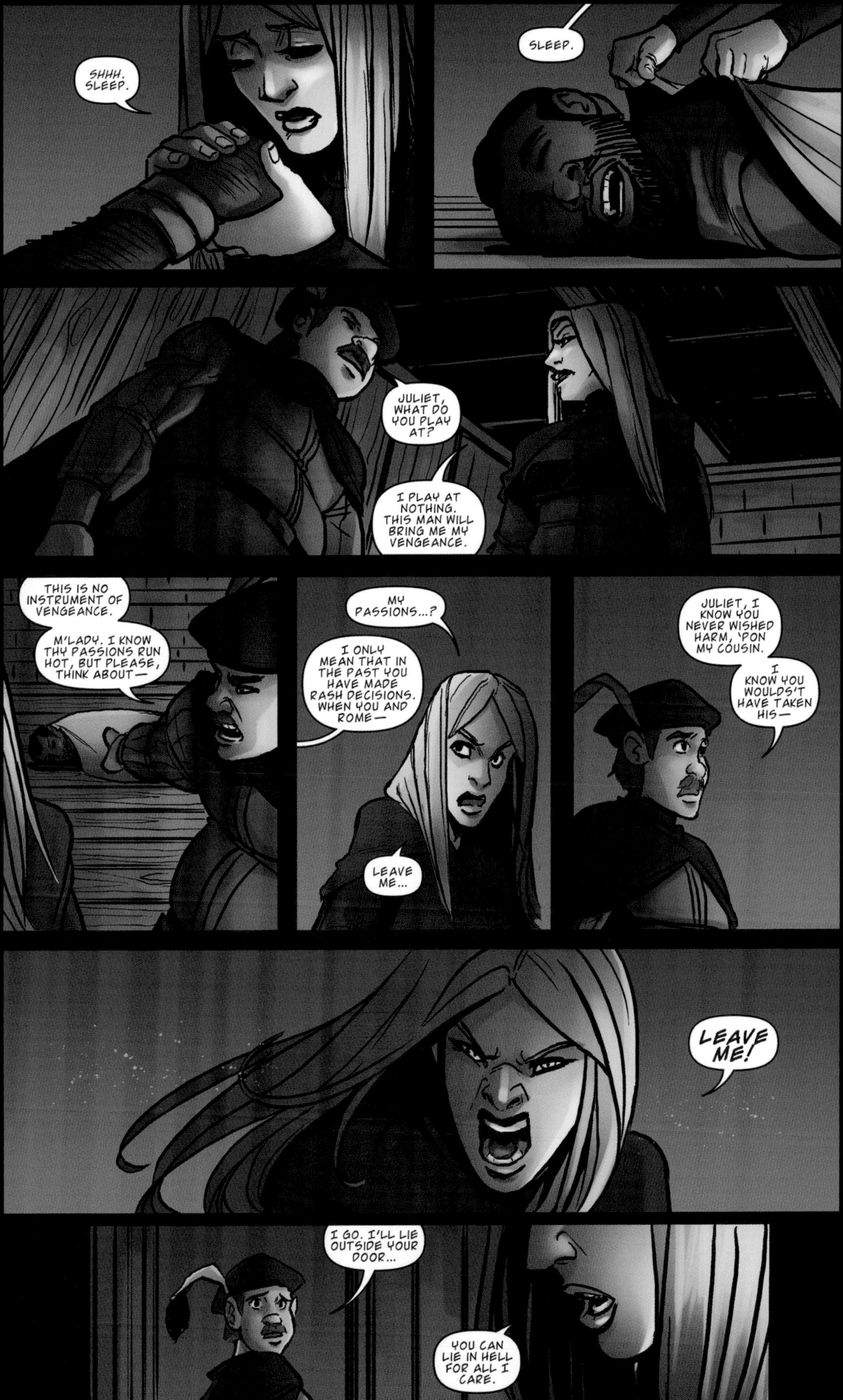
SHHH. SLEEP.
SLEEP.
JULIET, WHAT DO YOU PLAY AT?
I PLAY AT NOTHING. THIS MAN WILL BRING ME MY VENGEANCE.
THIS IS NO INSTRUMENT OF VENGEANCE.
M'LADY. I KNOW THY PASSIONS RUN HOT, BUT PLEASE, THINK ABOUT—
MY PASSIONS...?
I ONLY MEAN THAT IN THE PAST YOU HAVE MADE RASH DECISIONS. WHEN YOU AND ROME—
LEAVE ME...
JULIET, I KNOW YOU NEVER WISHED HARM, 'PON MY COUSIN.
I KNOW YOU WOULDS'T HAVE TAKEN HIS—
LEAVE ME!
I GO. I'LL LIE OUTSIDE YOUR DOOR...
YOU CAN LIE IN HELL FOR ALL I CARE.

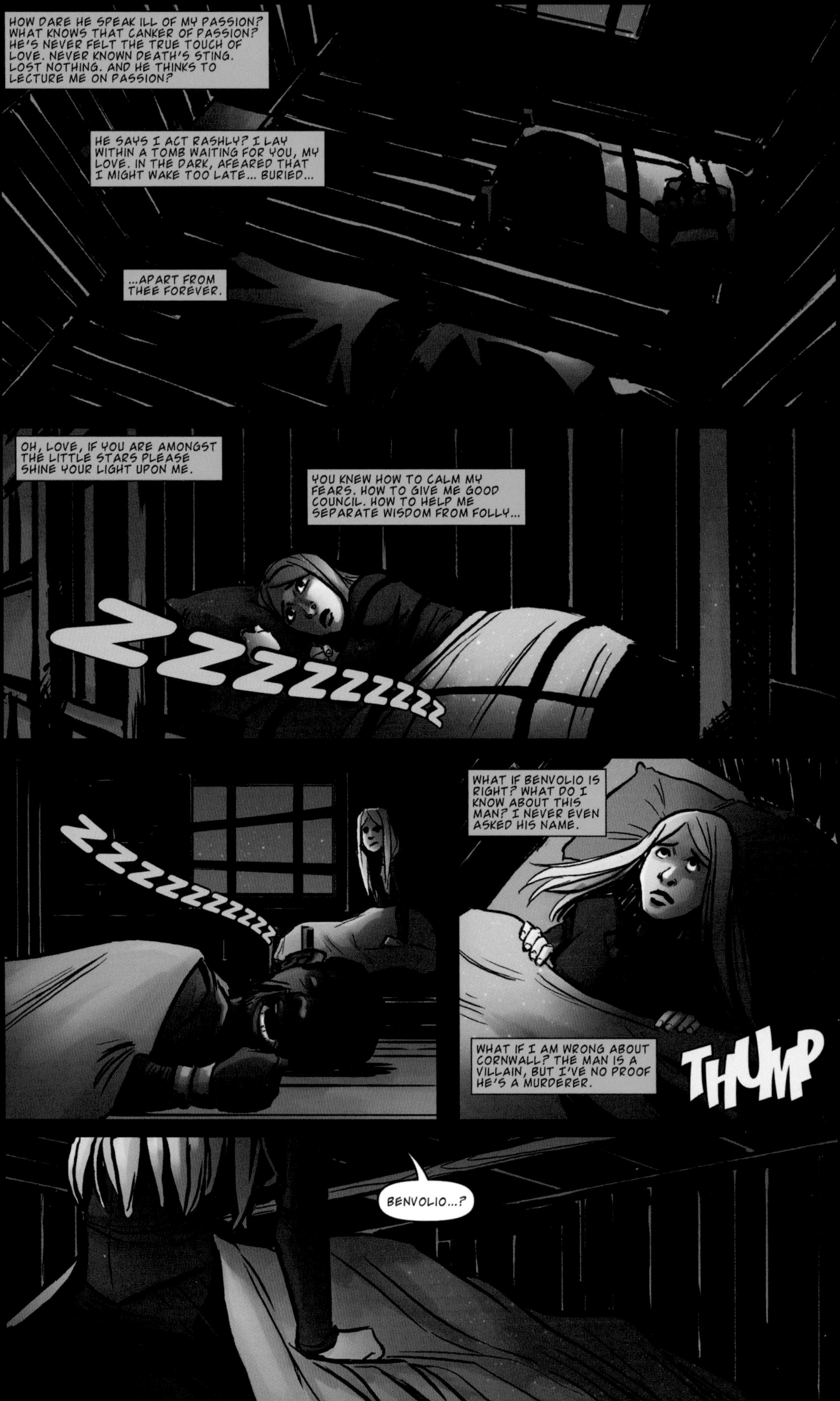
HOW DARE HE SPEAK ILL OF MY PASSION? WHAT KNOWS THAT CANKER OF PASSION? HE'S NEVER FELT THE TRUE TOUCH OF LOVE. NEVER KNOWN DEATH'S STING. LOST NOTHING. AND HE THINKS TO LECTURE ME ON PASSION?
HE SAYS I ACT RASHLY? I LAY WITHIN A TOMB WAITING FOR YOU, MY LOVE. IN THE DARK, AFEARED THAT I MIGHT WAKE TOO LATE... BURIED...
...APART FROM THEE FOREVER.
OH, LOVE, IF YOU ARE AMONGST THE LITTLE STARS PLEASE SHINE YOUR LIGHT UPON ME.
YOU KNEW HOW TO CALM MY FEARS. HOW TO GIVE ME GOOD COUNCIL. HOW TO HELP ME SEPARATE WISDOM FROM FOLLY...
ZZZZZZZZZZ
ZZZZZZZZZZZZ
WHAT IF BENVOLIO IS RIGHT? WHAT DO I KNOW ABOUT THIS MAN? I NEVER EVEN ASKED HIS NAME.
WHAT IF I AM WRONG ABOUT CORNWALL? THE MAN IS A VILLAIN, BUT I'VE NO PROOF HE'S A MURDERER.
THUMP
BENVOLIO...?

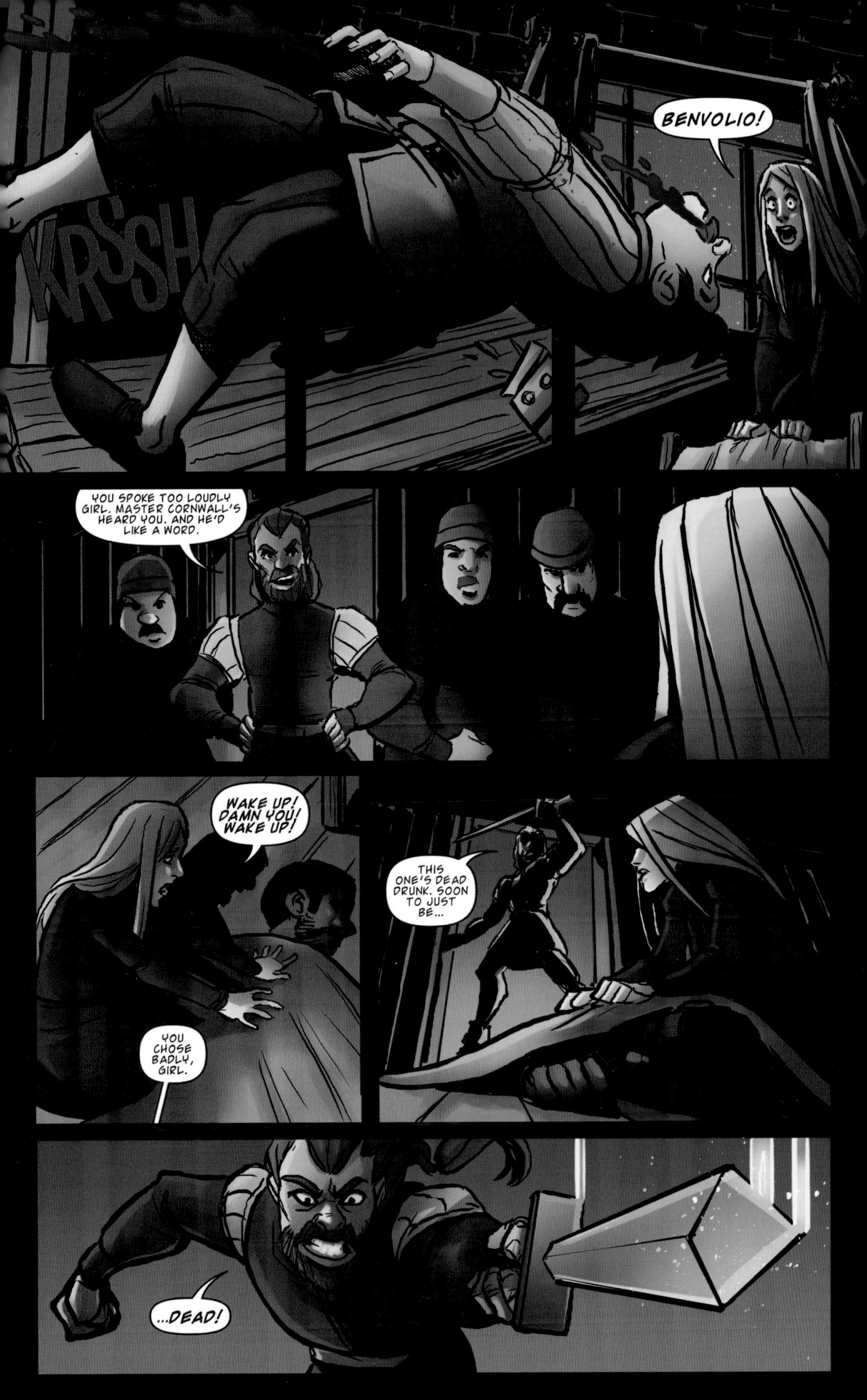
KRSSH
BENVOLIO!
YOU SPOKE TOO LOUDLY GIRL. MASTER CORNWALL'S HEARD YOU. AND HE'D LIKE A WORD.
WAKE UP! DAMN YOU! WAKE UP!
YOU CHOSE BADLY, GIRL.
THIS ONE'S DEAD DRUNK. SOON TO JUST BE...
...DEAD!

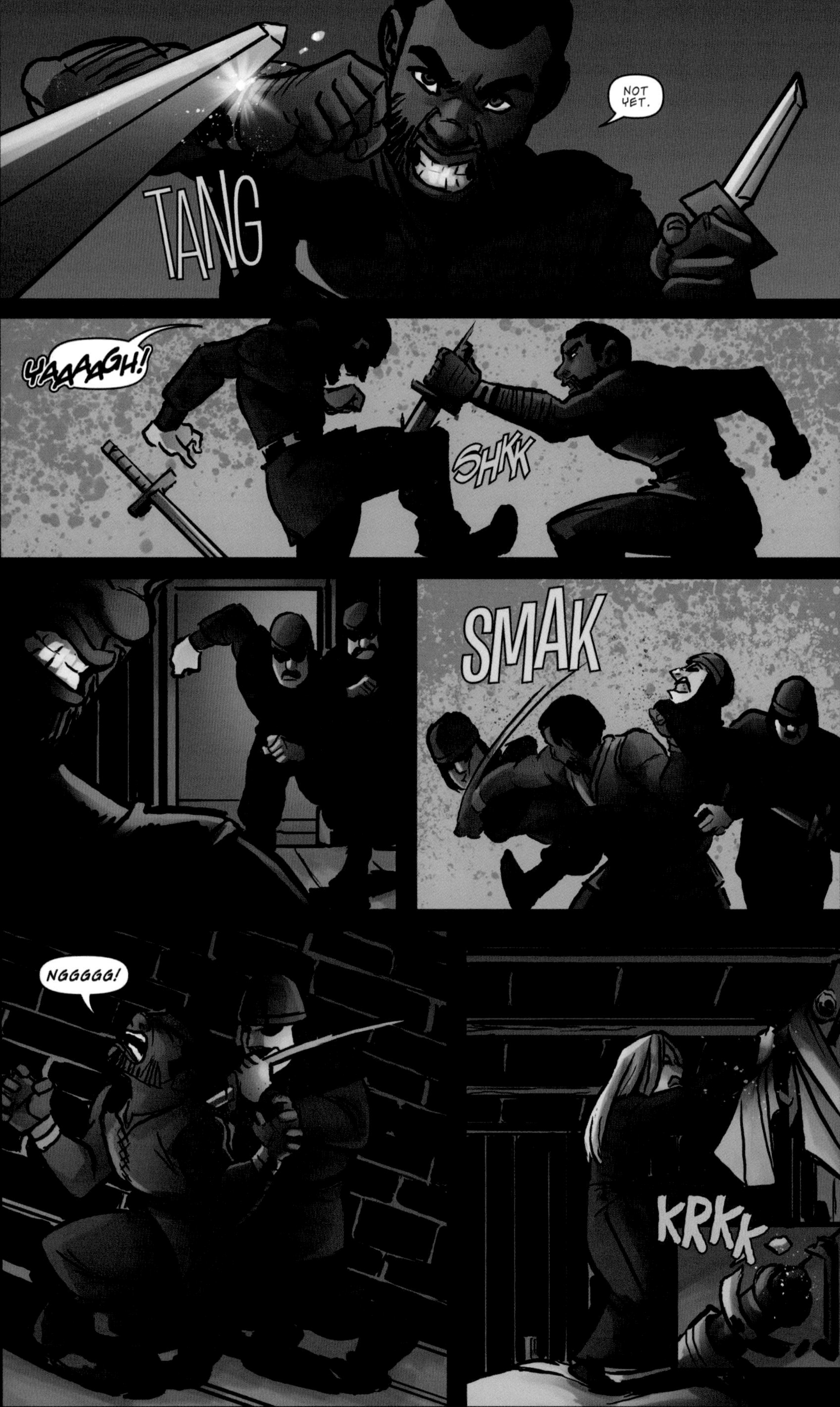
NOT YET.
TANG
YAAAAAGH!
SHKK
SMAK
NGGGGG!
KRKK

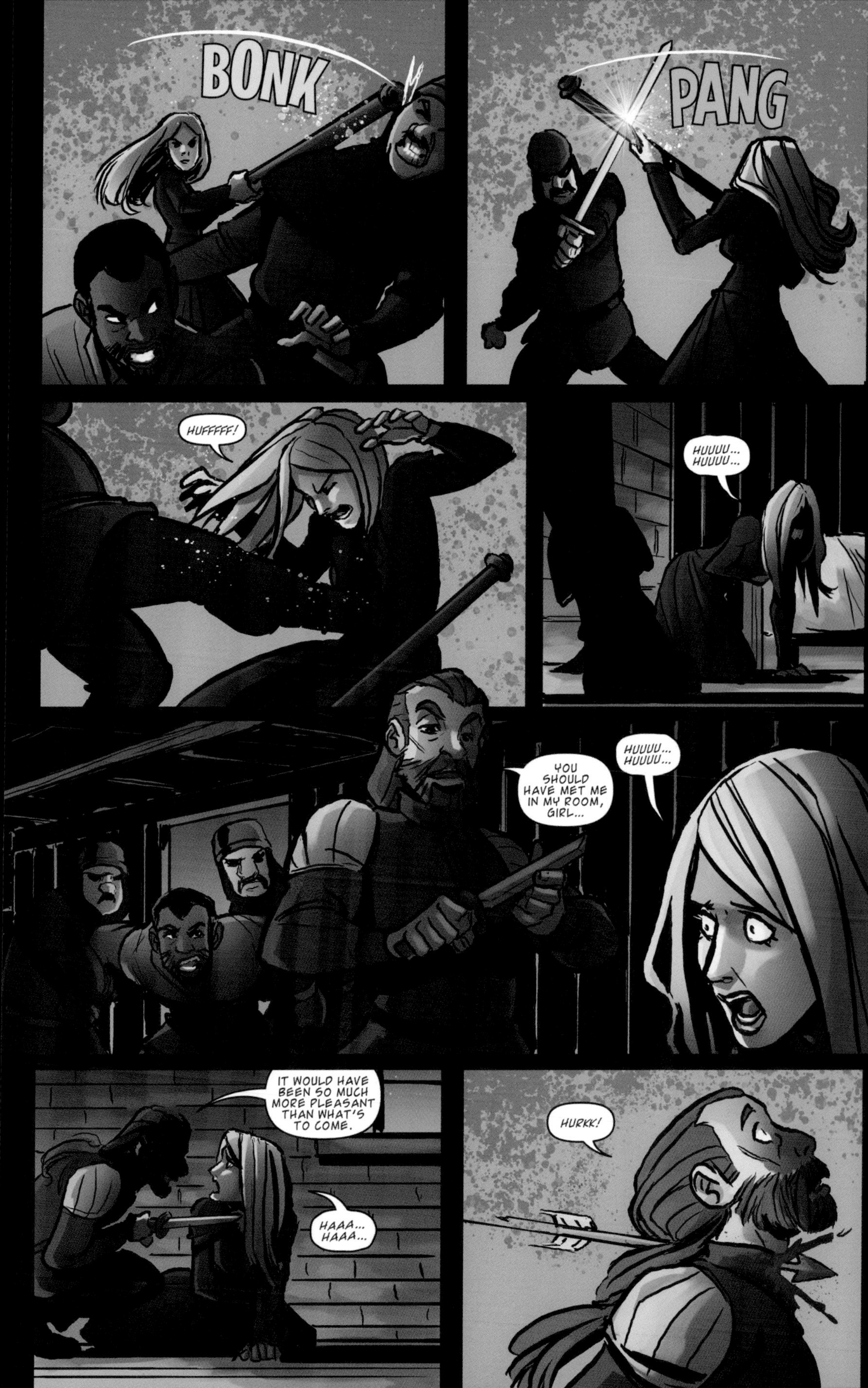
BONK
PANG
HUFFFFF!
HUUUU... HUUUU...
YOU SHOULD HAVE MET ME IN MY ROOM, GIRL...
HUUUU... HUUUU...
IT WOULD HAVE BEEN SO MUCH MORE PLEASANT THAN WHAT'S TO COME.
HAAA... HAAA...
HURKK!

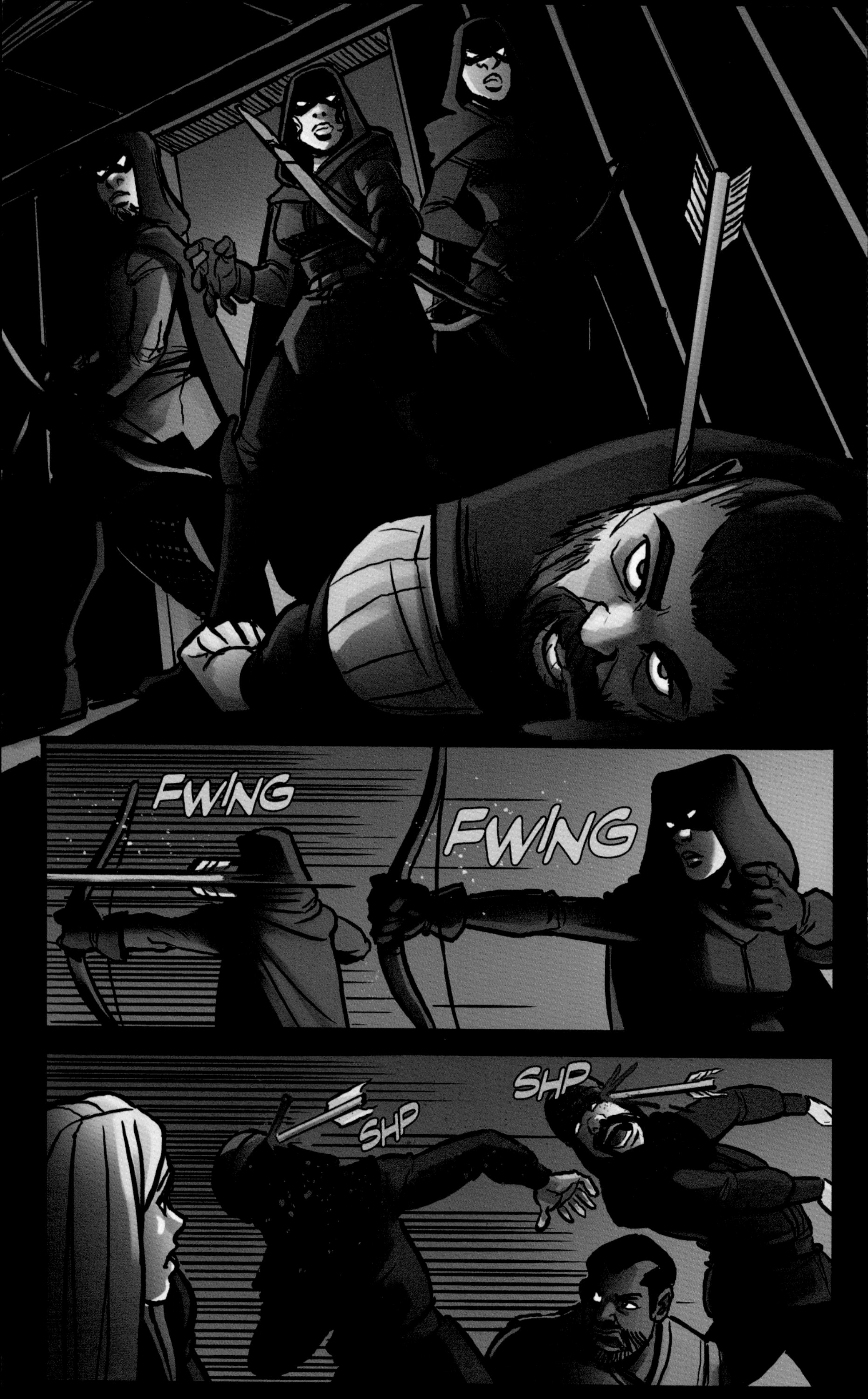
FWING
FWING
SHP
SHP

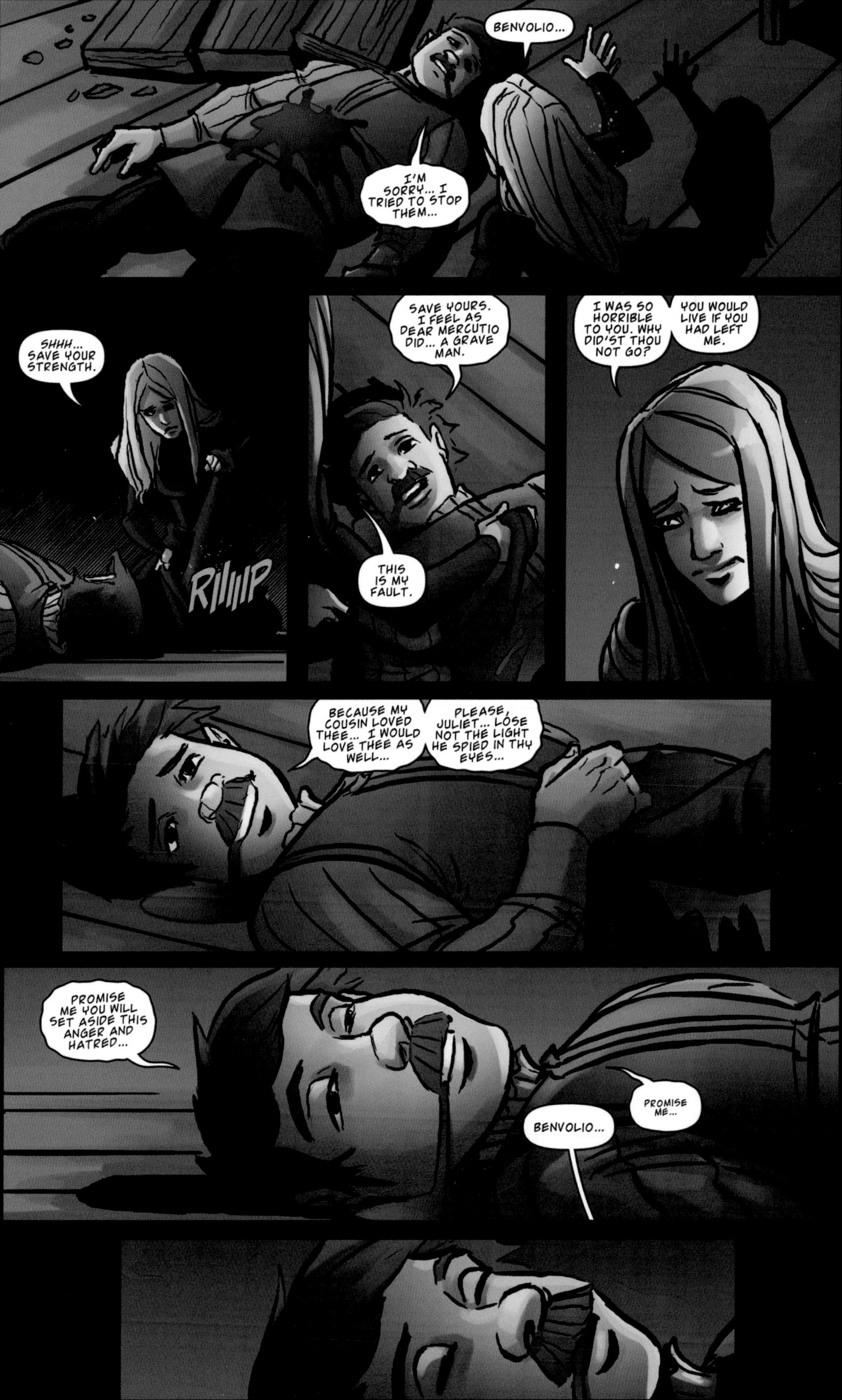
BENVOLIO...
I'M SORRY... I TRIED TO STOP THEM...
SHHH... SAVE YOUR STRENGTH.
RIIIIP
SAVE YOURS. I FEEL AS DEAR MERCUTIO DID... A GRAVE MAN.
THIS IS MY FAULT.
I WAS SO HORRIBLE TO YOU. WHY DID'ST THOU NOT GO?
YOU WOULD LIVE IF YOU HAD LEFT ME.
BECAUSE MY COUSIN LOVED THEE... I WOULD LOVE THEE AS WELL...
PLEASE, JULIET... LOSE NOT THE LIGHT HE SPIED IN THY EYES...
PROMISE ME YOU WILL SET ASIDE THIS ANGER AND HATRED...
PROMISE ME...
BENVOLIO...

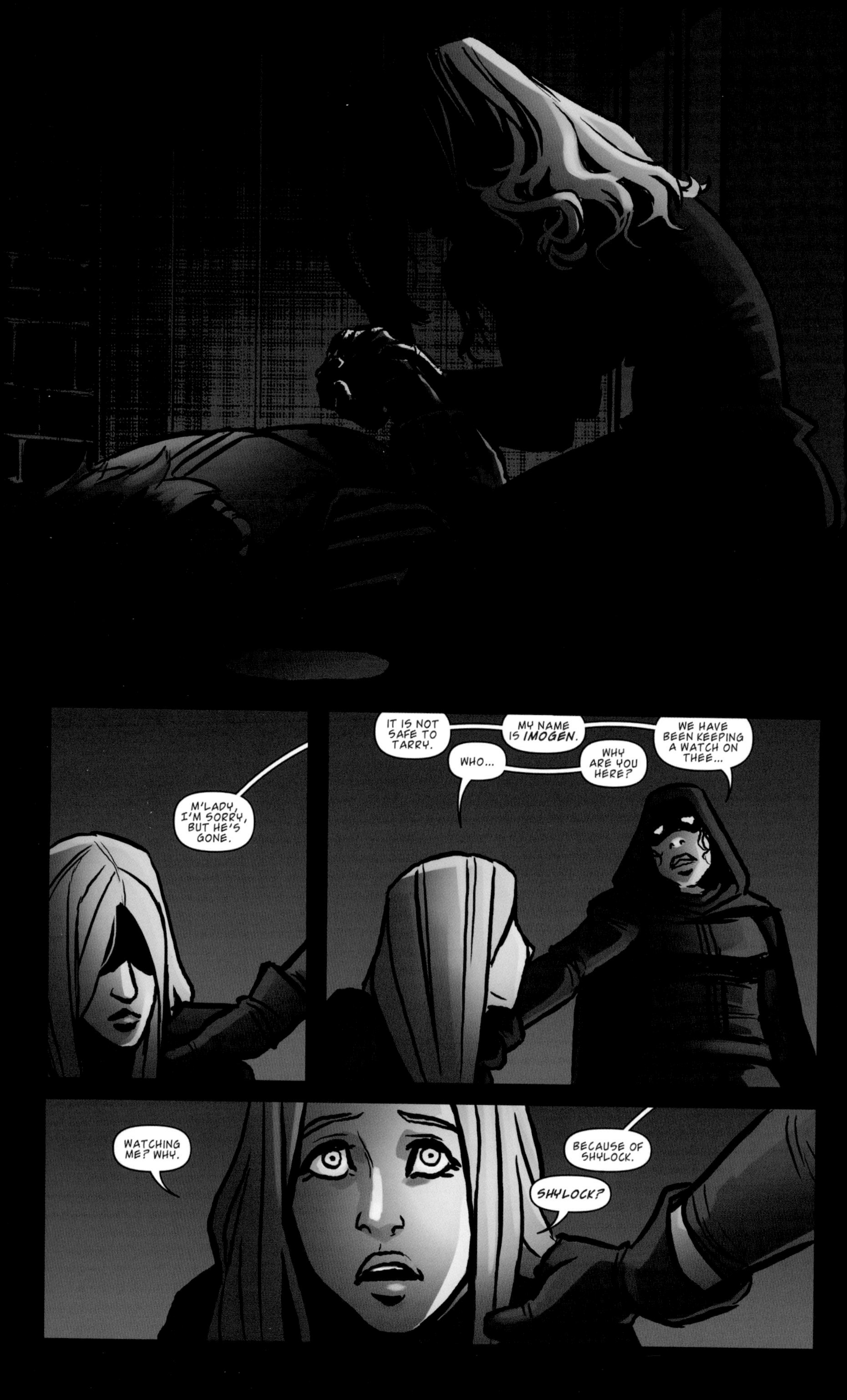
M'LADY, I'M SORRY, BUT HE'S GONE.
IT IS NOT SAFE TO TARRY.
WHO...
MY NAME IS IMOGEN.
WHY ARE YOU HERE?
WE HAVE BEEN KEEPING A WATCH ON THEE...
WATCHING ME? WHY.
BECAUSE OF SHYLOCK.
SHYLOCK?

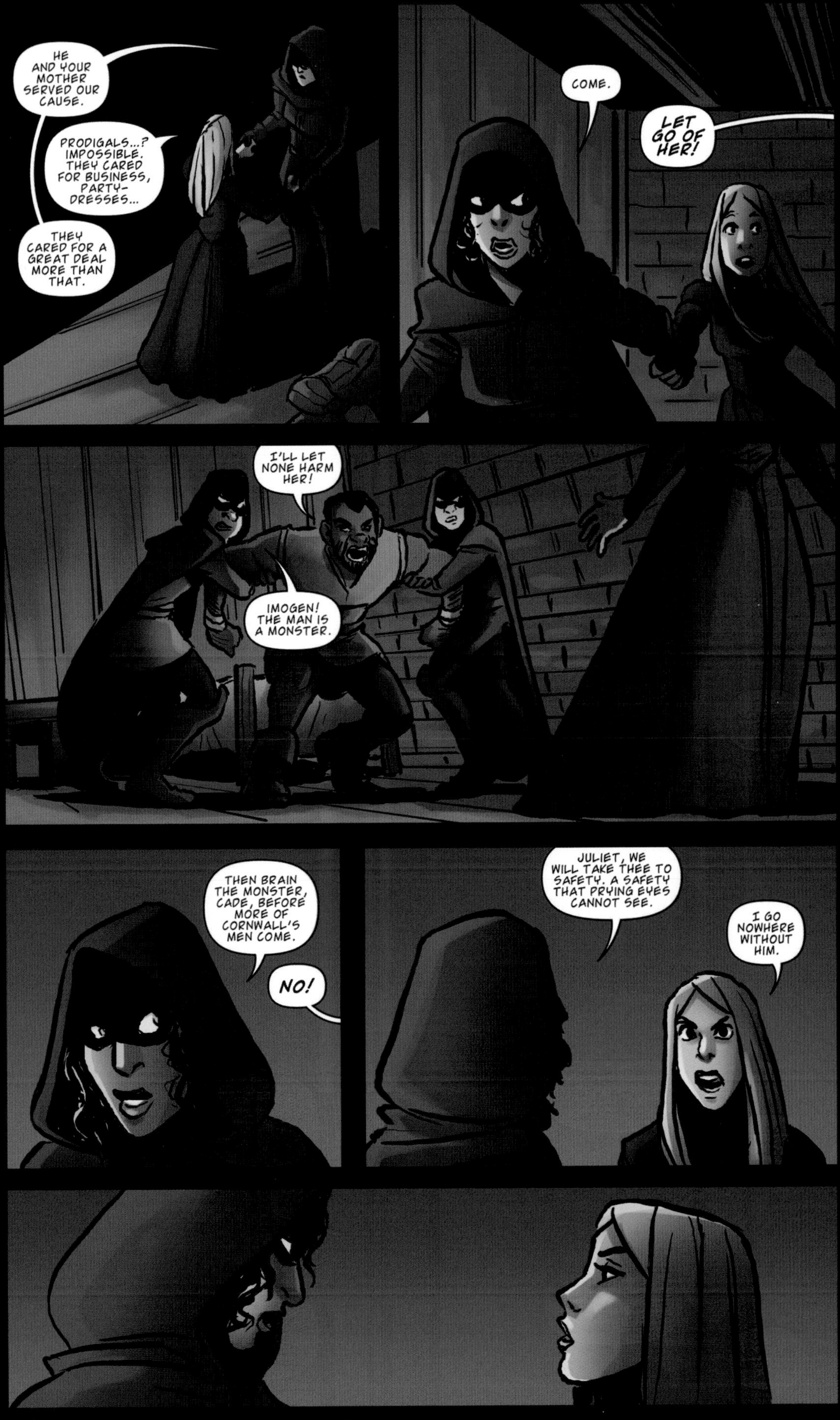
HE AND YOUR MOTHER SERVED OUR CAUSE.
PRODIGALS...? IMPOSSIBLE. THEY CARED FOR BUSINESS, PARTY-DRESSES...
THEY CARED FOR A GREAT DEAL MORE THAN THAT.
COME.
LET GO OF HER!
I'LL LET NONE HARM HER!
IMOGEN! THE MAN IS A MONSTER.
THEN BRAIN THE MONSTER, CADE, BEFORE MORE OF CORNWALL'S MEN COME.
NO!
JULIET, WE WILL TAKE THEE TO SAFETY. A SAFETY THAT PRYING EYES CANNOT SEE.
I GO NOWHERE WITHOUT HIM.

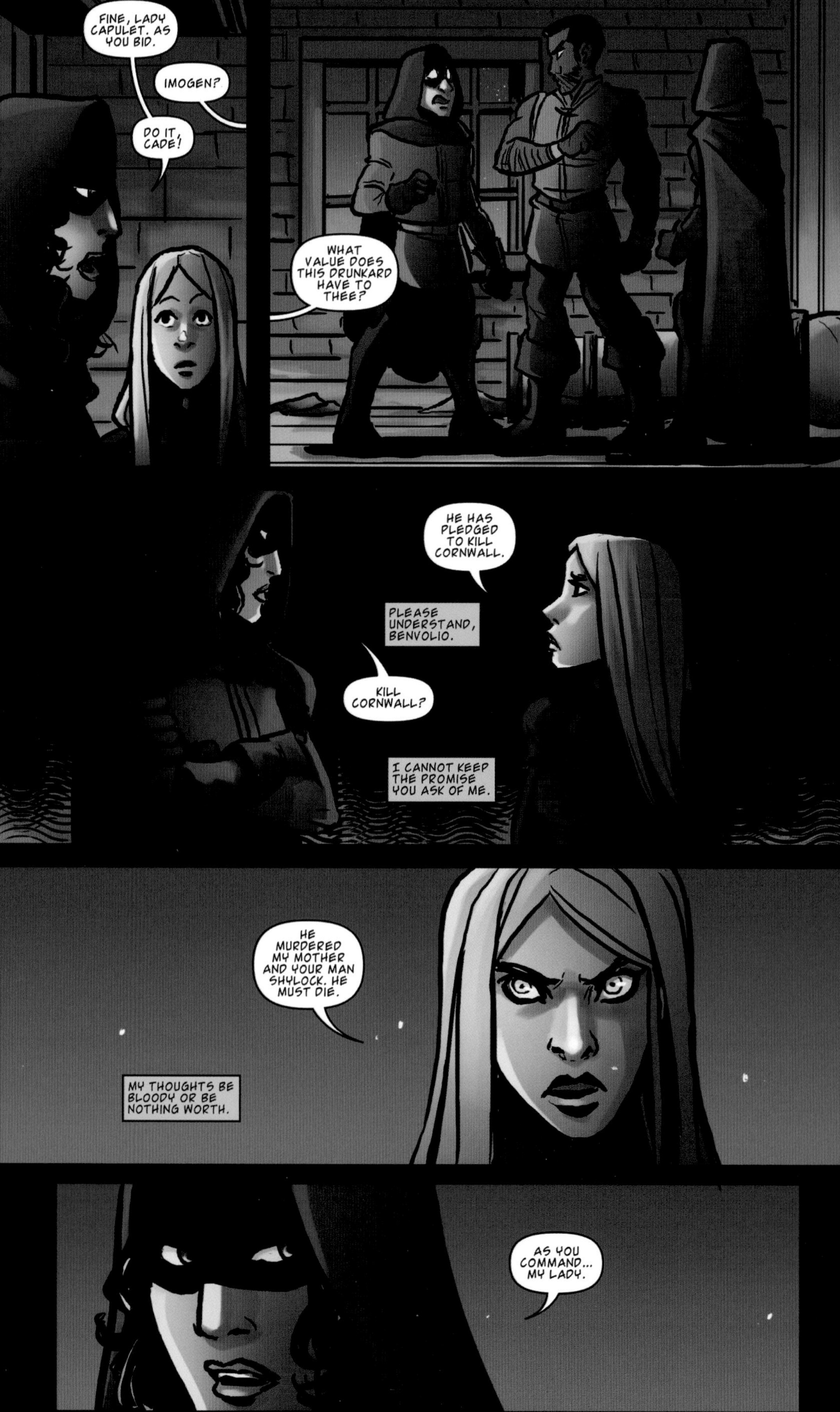
FINE, LADY CAPULET. AS YOU BID.
IMOGEN?
DO IT, CADE!
WHAT VALUE DOES THIS DRUNKARD HAVE TO THEE?
HE HAS PLEDGED TO KILL CORNWALL.
PLEASE UNDERSTAND, BENVOLIO.
KILL CORNWALL?
I CANNOT KEEP THE PROMISE YOU ASK OF ME.
HE MURDERED MY MOTHER AND YOUR MAN SHYLOCK. HE MUST DIE.
MY THOUGHTS BE BLOODY OR BE NOTHING WORTH.
AS YOU COMMAND... MY LADY.

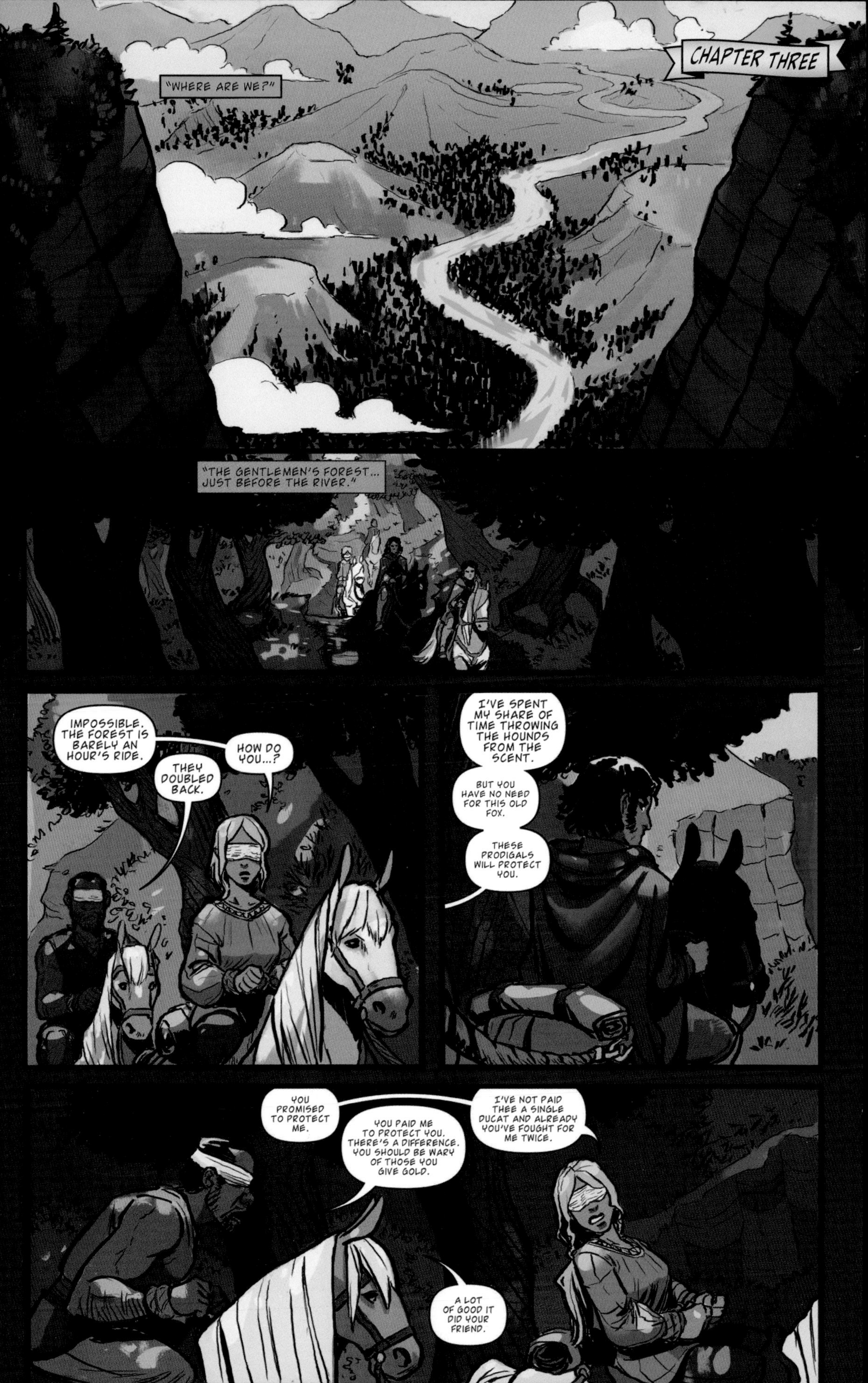
CHAPTER THREE
"WHERE ARE WE?"
"THE GENTLEMEN'S FOREST... JUST BEFORE THE RIVER."
IMPOSSIBLE. THE FOREST IS BARELY AN HOUR'S RIDE.
HOW DO YOU...?
THEY DOUBLED BACK.
I'VE SPENT MY SHARE OF TIME THROWING THE HOUNDS FROM THE SCENT.
BUT YOU HAVE NO NEED FOR THIS OLD FOX.
THESE PRODIGALS WILL PROTECT YOU.
YOU PROMISED TO PROTECT ME.
I'VE NOT PAID THEE A SINGLE DUCAT AND ALREADY YOU'VE FOUGHT FOR ME TWICE.
YOU PAID ME TO PROTECT YOU. THERE'S A DIFFERENCE. YOU SHOULD BE WARY OF THOSE YOU GIVE GOLD.
A LOT OF GOOD IT DID YOUR FRIEND.

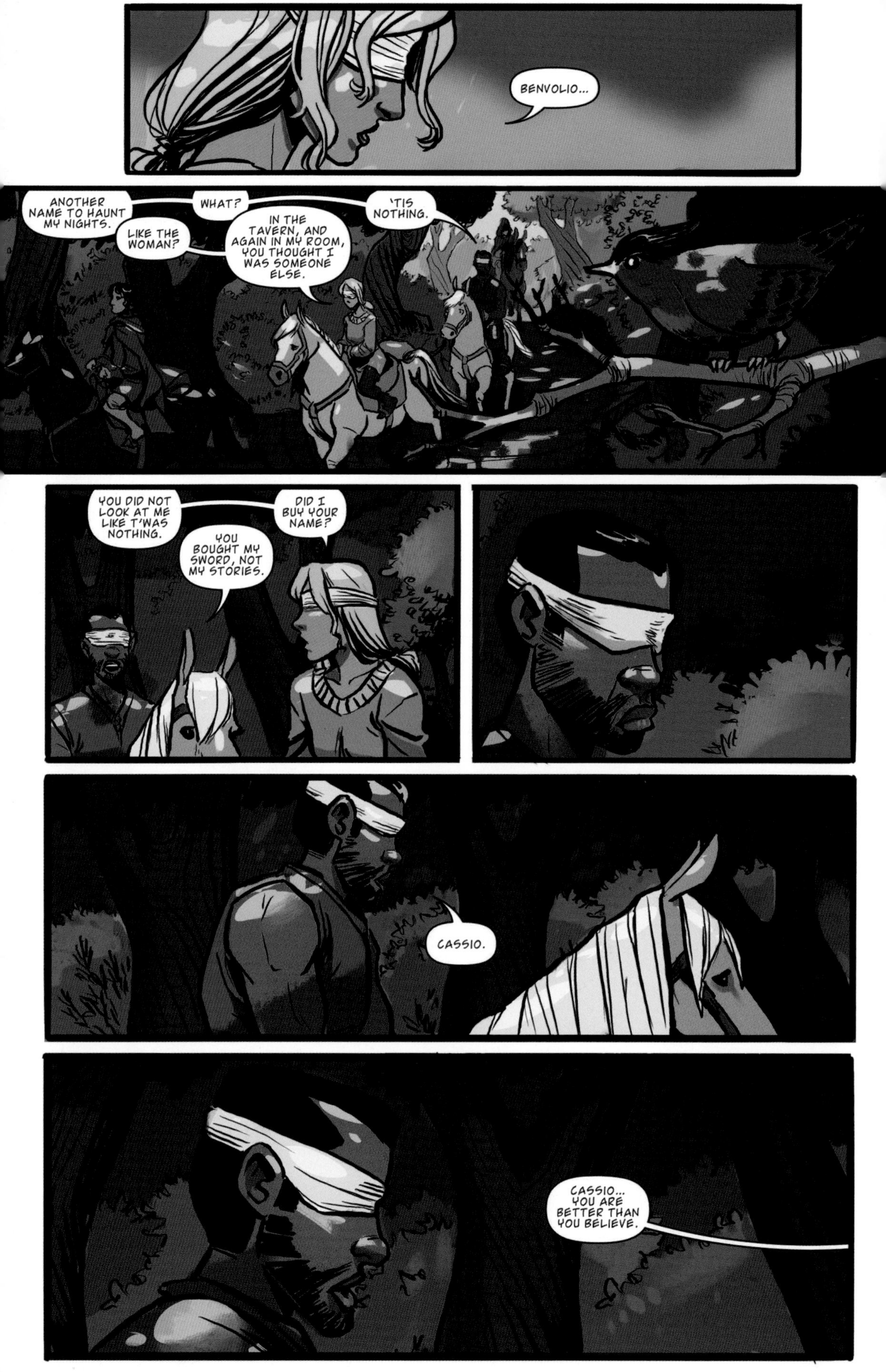
BENVOLIO...
ANOTHER NAME TO HAUNT MY NIGHTS.
WHAT?
'TIS NOTHING.
LIKE THE WOMAN?
IN THE TAVERN, AND AGAIN IN MY ROOM, YOU THOUGHT I WAS SOMEONE ELSE.
YOU DID NOT LOOK AT ME LIKE T'WAS NOTHING.
DID I BUY YOUR NAME?
YOU BOUGHT MY SWORD, NOT MY STORIES.
CASSIO.
CASSIO... YOU ARE BETTER THAN YOU BELIEVE.

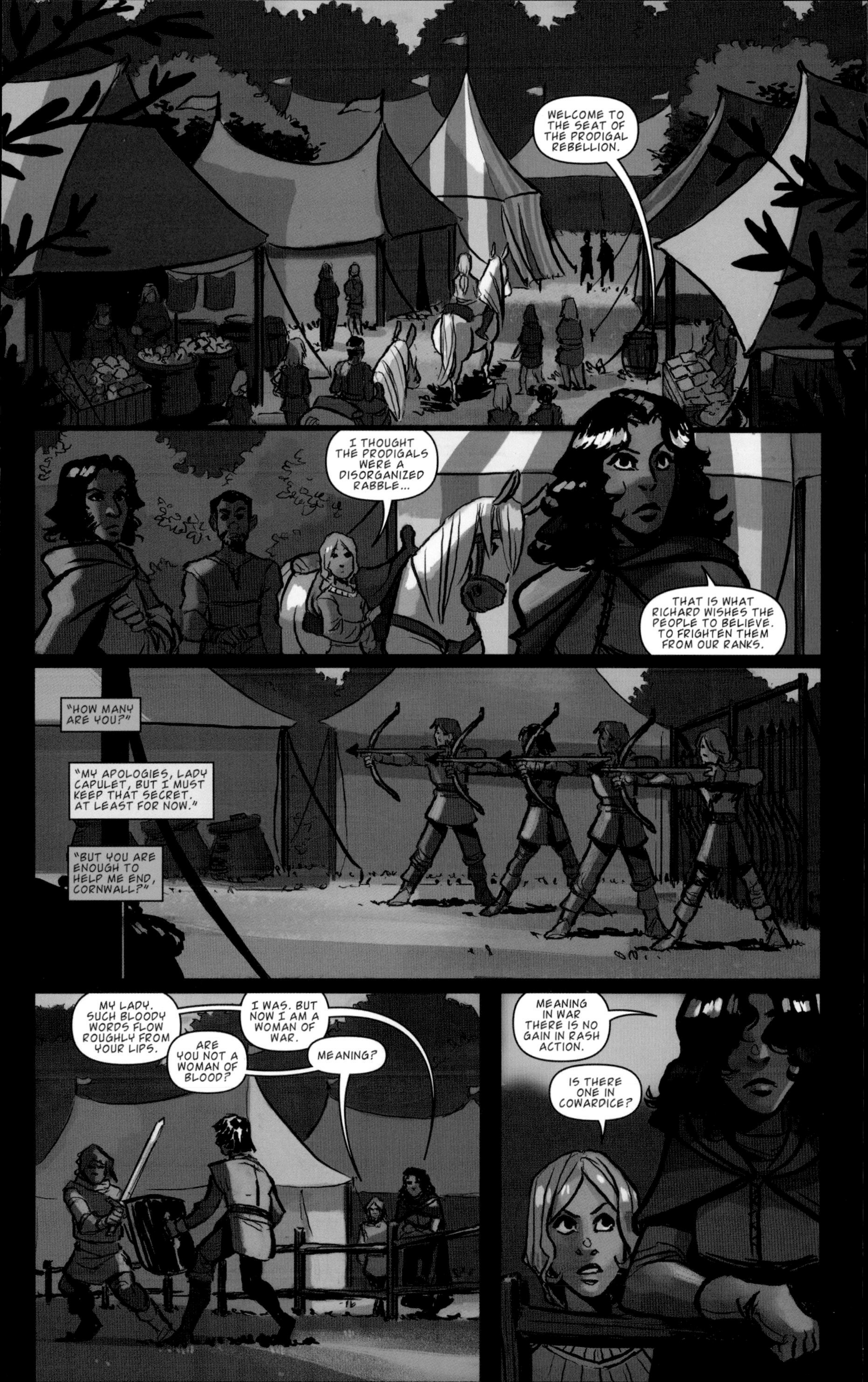
WELCOME TO THE SEAT OF THE PRODIGAL REBELLION.
I THOUGHT THE PRODIGALS WERE A DISORGANIZED RABBLE...
THAT IS WHAT RICHARD WISHES THE PEOPLE TO BELIEVE. TO FRIGHTEN THEM FROM OUR RANKS.
"HOW MANY ARE YOU?"
"MY APOLOGIES, LADY CAPULET, BUT I MUST KEEP THAT SECRET. AT LEAST FOR NOW."
"BUT YOU ARE ENOUGH TO HELP ME END, CORNWALL?"
MY LADY. SUCH BLOODY WORDS FLOW ROUGHLY FROM YOUR LIPS.
ARE YOU NOT A WOMAN OF BLOOD?
I WAS. BUT NOW I AM A WOMAN OF WAR.
MEANING?
MEANING IN WAR THERE IS NO GAIN IN RASH ACTION.
IS THERE ONE IN COWARDICE?

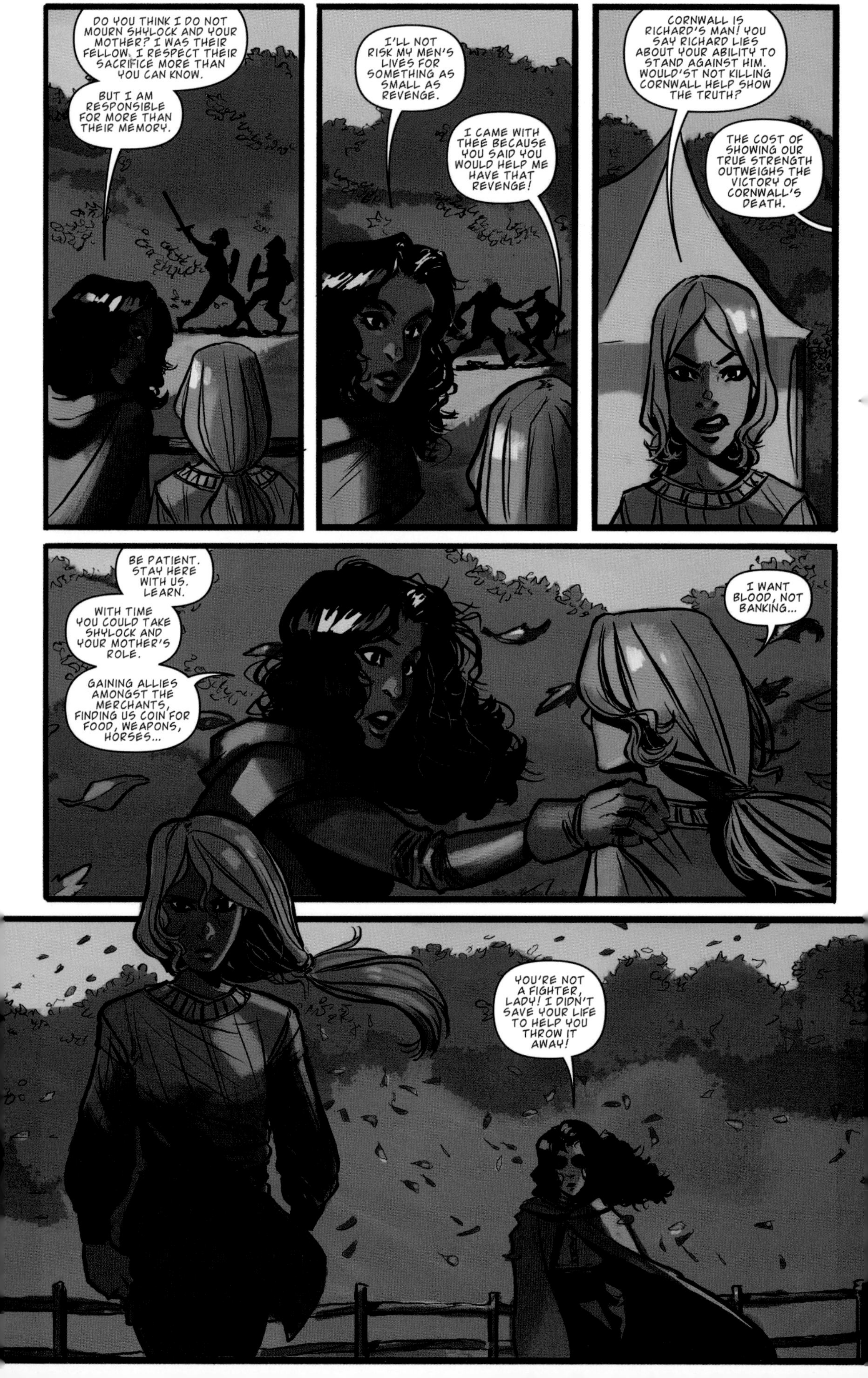
DO YOU THINK I DO NOT MOURN SHYLOCK AND YOUR MOTHER? I WAS THEIR FELLOW. I RESPECT THEIR SACRIFICE MORE THAN YOU CAN KNOW.
BUT I AM RESPONSIBLE FOR MORE THAN THEIR MEMORY.
I'LL NOT RISK MY MEN'S LIVES FOR SOMETHING AS SMALL AS REVENGE.
I CAME WITH THEE BECAUSE YOU SAID YOU WOULD HELP ME HAVE THAT REVENGE!
CORNWALL IS RICHARD'S MAN! YOU SAY RICHARD LIES ABOUT YOUR ABILITY TO STAND AGAINST HIM. WOULD'ST NOT KILLING CORNWALL HELP SHOW THE TRUTH?
THE COST OF SHOWING OUR TRUE STRENGTH OUTWEIGHS THE VICTORY OF CORNWALL'S DEATH.
BE PATIENT. STAY HERE WITH US. LEARN.
WITH TIME YOU COULD TAKE SHYLOCK AND YOUR MOTHER'S ROLE.
GAINING ALLIES AMONGST THE MERCHANTS, FINDING US COIN FOR FOOD, WEAPONS, HORSES...
I WANT BLOOD, NOT BANKING...
YOU'RE NOT A FIGHTER, LADY! I DIDN'T SAVE YOUR LIFE TO HELP YOU THROW IT AWAY!

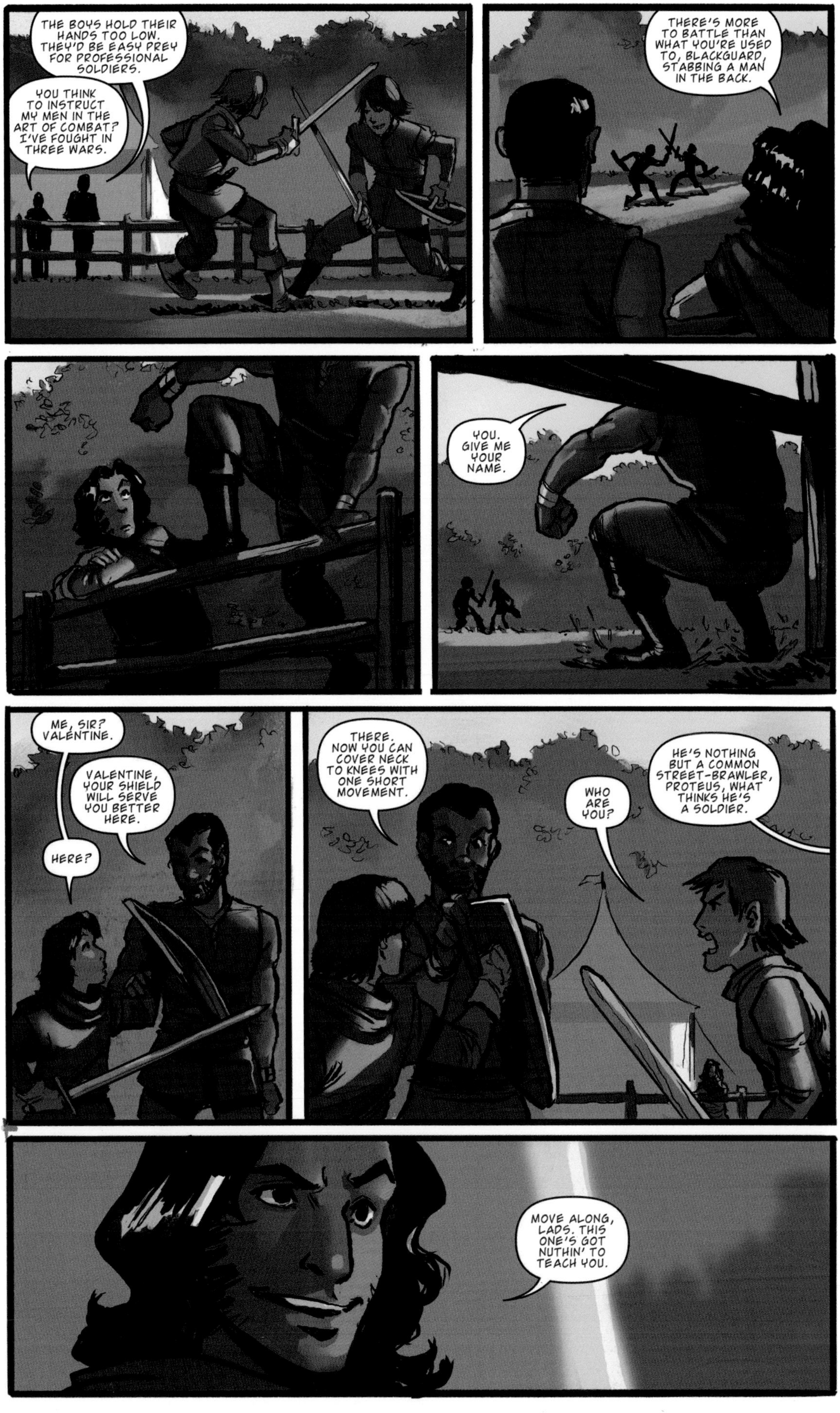
THE BOYS HOLD THEIR HANDS TOO LOW. THEY'D BE EASY PREY FOR PROFESSIONAL SOLDIERS.
YOU THINK TO INSTRUCT MY MEN IN THE ART OF COMBAT? I'VE FOUGHT IN THREE WARS.
THERE'S MORE TO BATTLE THAN WHAT YOU'RE USED TO, BLACKGUARD, STABBING A MAN IN THE BACK.
YOU. GIVE ME YOUR NAME.
ME, SIR? VALENTINE.
VALENTINE, YOUR SHIELD WILL SERVE YOU BETTER HERE.
HERE?
THERE. NOW YOU CAN COVER NECK TO KNEES WITH ONE SHORT MOVEMENT.
WHO ARE YOU?
HE'S NOTHING BUT A COMMON STREET-BRAWLER, PROTEUS, WHAT THINKS HE'S A SOLDIER.
MOVE ALONG, LADS. THIS ONE'S GOT NUTHIN' TO TEACH YOU.

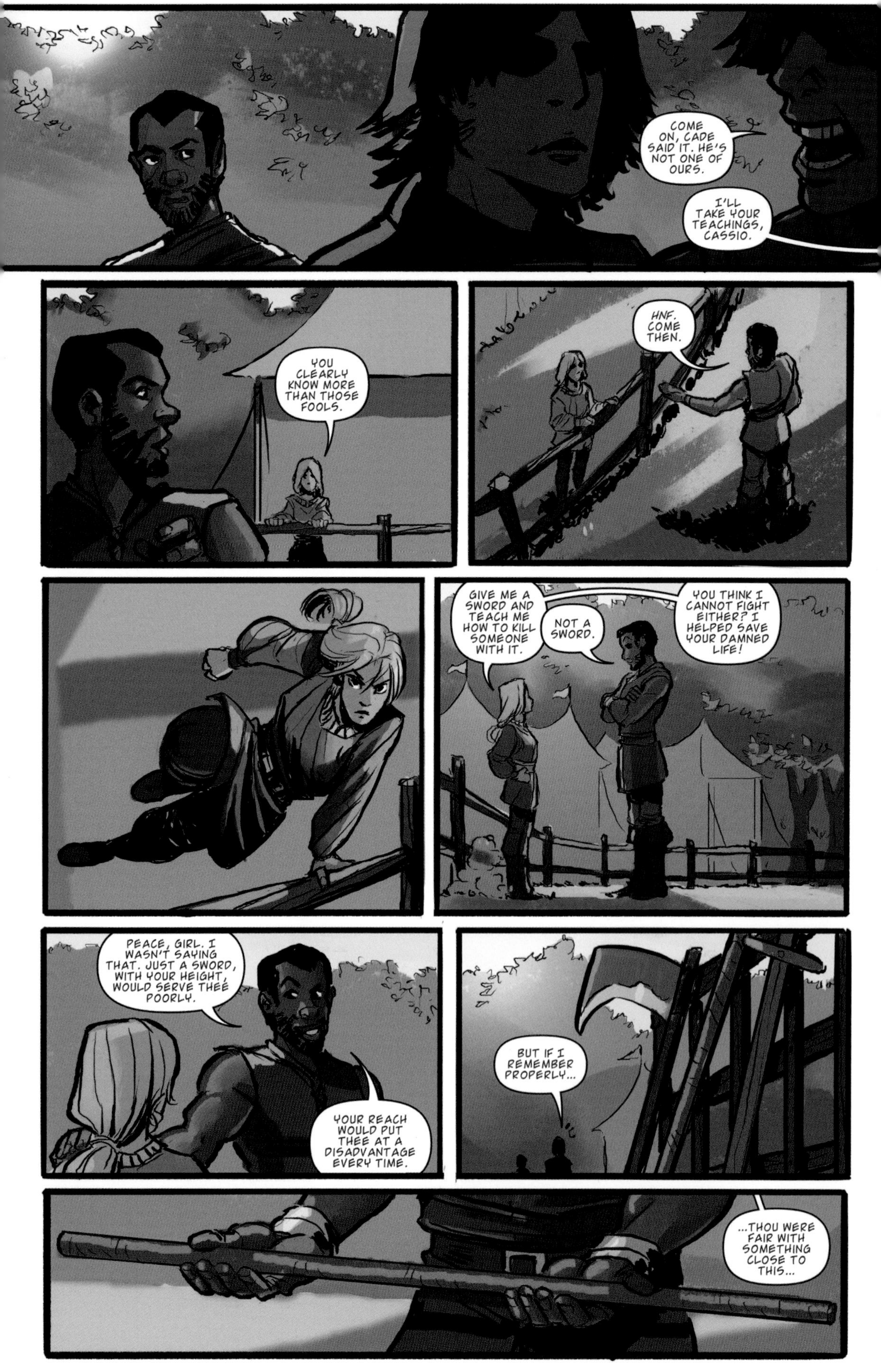
COME ON, CADE SAID IT. HE'S NOT ONE OF OURS.
I'LL TAKE YOUR TEACHINGS, CASSIO.
YOU CLEARLY KNOW MORE THAN THOSE FOOLS.
HNF. COME THEN.
GIVE ME A SWORD AND TEACH ME HOW TO KILL SOMEONE WITH IT.
NOT A SWORD.
YOU THINK I CANNOT FIGHT EITHER? I HELPED SAVE YOUR DAMNED LIFE!
PEACE, GIRL. I WASN'T SAYING THAT. JUST A SWORD, WITH YOUR HEIGHT, WOULD SERVE THEE POORLY.
YOUR REACH WOULD PUT THEE AT A DISADVANTAGE EVERY TIME.
BUT IF I REMEMBER PROPERLY...
...THOU WERE FAIR WITH SOMETHING CLOSE TO THIS...

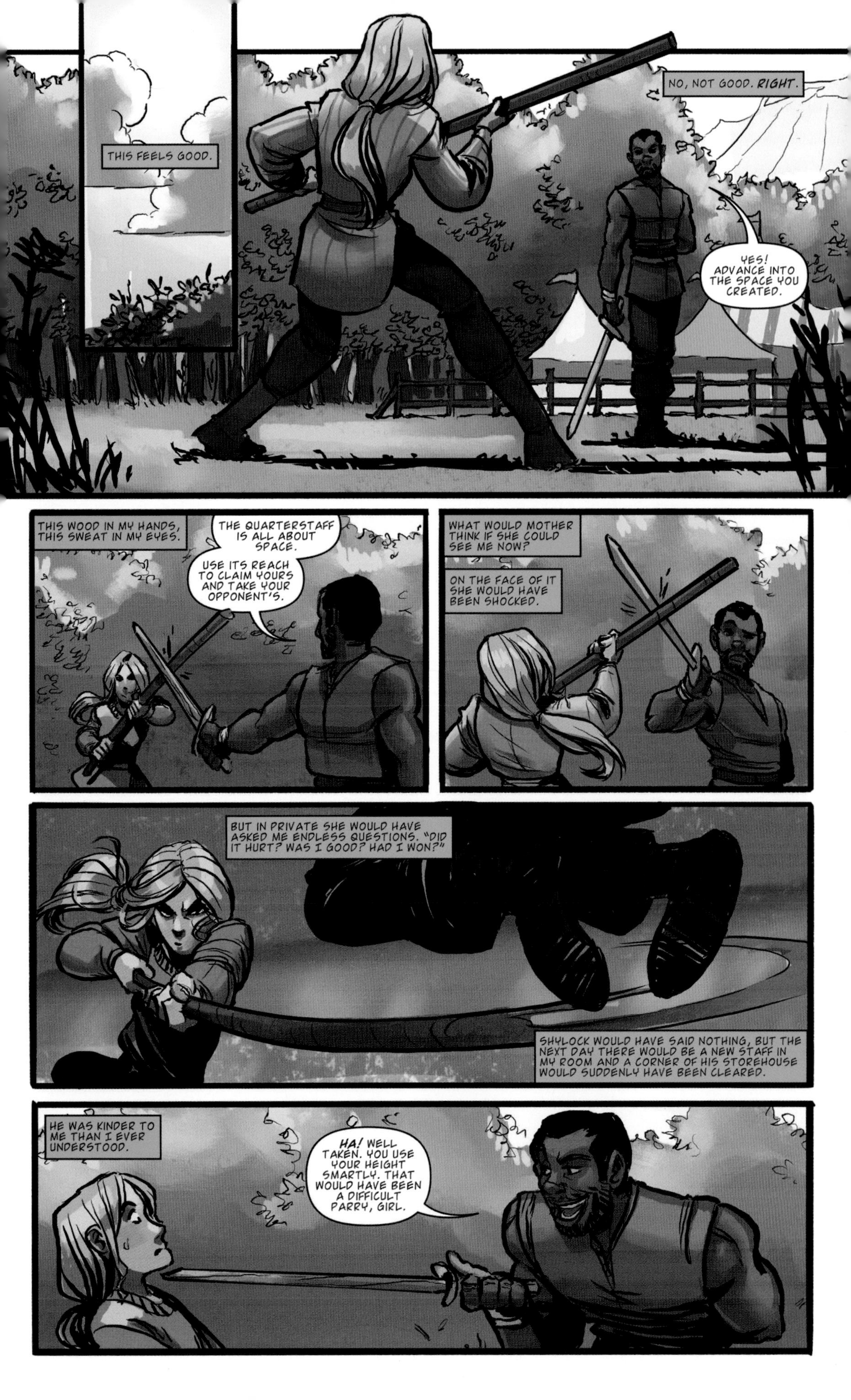
THIS FEELS GOOD.
NO, NOT GOOD. RIGHT.
YES! ADVANCE INTO THE SPACE YOU CREATED.
THIS WOOD IN MY HANDS, THIS SWEAT IN MY EYES.
THE QUARTERSTAFF IS ALL ABOUT SPACE.
USE ITS REACH TO CLAIM YOURS AND TAKE YOUR OPPONENT'S.
WHAT WOULD MOTHER THINK IF SHE COULD SEE ME NOW?
ON THE FACE OF IT SHE WOULD HAVE BEEN SHOCKED.
BUT IN PRIVATE SHE WOULD HAVE ASKED ME ENDLESS QUESTIONS. "DID IT HURT? WAS I GOOD? HAD I WON?"
SHYLOCK WOULD HAVE SAID NOTHING, BUT THE NEXT DAY THERE WOULD BE A NEW STAFF IN MY ROOM AND A CORNER OF HIS STOREHOUSE WOULD SUDDENLY HAVE BEEN CLEARED.
HE WAS KINDER TO ME THAN I EVER UNDERSTOOD.
HA! WELL TAKEN. YOU USE YOUR HEIGHT SMARTLY. THAT WOULD HAVE BEEN A DIFFICULT PARRY, GIRL.

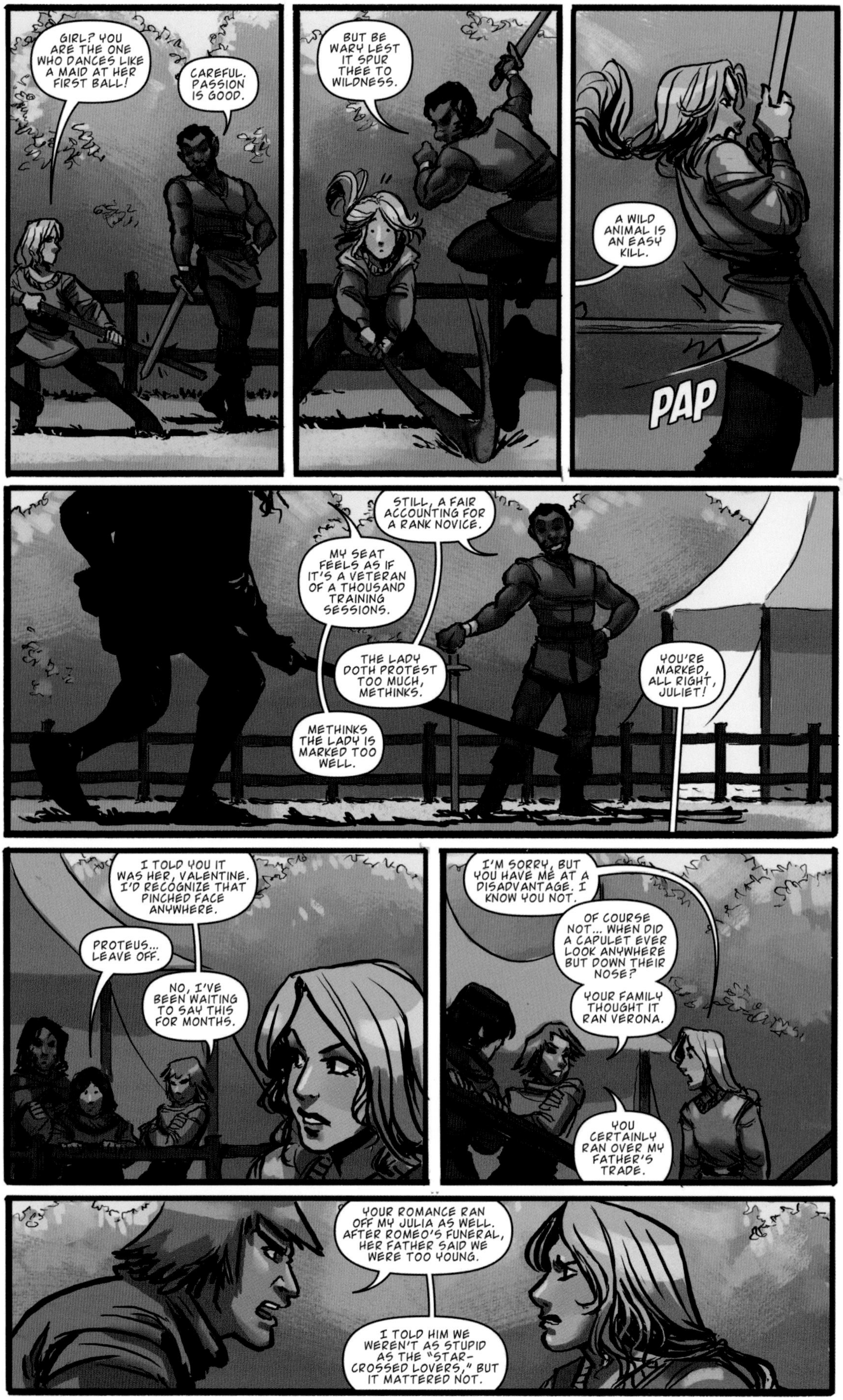
GIRL? YOU ARE THE ONE WHO DANCES LIKE A MAID AT HER FIRST BALL!
CAREFUL. PASSION IS GOOD.
BUT BE WARY LEST IT SPUR THEE TO WILDNESS.
A WILD ANIMAL IS AN EASY KILL.
PAP
STILL, A FAIR ACCOUNTING FOR A RANK NOVICE.
MY SEAT FEELS AS IF IT'S A VETERAN OF A THOUSAND TRAINING SESSIONS.
THE LADY DOTH PROTEST TOO MUCH, METHINKS.
METHINKS THE LADY IS MARKED TOO WELL.
YOU'RE MARKED, ALL RIGHT, JULIET!
I TOLD YOU IT WAS HER, VALENTINE. I'D RECOGNIZE THAT PINCHED FACE ANYWHERE.
PROTEUS... LEAVE OFF.
NO, I'VE BEEN WAITING TO SAY THIS FOR MONTHS.
I'M SORRY, BUT YOU HAVE ME AT A DISADVANTAGE. I KNOW YOU NOT.
OF COURSE NOT... WHEN DID A CAPULET EVER LOOK ANYWHERE BUT DOWN THEIR NOSE?
YOUR FAMILY THOUGHT IT RAN VERONA.
YOU CERTAINLY RAN OVER MY FATHER'S TRADE.
YOUR ROMANCE RAN OFF MY JULIA AS WELL. AFTER ROMEO'S FUNERAL, HER FATHER SAID WE WERE TOO YOUNG.
I TOLD HIM WE WEREN'T AS STUPID AS THE "STAR-CROSSED LOVERS," BUT IT MATTERED NOT.

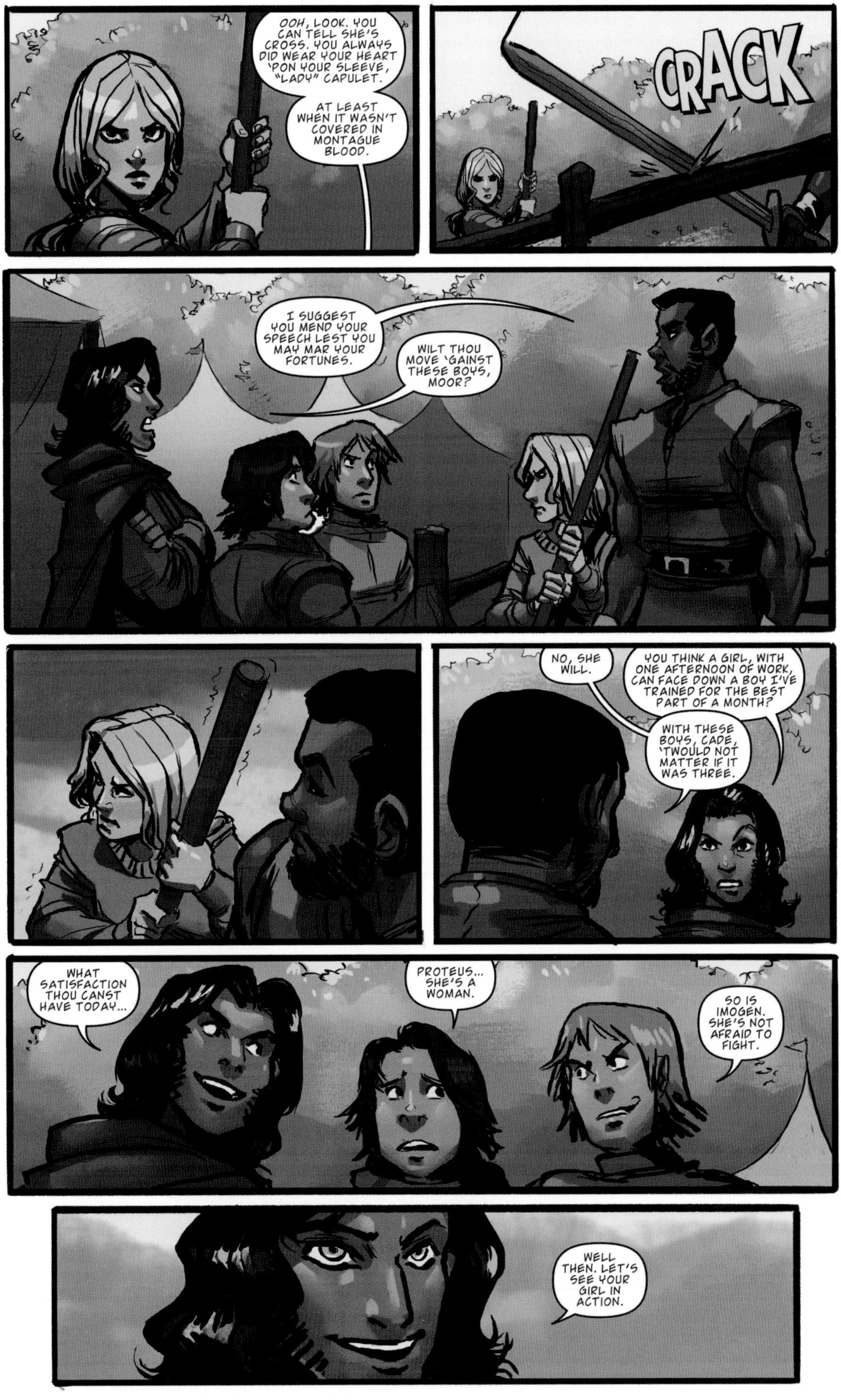
OOH, LOOK. YOU CAN TELL SHE'S CROSS. YOU ALWAYS DID WEAR YOUR HEART 'PON YOUR SLEEVE, "LADY" CAPULET.
AT LEAST WHEN IT WASN'T COVERED IN MONTAGUE BLOOD.
CRACK
I SUGGEST YOU MEND YOUR SPEECH LEST YOU MAY MAR YOUR FORTUNES.
WILT THOU MOVE 'GAINST THESE BOYS, MOOR?
NO, SHE WILL.
YOU THINK A GIRL, WITH ONE AFTERNOON OF WORK, CAN FACE DOWN A BOY I'VE TRAINED FOR THE BEST PART OF A MONTH?
WITH THESE BOYS, CADE, 'TWOULD NOT MATTER IF IT WAS THREE.
WHAT SATISFACTION THOU CANST HAVE TODAY...
PROTEUS... SHE'S A WOMAN.
SO IS IMOGEN. SHE'S NOT AFRAID TO FIGHT.
WELL THEN. LET'S SEE YOUR GIRL IN ACTION.

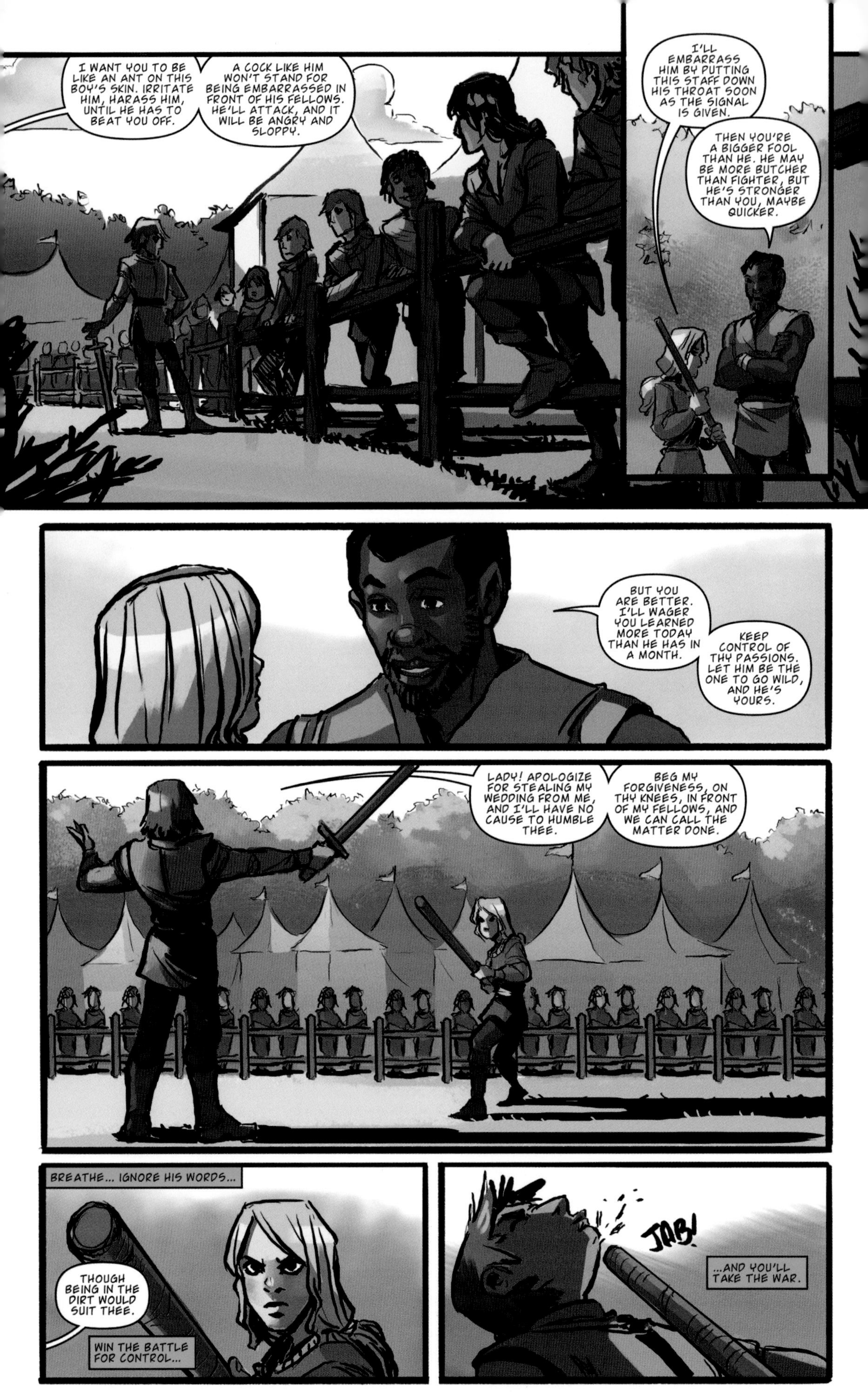
I WANT YOU TO BE LIKE AN ANT ON THIS BOY'S SKIN. IRRITATE HIM, HARASS HIM, UNTIL HE HAS TO BEAT YOU OFF.
A COCK LIKE HIM WON'T STAND FOR BEING EMBARRASSED IN FRONT OF HIS FELLOWS. HE'LL ATTACK, AND IT WILL BE ANGRY AND SLOPPY.
I'LL EMBARRASS HIM BY PUTTING THIS STAFF DOWN HIS THROAT SOON AS THE SIGNAL IS GIVEN.
THEN YOU'RE A BIGGER FOOL THAN HE. HE MAY BE MORE BUTCHER THAN FIGHTER, BUT HE'S STRONGER THAN YOU, MAYBE QUICKER.
BUT YOU ARE BETTER. I'LL WAGER YOU LEARNED MORE TODAY THAN HE HAS IN A MONTH.
KEEP CONTROL OF THY PASSIONS. LET HIM BE THE ONE TO GO WILD, AND HE'S YOURS.
LADY! APOLOGIZE FOR STEALING MY WEDDING FROM ME, AND I'LL HAVE NO CAUSE TO HUMBLE THEE.
BEG MY FORGIVENESS, ON THY KNEES, IN FRONT OF MY FELLOWS, AND WE CAN CALL THE MATTER DONE.
BREATHE... IGNORE HIS WORDS...
THOUGH BEING IN THE DIRT WOULD SUIT THEE.
WIN THE BATTLE FOR CONTROL...
JAB!
...AND YOU'LL TAKE THE WAR.

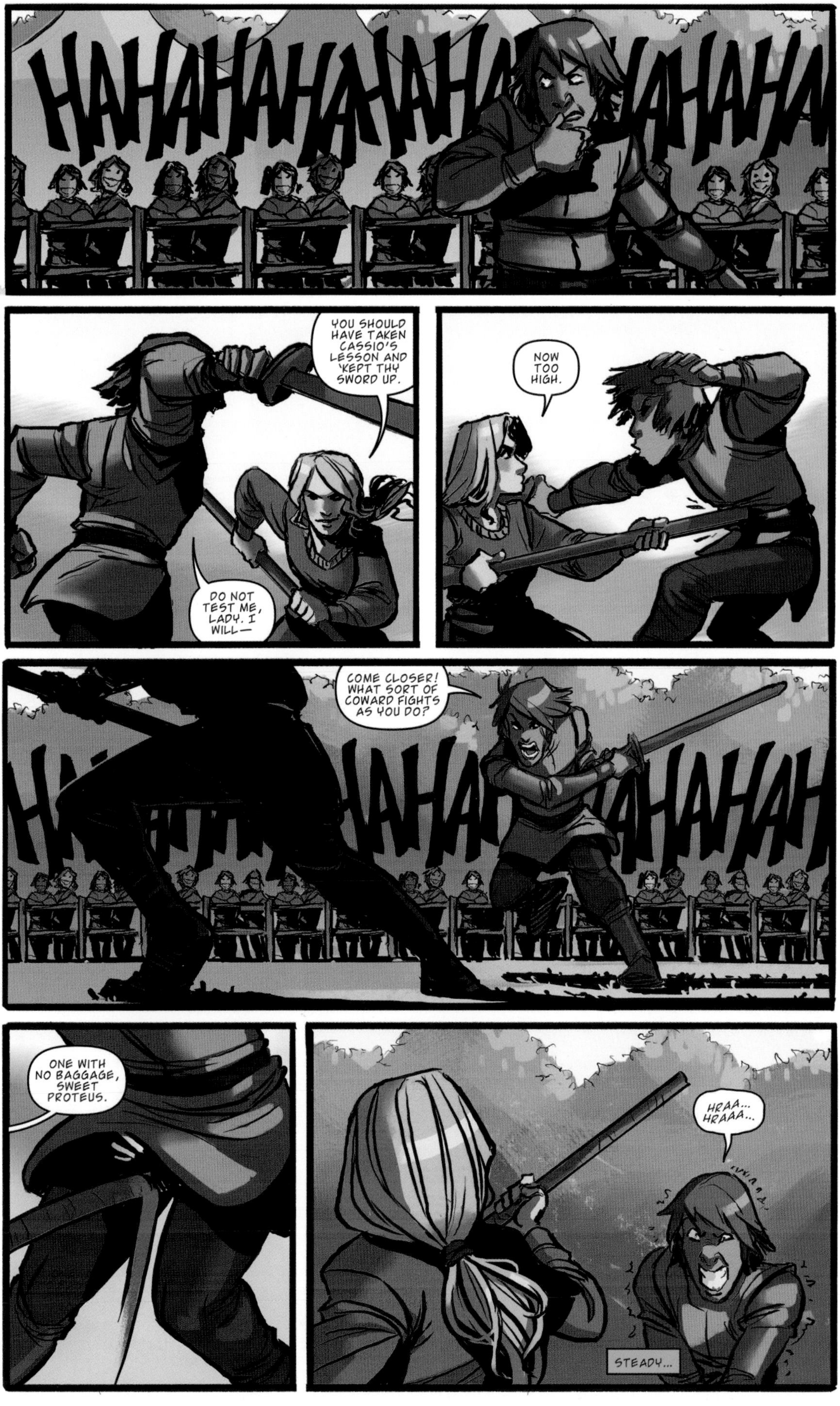
HAHAHAHAHAHAHAHAHAHAHA
YOU SHOULD HAVE TAKEN CASSIO'S LESSON AND 'KEPT THY SWORD UP.
DO NOT TEST ME, LADY. I WILL—
NOW TOO HIGH.
COME CLOSER! WHAT SORT OF COWARD FIGHTS AS YOU DO?
HAHAHAHAHAHAH
ONE WITH NO BAGGAGE, SWEET PROTEUS.
HRAA... HRAAA...
STEADY...

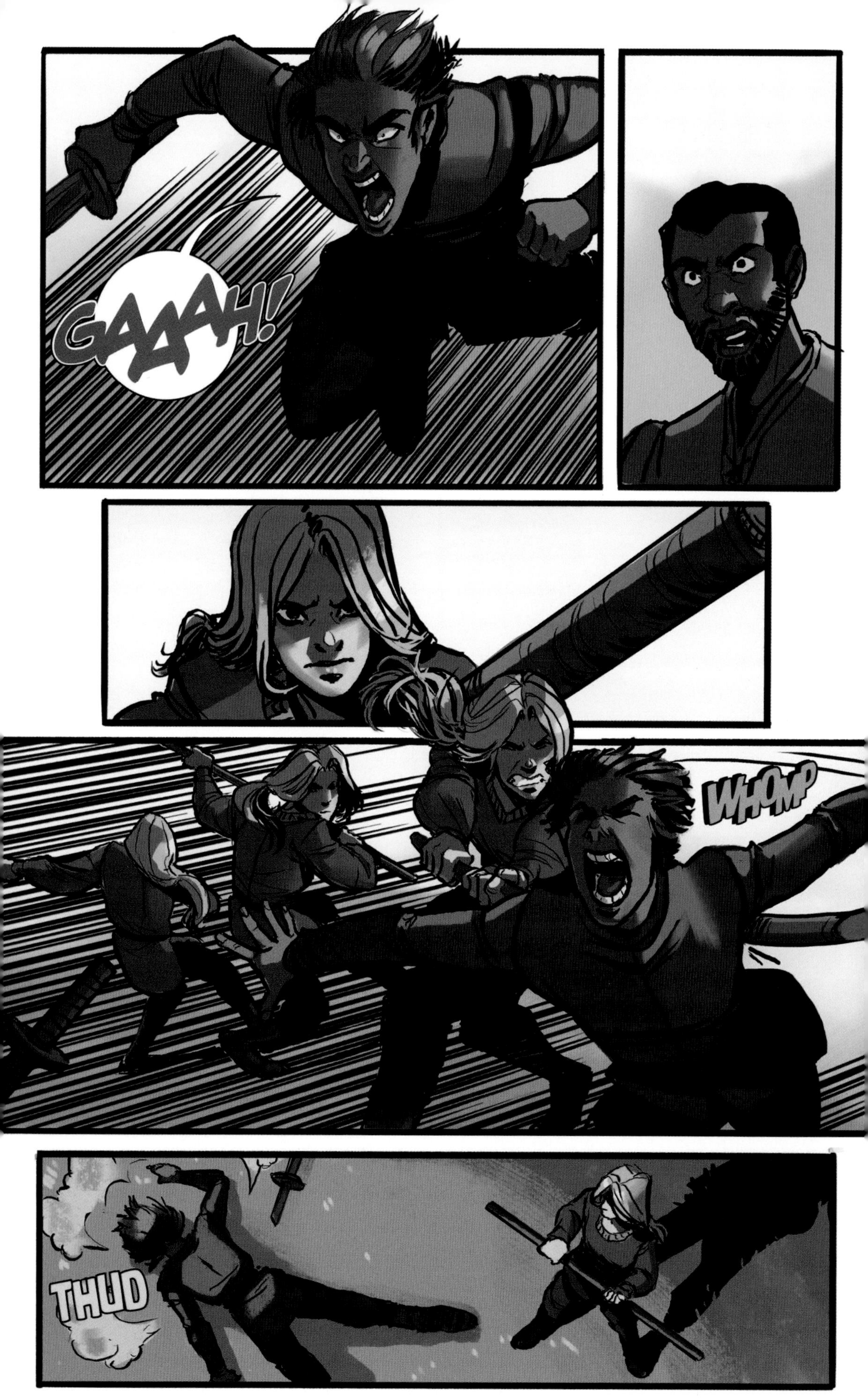
GAAAH!
WHOMP
THUD

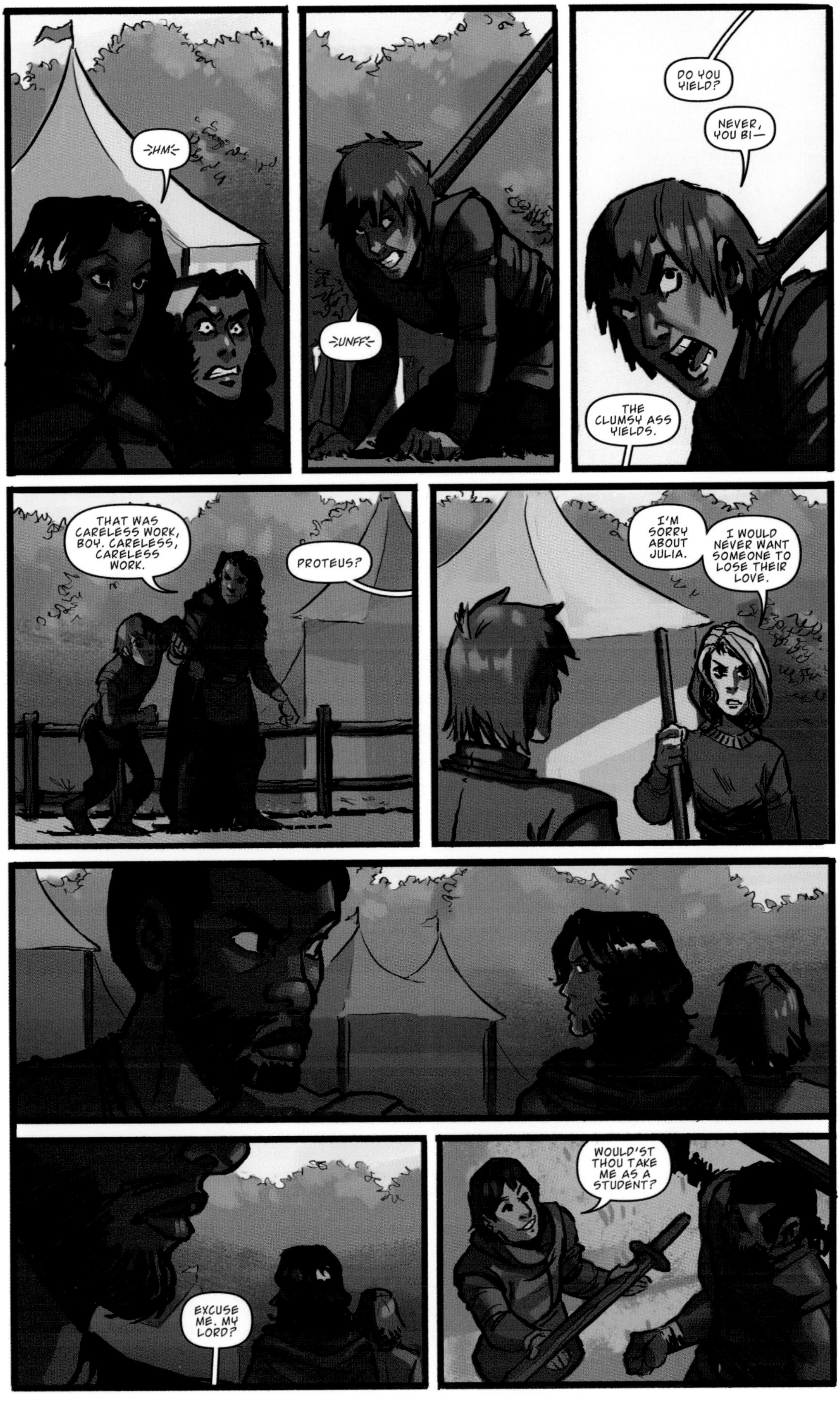
HM
UNFF
DO YOU YIELD?
NEVER, YOU BI—
THE CLUMSY ASS YIELDS.
THAT WAS CARELESS WORK, BOY. CARELESS, CARELESS WORK.
PROTEUS?
I'M SORRY ABOUT JULIA.
I WOULD NEVER WANT SOMEONE TO LOSE THEIR LOVE.
EXCUSE ME. MY LORD?
WOULD'ST THOU TAKE ME AS A STUDENT?

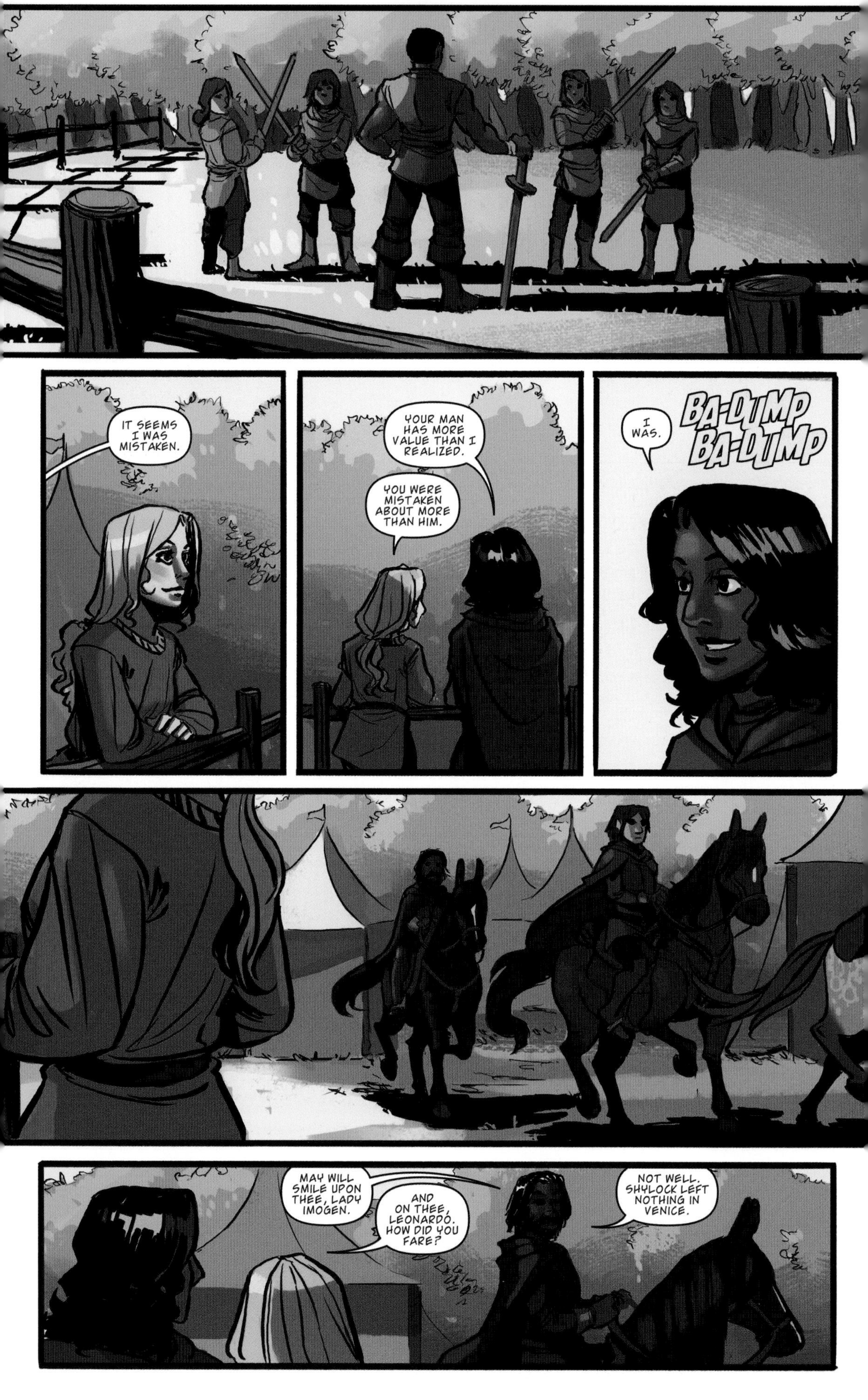
IT SEEMS I WAS MISTAKEN.
YOUR MAN HAS MORE VALUE THAN I REALIZED.
YOU WERE MISTAKEN ABOUT MORE THAN HIM.
I WAS.
BA-DUMP BA-DUMP
MAY WILL SMILE UPON THEE, LADY IMOGEN.
AND ON THEE, LEONARDO. HOW DID YOU FARE?
NOT WELL. SHYLOCK LEFT NOTHING IN VENICE.

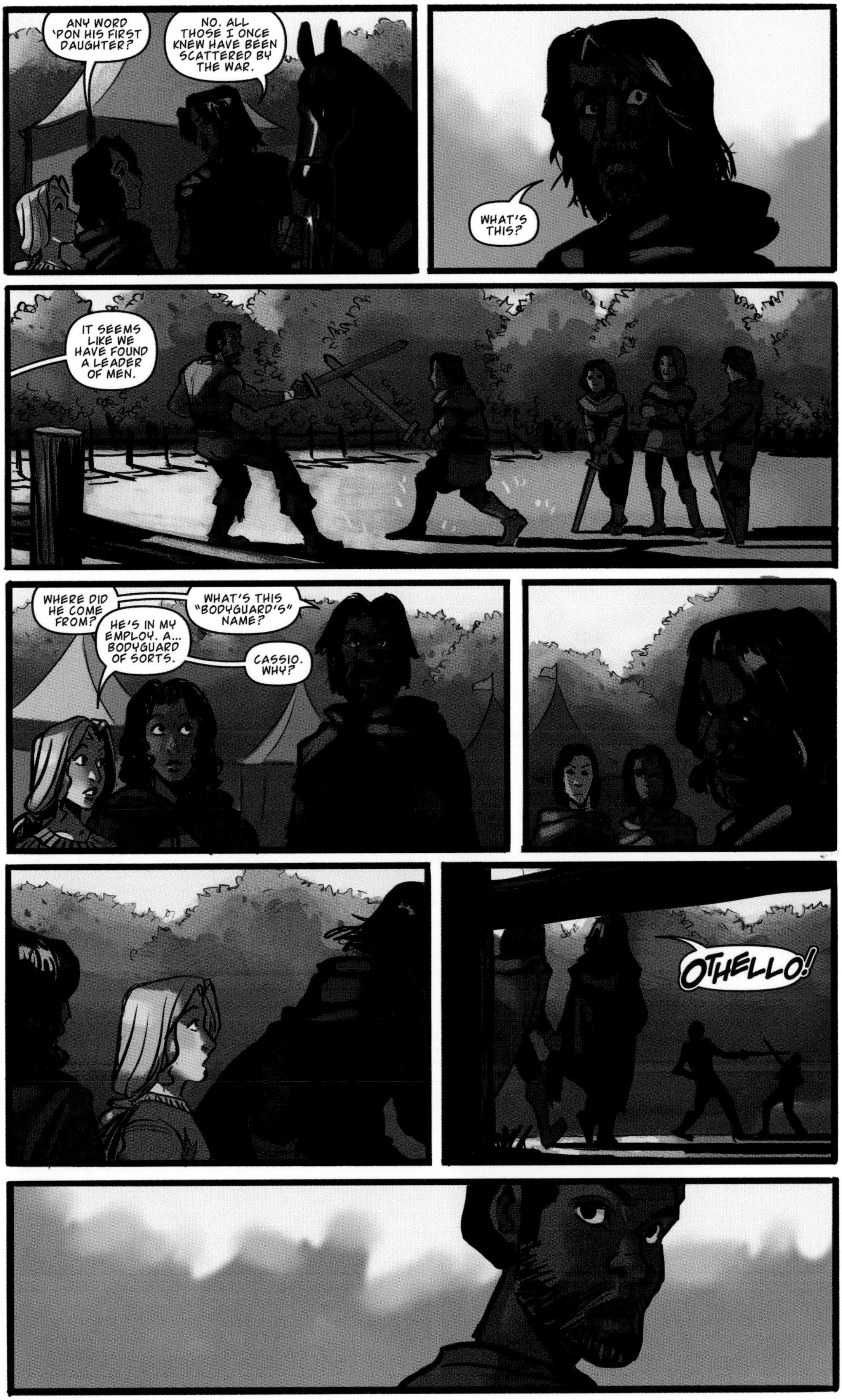
ANY WORD 'PON HIS FIRST DAUGHTER?
NO. ALL THOSE I ONCE KNEW HAVE BEEN SCATTERED BY THE WAR.
WHAT'S THIS?
IT SEEMS LIKE WE HAVE FOUND A LEADER OF MEN.
WHERE DID HE COME FROM?
HE'S IN MY EMPLOY. A... BODYGUARD OF SORTS.
WHAT'S THIS "BODYGUARD'S" NAME?
CASSIO. WHY?
OTHELLO!

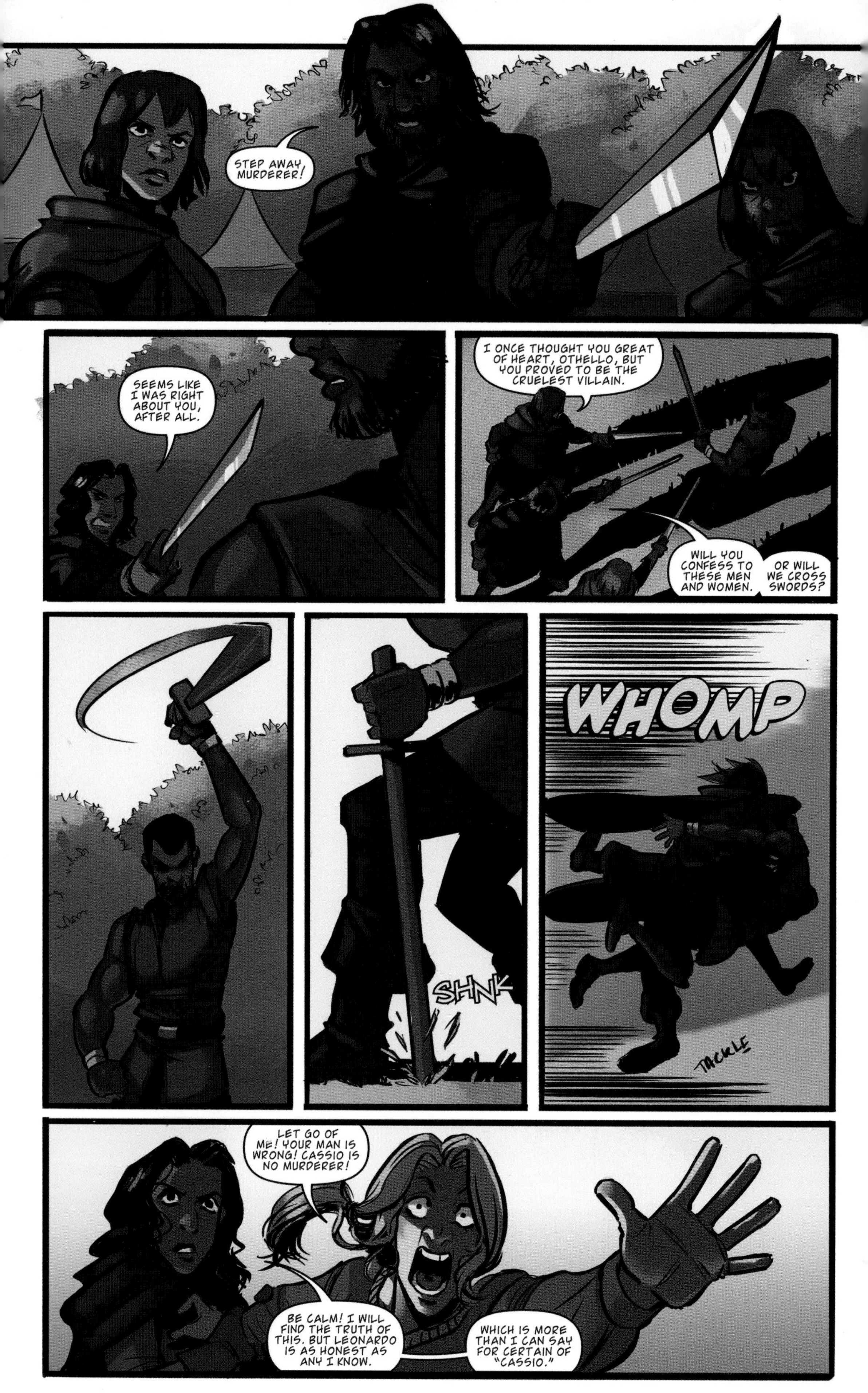
STEP AWAY MURDERER!
SEEMS LIKE I WAS RIGHT ABOUT YOU, AFTER ALL.
I ONCE THOUGHT YOU GREAT OF HEART, OTHELLO, BUT YOU PROVED TO BE THE CRUELEST VILLAIN.
WILL YOU CONFESS TO THESE MEN AND WOMEN.
OR WILL WE CROSS SWORDS?
SHNK
WHOMP
TACKLE
LET GO OF ME! YOUR MAN IS WRONG! CASSIO IS NO MURDERER!
BE CALM! I WILL FIND THE TRUTH OF THIS. BUT LEONARDO IS AS HONEST AS ANY I KNOW.
WHICH IS MORE THAN I CAN SAY FOR CERTAIN OF "CASSIO."

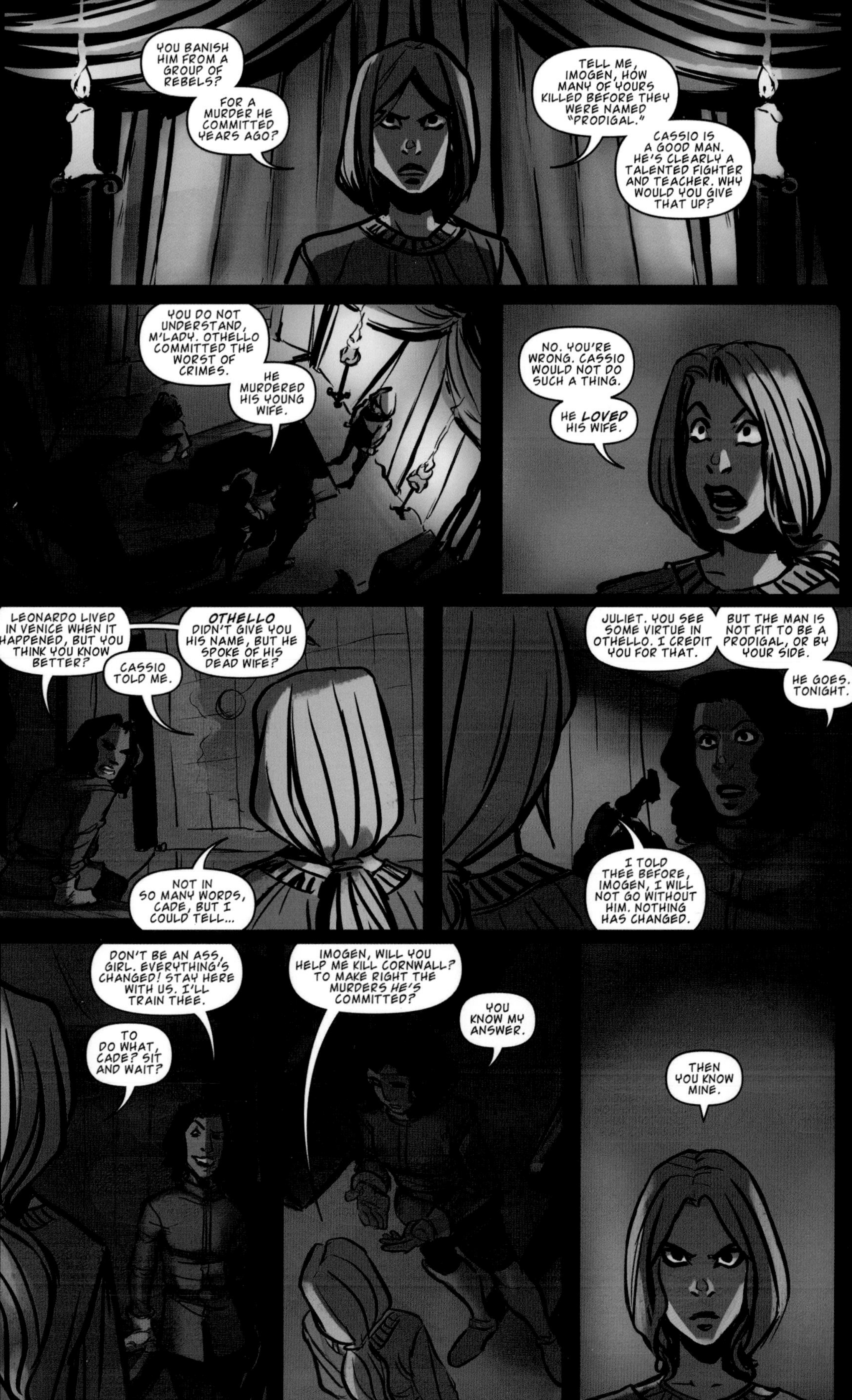
YOU BANISH HIM FROM A GROUP OF REBELS?
FOR A MURDER HE COMMITTED YEARS AGO?
TELL ME, IMOGEN, HOW MANY OF YOURS KILLED BEFORE THEY WERE NAMED "PRODIGAL."
CASSIO IS A GOOD MAN. HE'S CLEARLY A TALENTED FIGHTER AND TEACHER. WHY WOULD YOU GIVE THAT UP?
YOU DO NOT UNDERSTAND, M'LADY. OTHELLO COMMITTED THE WORST OF CRIMES.
HE MURDERED HIS YOUNG WIFE.
NO. YOU'RE WRONG. CASSIO WOULD NOT DO SUCH A THING.
HE ***LOVED*** HIS WIFE.
LEONARDO LIVED IN VENICE WHEN IT HAPPENED, BUT YOU THINK YOU KNOW BETTER?
CASSIO TOLD ME.
OTHELLO DIDN'T GIVE YOU HIS NAME, BUT HE SPOKE OF HIS DEAD WIFE?
NOT IN SO MANY WORDS, CADE, BUT I COULD TELL...
JULIET. YOU SEE SOME VIRTUE IN OTHELLO. I CREDIT YOU FOR THAT.
BUT THE MAN IS NOT FIT TO BE A PRODIGAL, OR BY YOUR SIDE.
HE GOES. TONIGHT.
I TOLD THEE BEFORE, IMOGEN, I WILL NOT GO WITHOUT HIM. NOTHING HAS CHANGED.
DON'T BE AN ASS, GIRL. EVERYTHING'S CHANGED! STAY HERE WITH US. I'LL TRAIN THEE.
TO DO WHAT, CADE? SIT AND WAIT?
IMOGEN, WILL YOU HELP ME KILL CORNWALL? TO MAKE RIGHT THE MURDERS HE'S COMMITTED?
YOU KNOW MY ANSWER.
THEN YOU KNOW MINE.

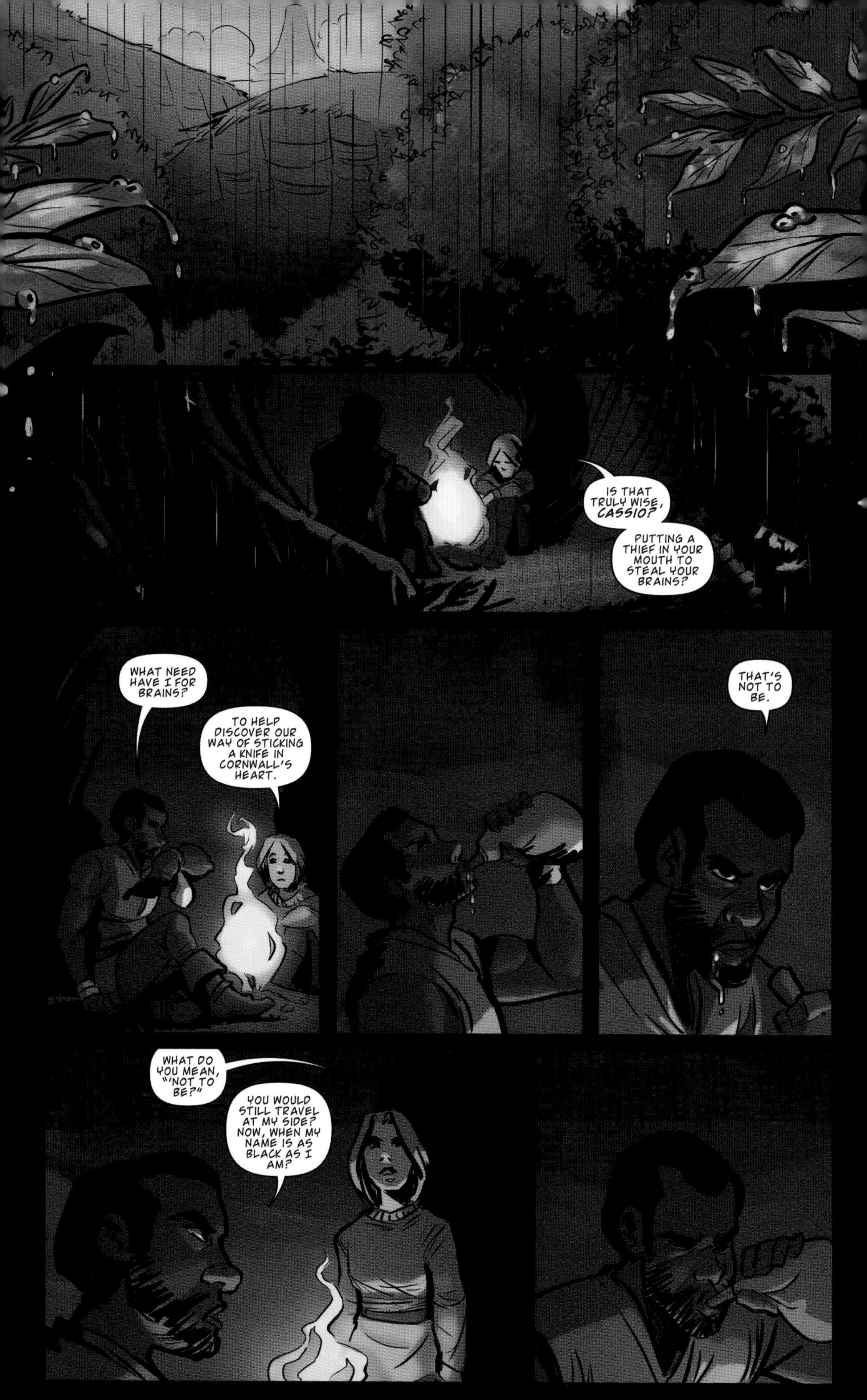
IS THAT TRULY WISE, CASSIO?
PUTTING A THIEF IN YOUR MOUTH TO STEAL YOUR BRAINS?
WHAT NEED HAVE I FOR BRAINS?
TO HELP DISCOVER OUR WAY OF STICKING A KNIFE IN CORNWALL'S HEART.
THAT'S NOT TO BE.
WHAT DO YOU MEAN, "NOT TO BE?"
YOU WOULD STILL TRAVEL AT MY SIDE? NOW, WHEN MY NAME IS AS BLACK AS I AM?

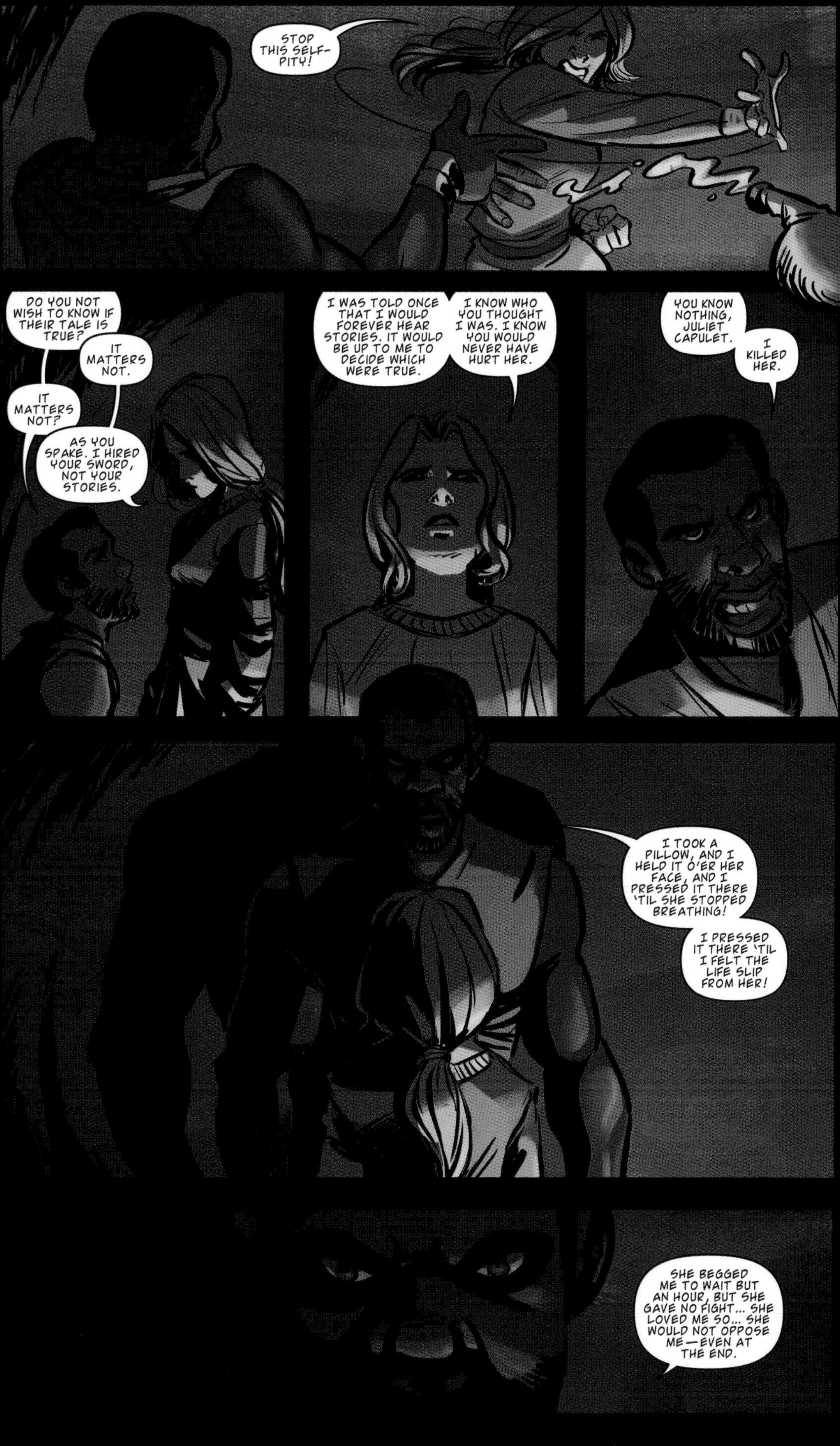
STOP THIS SELF-PITY!
DO YOU NOT WISH TO KNOW IF THEIR TALE IS TRUE?
IT MATTERS NOT.
IT MATTERS NOT?
AS YOU SPAKE. I HIRED YOUR SWORD, NOT YOUR STORIES.
I WAS TOLD ONCE THAT I WOULD FOREVER HEAR STORIES. IT WOULD BE UP TO ME TO DECIDE WHICH WERE TRUE.
I KNOW WHO YOU THOUGHT I WAS. I KNOW YOU WOULD NEVER HAVE HURT HER.
YOU KNOW NOTHING, JULIET CAPULET.
I KILLED HER.
I TOOK A PILLOW, AND I HELD IT O'ER HER FACE, AND I PRESSED IT THERE 'TIL SHE STOPPED BREATHING!
I PRESSED IT THERE 'TIL I FELT THE LIFE SLIP FROM HER!
SHE BEGGED ME TO WAIT BUT AN HOUR, BUT SHE GAVE NO FIGHT... SHE LOVED ME SO... SHE WOULD NOT OPPOSE ME—EVEN AT THE END.

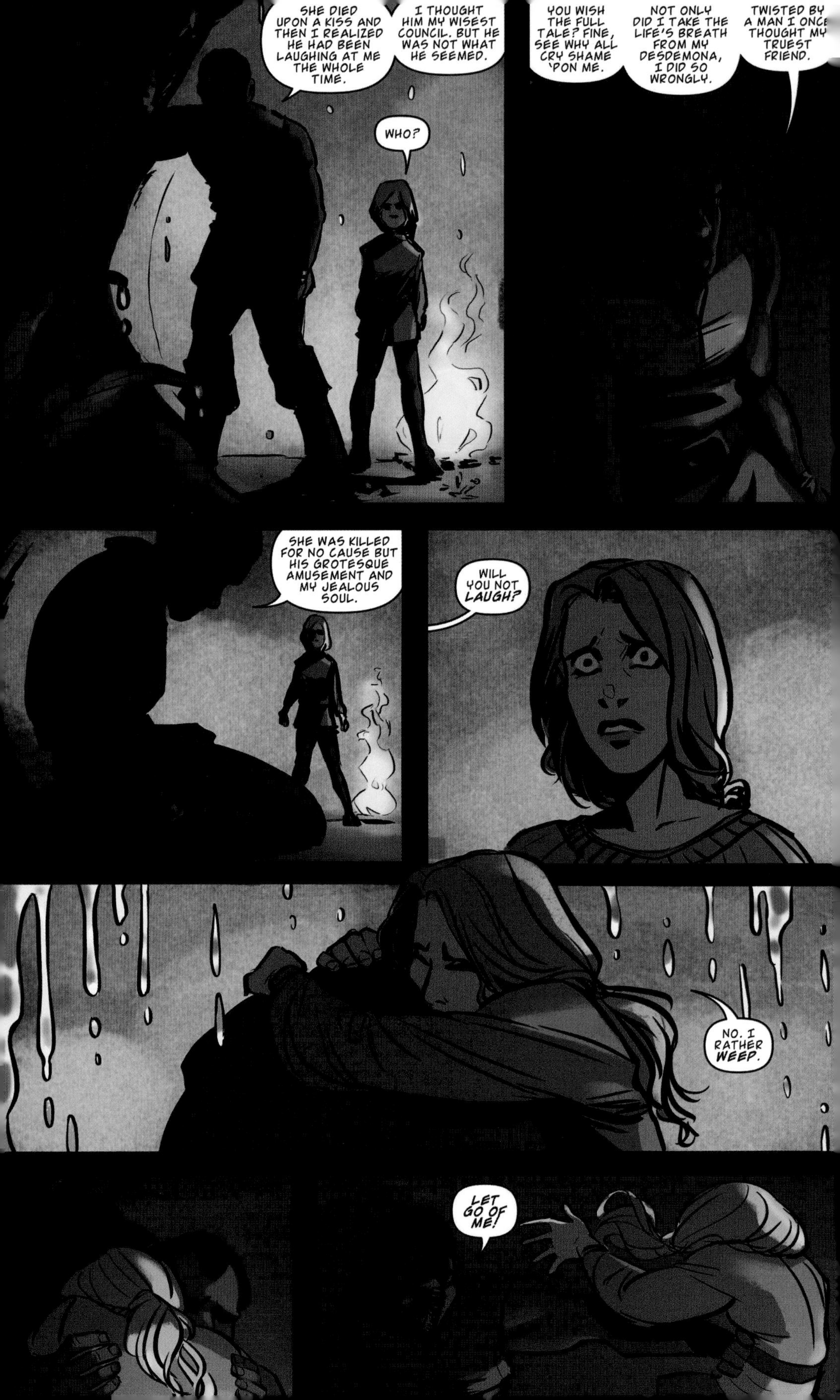
SHE DIED UPON A KISS AND THEN I REALIZED HE HAD BEEN LAUGHING AT ME THE WHOLE TIME.
I THOUGHT HIM MY WISEST COUNCIL. BUT HE WAS NOT WHAT HE SEEMED.
WHO?
YOU WISH THE FULL TALE? FINE, SEE WHY ALL CRY SHAME 'PON ME.
NOT ONLY DID I TAKE THE LIFE'S BREATH FROM MY DESDEMONA, I DID SO WRONGLY.
TWISTED BY A MAN I ONCE THOUGHT MY TRUEST FRIEND.
SHE WAS KILLED FOR NO CAUSE BUT HIS GROTESQUE AMUSEMENT AND MY JEALOUS SOUL.
WILL YOU NOT LAUGH?
NO. I RATHER WEEP.
LET GO OF ME!

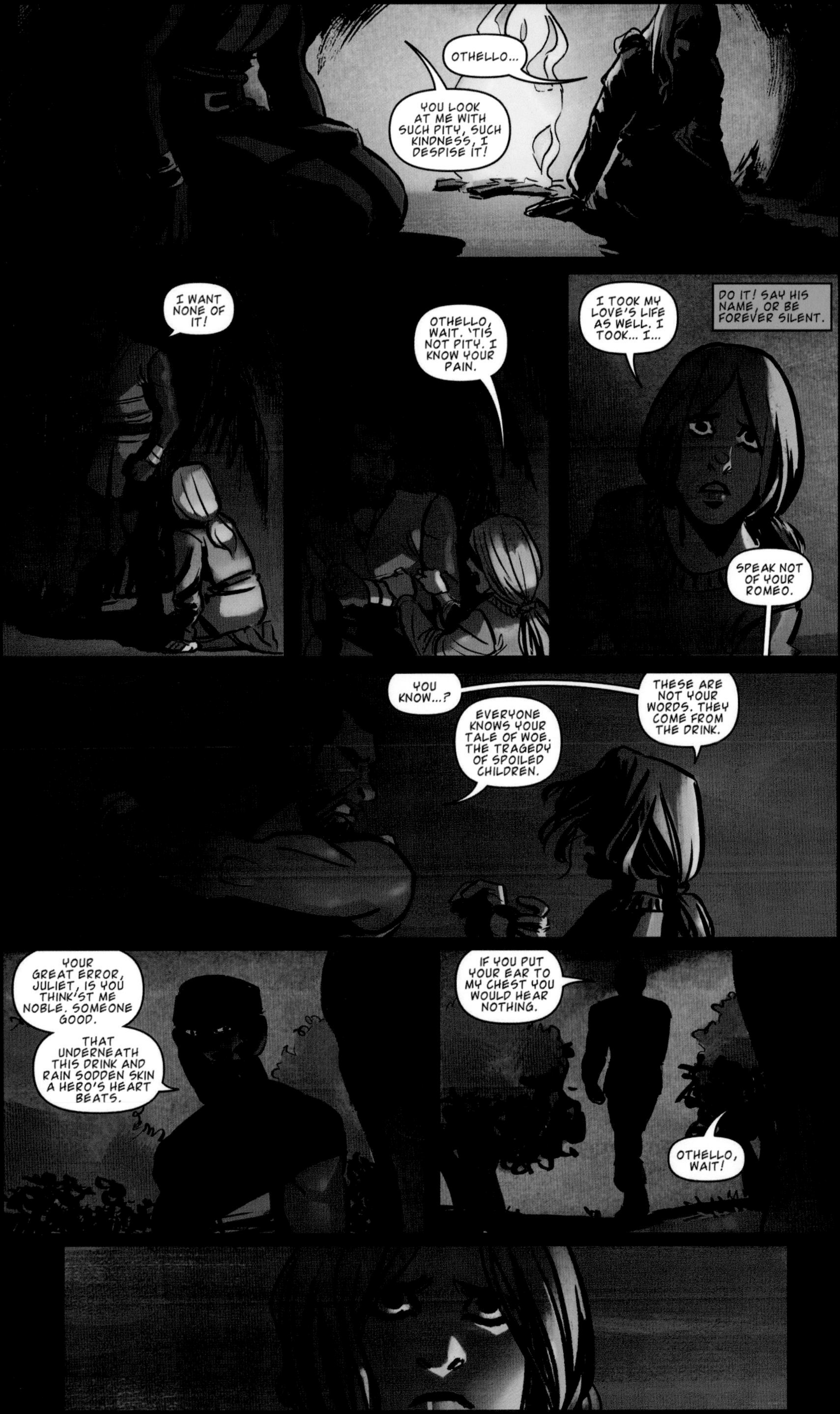

OTHELLO...
YOU LOOK AT ME WITH SUCH PITY, SUCH KINDNESS, I DESPISE IT!
I WANT NONE OF IT!
OTHELLO, WAIT. 'TIS NOT PITY. I KNOW YOUR PAIN.
I TOOK MY LOVE'S LIFE AS WELL. I TOOK... I...
DO IT! SAY HIS NAME, OR BE FOREVER SILENT.
SPEAK NOT OF YOUR ROMEO.
YOU KNOW...?
EVERYONE KNOWS YOUR TALE OF WOE. THE TRAGEDY OF SPOILED CHILDREN.
THESE ARE NOT YOUR WORDS. THEY COME FROM THE DRINK.
YOUR GREAT ERROR, JULIET, IS YOU THINK'ST ME NOBLE. SOMEONE GOOD.
THAT UNDERNEATH THIS DRINK AND RAIN SODDEN SKIN A HERO'S HEART BEATS.
IF YOU PUT YOUR EAR TO MY CHEST YOU WOULD HEAR NOTHING.
OTHELLO, WAIT!

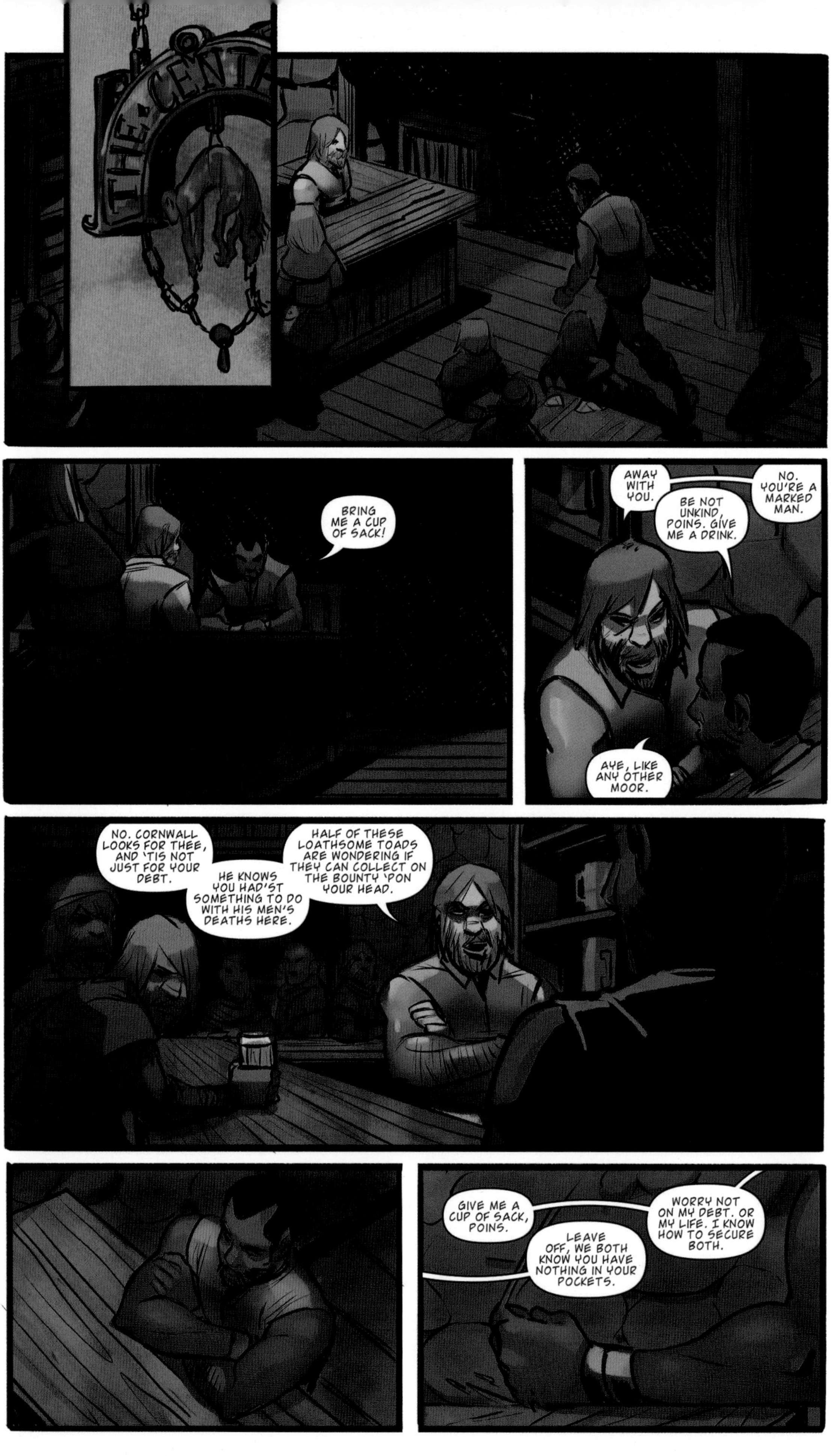
THE CENTA
BRING ME A CUP OF SACK!
AWAY WITH YOU.
BE NOT UNKIND, POINS. GIVE ME A DRINK.
NO. YOU'RE A MARKED MAN.
AYE, LIKE ANY OTHER MOOR.
NO. CORNWALL LOOKS FOR THEE, AND 'TIS NOT JUST FOR YOUR DEBT.
HE KNOWS YOU HAD'ST SOMETHING TO DO WITH HIS MEN'S DEATHS HERE.
HALF OF THESE LOATHSOME TOADS ARE WONDERING IF THEY CAN COLLECT ON THE BOUNTY 'PON YOUR HEAD.
GIVE ME A CUP OF SACK, POINS.
LEAVE OFF, WE BOTH KNOW YOU HAVE NOTHING IN YOUR POCKETS.
WORRY NOT ON MY DEBT. OR MY LIFE. I KNOW HOW TO SECURE BOTH.

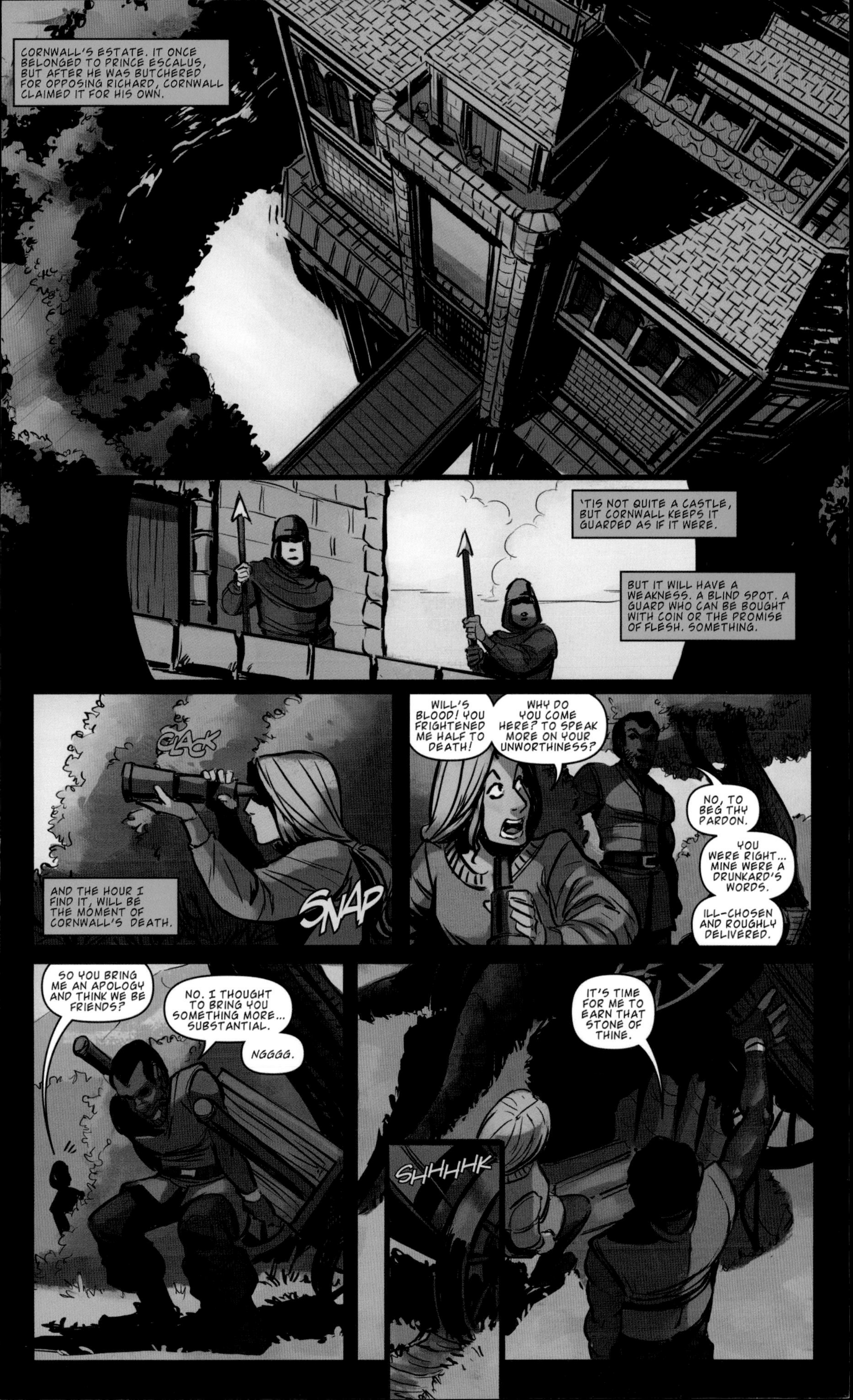
CORNWALL'S ESTATE. IT ONCE BELONGED TO PRINCE ESCALUS, BUT AFTER HE WAS BUTCHERED FOR OPPOSING RICHARD, CORNWALL CLAIMED IT FOR HIS OWN.
'TIS NOT QUITE A CASTLE, BUT CORNWALL KEEPS IT GUARDED AS IF IT WERE.
BUT IT WILL HAVE A WEAKNESS. A BLIND SPOT. A GUARD WHO CAN BE BOUGHT WITH COIN OR THE PROMISE OF FLESH. SOMETHING.
CLACK
AND THE HOUR I FIND IT, WILL BE THE MOMENT OF CORNWALL'S DEATH.
SNAP
WILL'S BLOOD! YOU FRIGHTENED ME HALF TO DEATH!
WHY DO YOU COME HERE? TO SPEAK MORE ON YOUR UNWORTHINESS?
NO, TO BEG THY PARDON.
YOU WERE RIGHT... MINE WERE A DRUNKARD'S WORDS.
ILL-CHOSEN AND ROUGHLY DELIVERED.
SO YOU BRING ME AN APOLOGY AND THINK WE BE FRIENDS?
NO. I THOUGHT TO BRING YOU SOMETHING MORE... SUBSTANTIAL.
NGGGG.
IT'S TIME FOR ME TO EARN THAT STONE OF THINE.
SHHHHK

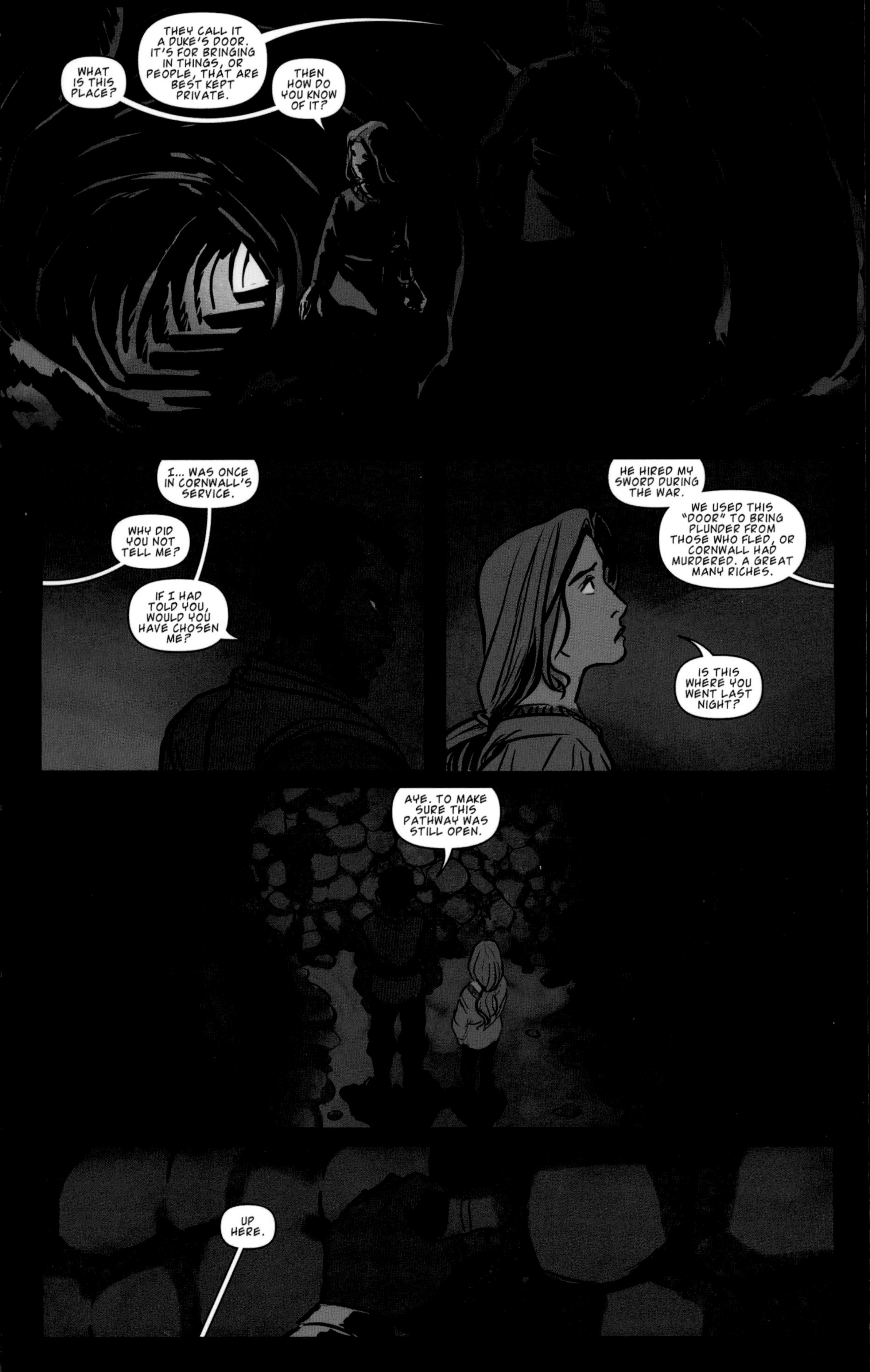
WHAT IS THIS PLACE?
THEY CALL IT A DUKE'S DOOR. IT'S FOR BRINGING IN THINGS, OR PEOPLE, THAT ARE BEST KEPT PRIVATE.
THEN HOW DO YOU KNOW OF IT?
I... WAS ONCE IN CORNWALL'S SERVICE.
WHY DID YOU NOT TELL ME?
IF I HAD TOLD YOU, WOULD YOU HAVE CHOSEN ME?
HE HIRED MY SWORD DURING THE WAR.
WE USED THIS "DOOR" TO BRING PLUNDER FROM THOSE WHO FLED, OR CORNWALL HAD MURDERED. A GREAT MANY RICHES.
IS THIS WHERE YOU WENT LAST NIGHT?
AYE. TO MAKE SURE THIS PATHWAY WAS STILL OPEN.
UP HERE.

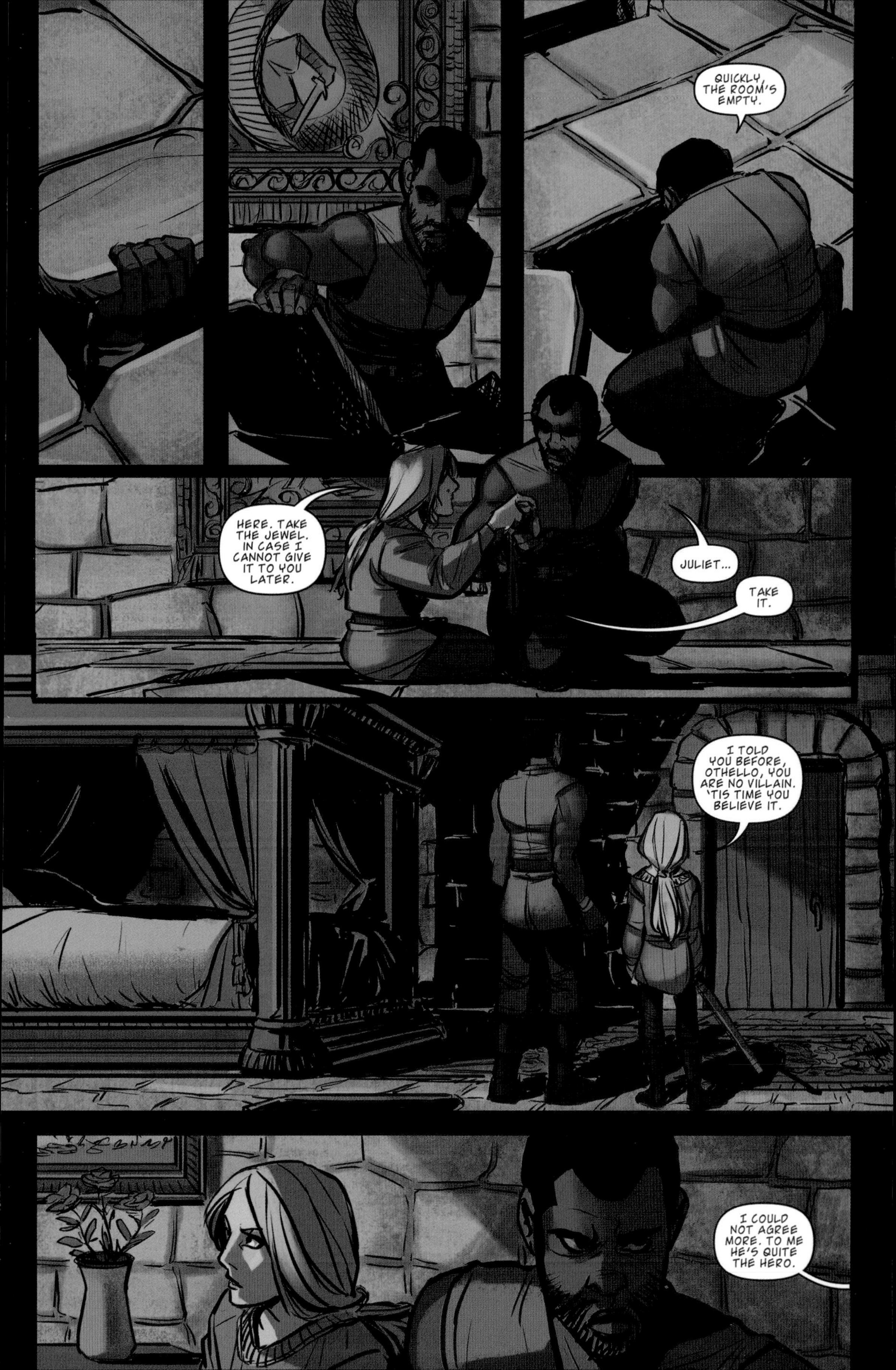
QUICKLY, THE ROOM'S EMPTY.
HERE. TAKE THE JEWEL. IN CASE I CANNOT GIVE IT TO YOU LATER.
JULIET...
TAKE IT.
I TOLD YOU BEFORE, OTHELLO, YOU ARE NO VILLAIN. 'TIS TIME YOU BELIEVE IT.
I COULD NOT AGREE MORE. TO ME HE'S QUITE THE HERO.

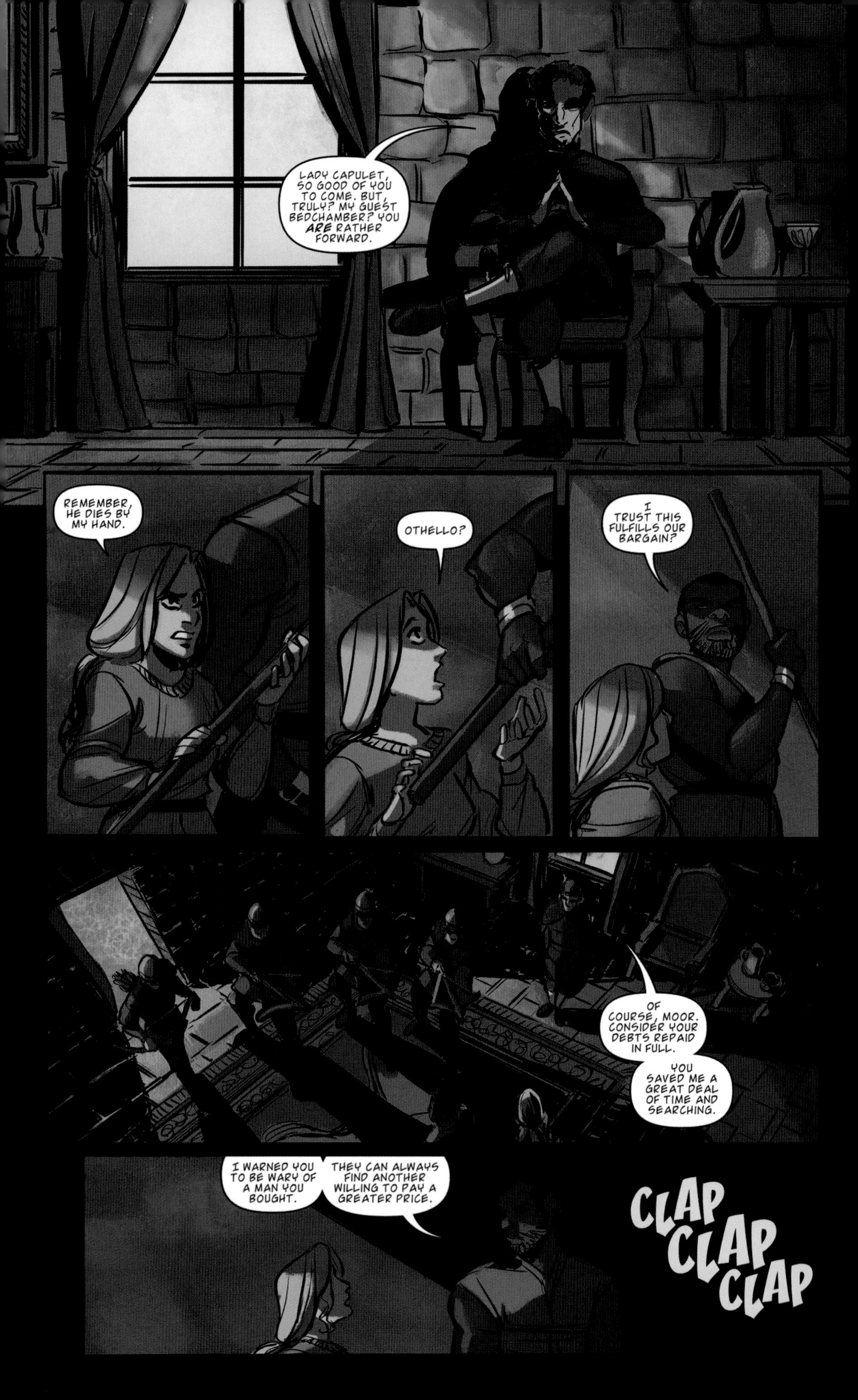
LADY CAPULET, SO GOOD OF YOU TO COME. BUT, TRULY? MY GUEST BEDCHAMBER? YOU *ARE* RATHER FORWARD.
REMEMBER, HE DIES BY MY HAND.
OTHELLO?
I TRUST THIS FULFILLS OUR BARGAIN?
OF COURSE, MOOR. CONSIDER YOUR DEBTS REPAID IN FULL.
YOU SAVED ME A GREAT DEAL OF TIME AND SEARCHING.
I WARNED YOU TO BE WARY OF A MAN YOU BOUGHT.
THEY CAN ALWAYS FIND ANOTHER WILLING TO PAY A GREATER PRICE.
CLAP CLAP CLAP

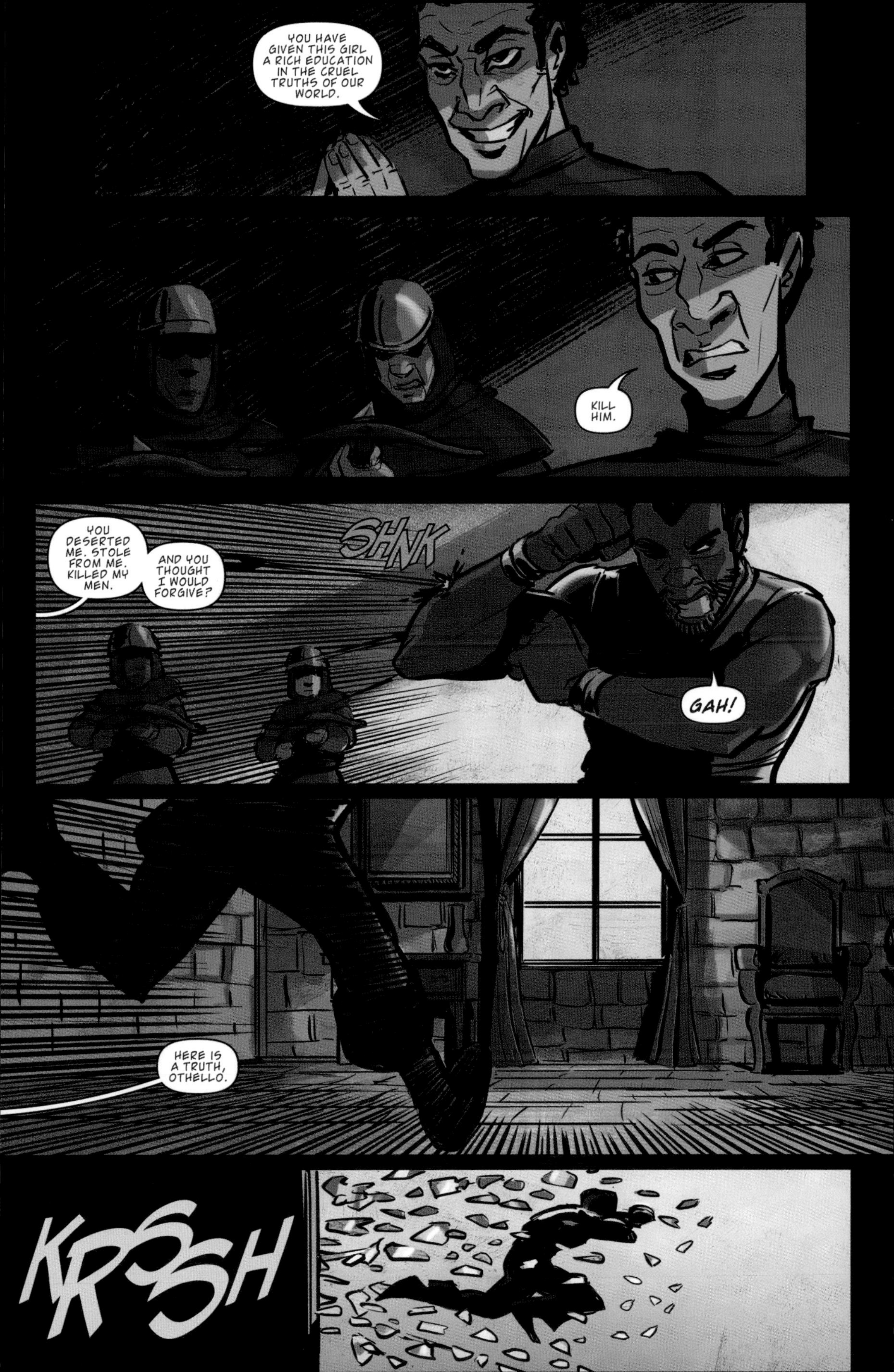
YOU HAVE GIVEN THIS GIRL A RICH EDUCATION IN THE CRUEL TRUTHS OF OUR WORLD.
KILL HIM.
SHNK
YOU DESERTED ME. STOLE FROM ME. KILLED MY MEN.
AND YOU THOUGHT I WOULD FORGIVE?
GAH!
HERE IS A TRUTH, OTHELLO.
KRSSH

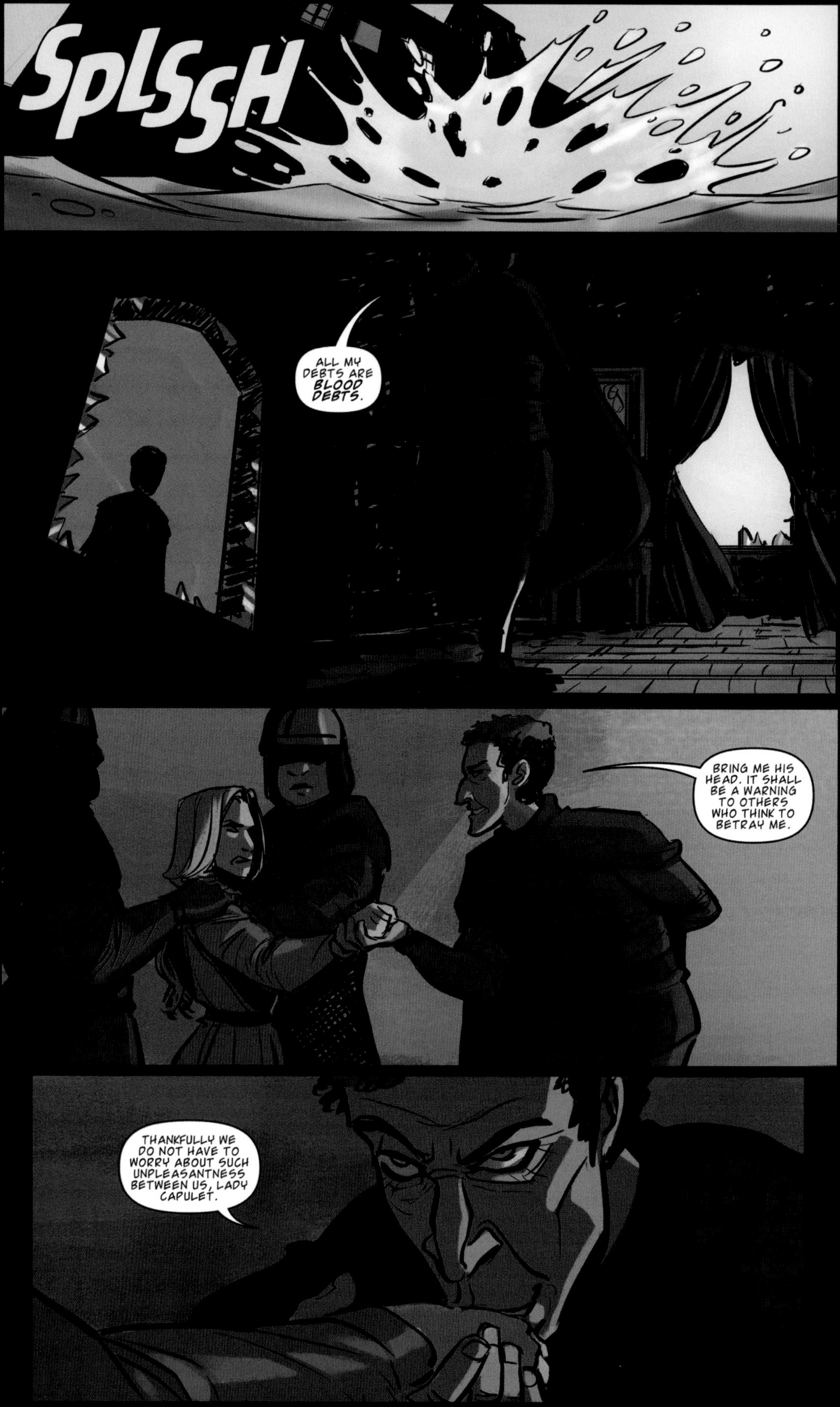
SPLSSH
ALL MY DEBTS ARE BLOOD DEBTS.
BRING ME HIS HEAD. IT SHALL BE A WARNING TO OTHERS WHO THINK TO BETRAY ME.
THANKFULLY WE DO NOT HAVE TO WORRY ABOUT SUCH UNPLEASANTNESS BETWEEN US, LADY CAPULET.

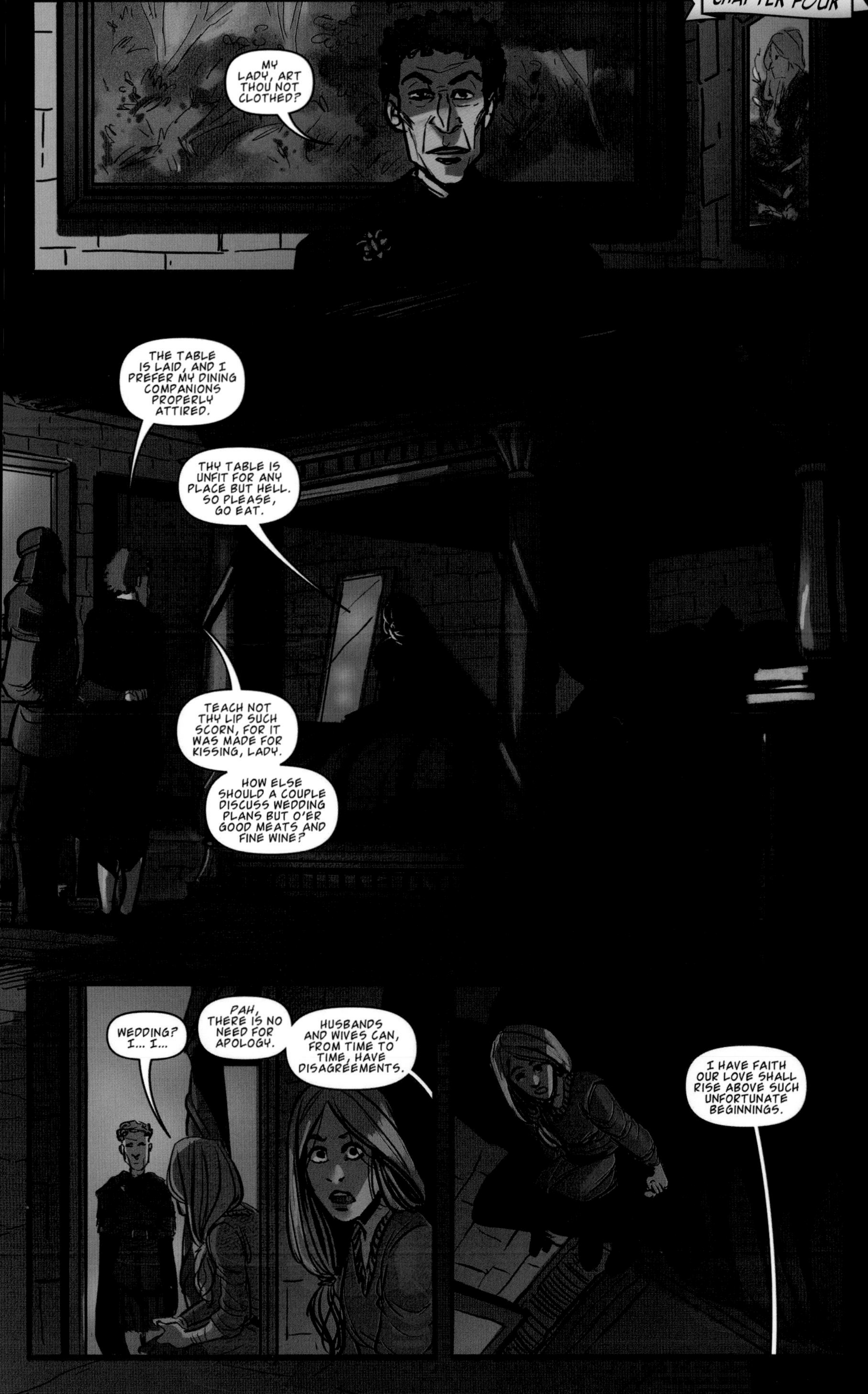
MY LADY, ART THOU NOT CLOTHED?
THE TABLE IS LAID, AND I PREFER MY DINING COMPANIONS PROPERLY ATTIRED.
THY TABLE IS UNFIT FOR ANY PLACE BUT HELL. SO PLEASE, GO EAT.
TEACH NOT THY LIP SUCH SCORN, FOR IT WAS MADE FOR KISSING, LADY.
HOW ELSE SHOULD A COUPLE DISCUSS WEDDING PLANS BUT O'ER GOOD MEATS AND FINE WINE?
WEDDING? I... I...
PAH, THERE IS NO NEED FOR APOLOGY.
HUSBANDS AND WIVES CAN, FROM TIME TO TIME, HAVE DISAGREEMENTS.
I HAVE FAITH OUR LOVE SHALL RISE ABOVE SUCH UNFORTUNATE BEGINNINGS.

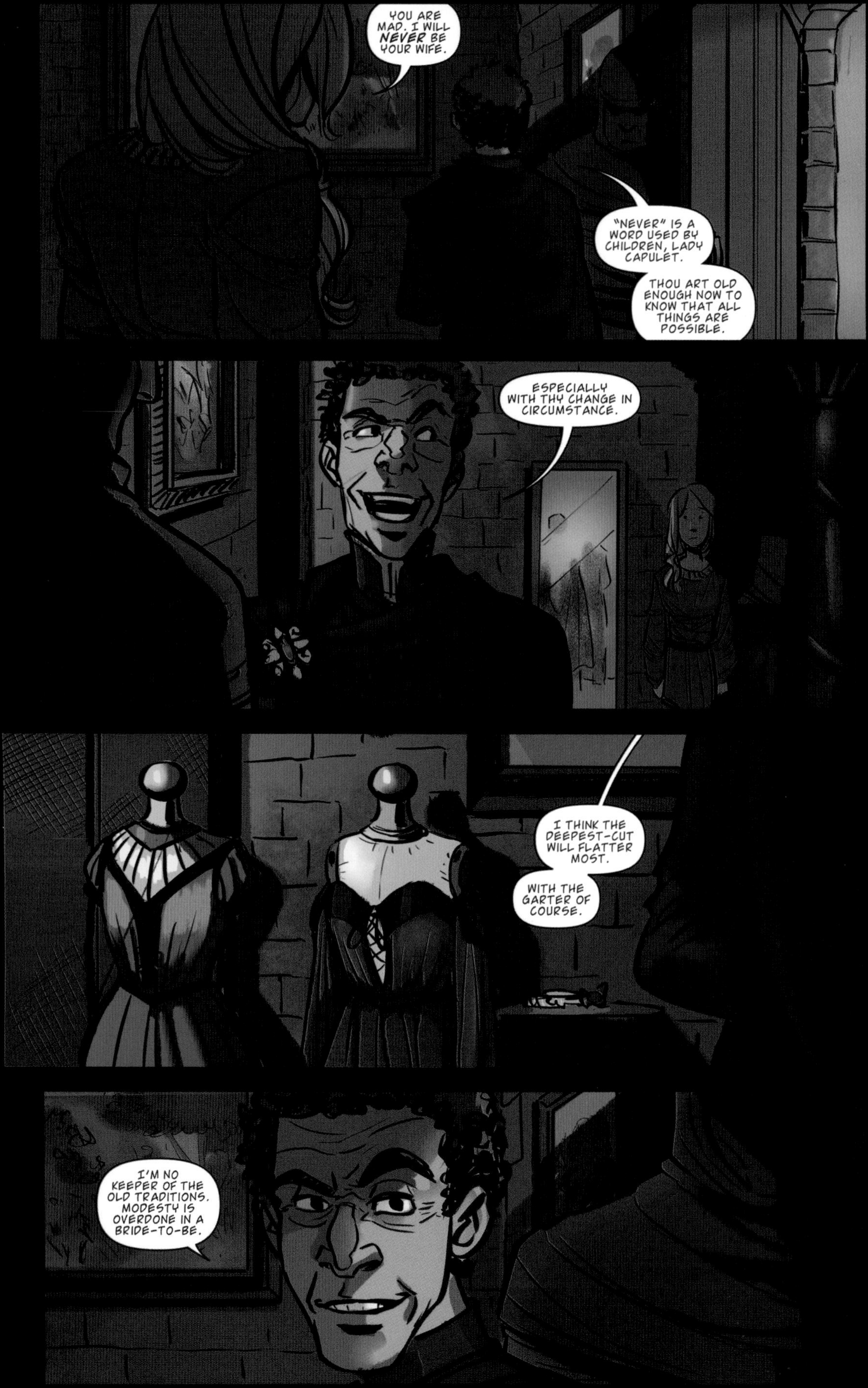
YOU ARE MAD. I WILL NEVER BE YOUR WIFE.
"NEVER" IS A WORD USED BY CHILDREN, LADY CAPULET.
THOU ART OLD ENOUGH NOW TO KNOW THAT ALL THINGS ARE POSSIBLE.
ESPECIALLY WITH THY CHANGE IN CIRCUMSTANCE.
I THINK THE DEEPEST-CUT WILL FLATTER MOST.
WITH THE GARTER OF COURSE.
I'M NO KEEPER OF THE OLD TRADITIONS. MODESTY IS OVERDONE IN A BRIDE-TO-BE.

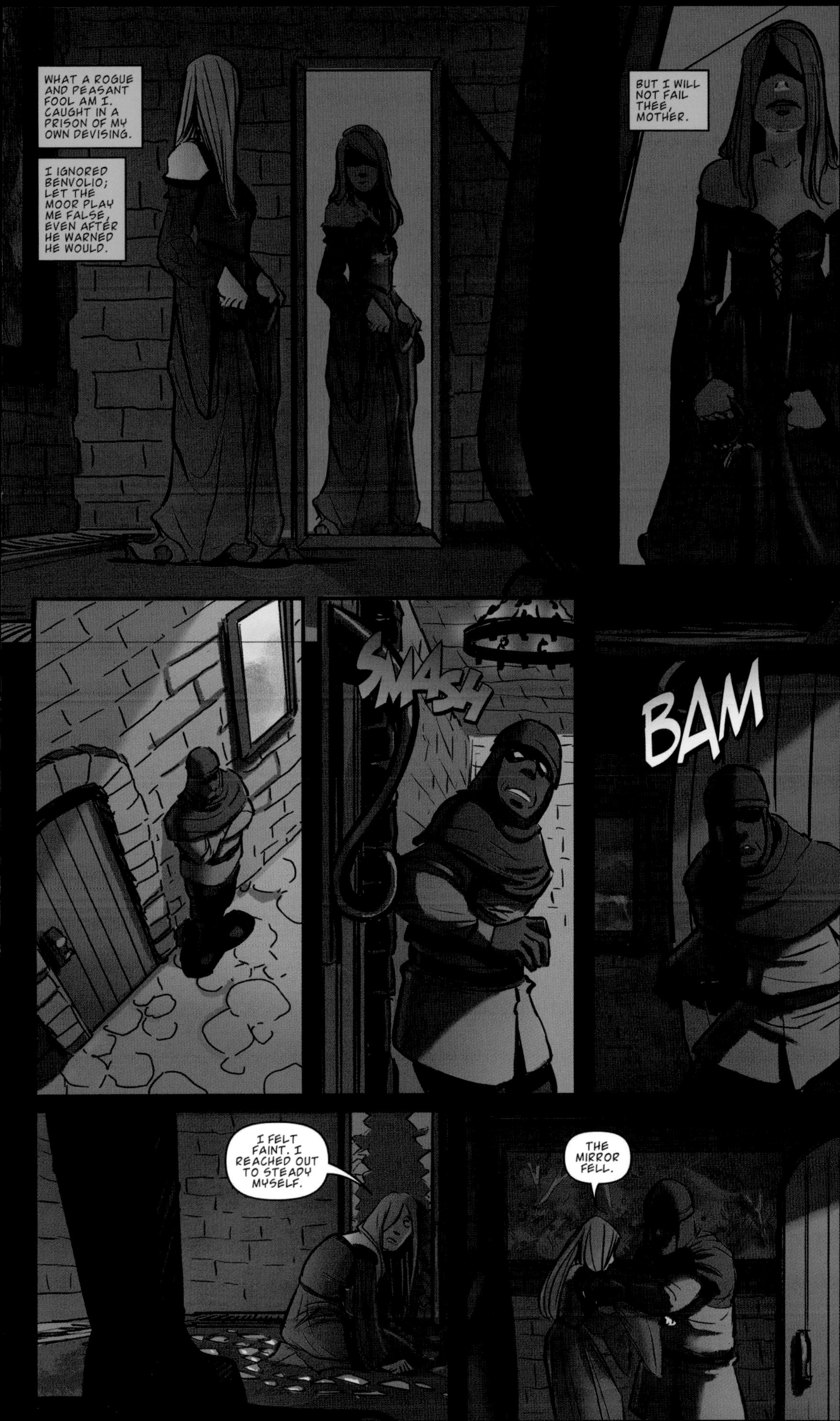
WHAT A ROGUE AND PEASANT FOOL AM I. CAUGHT IN A PRISON OF MY OWN DEVISING.
I IGNORED BENVOLIO; LET THE MOOR PLAY ME FALSE, EVEN AFTER HE WARNED HE WOULD.
BUT I WILL NOT FAIL THEE, MOTHER.
SMASH
BAM
I FELT FAINT. I REACHED OUT TO STEADY MYSELF.
THE MIRROR FELL.

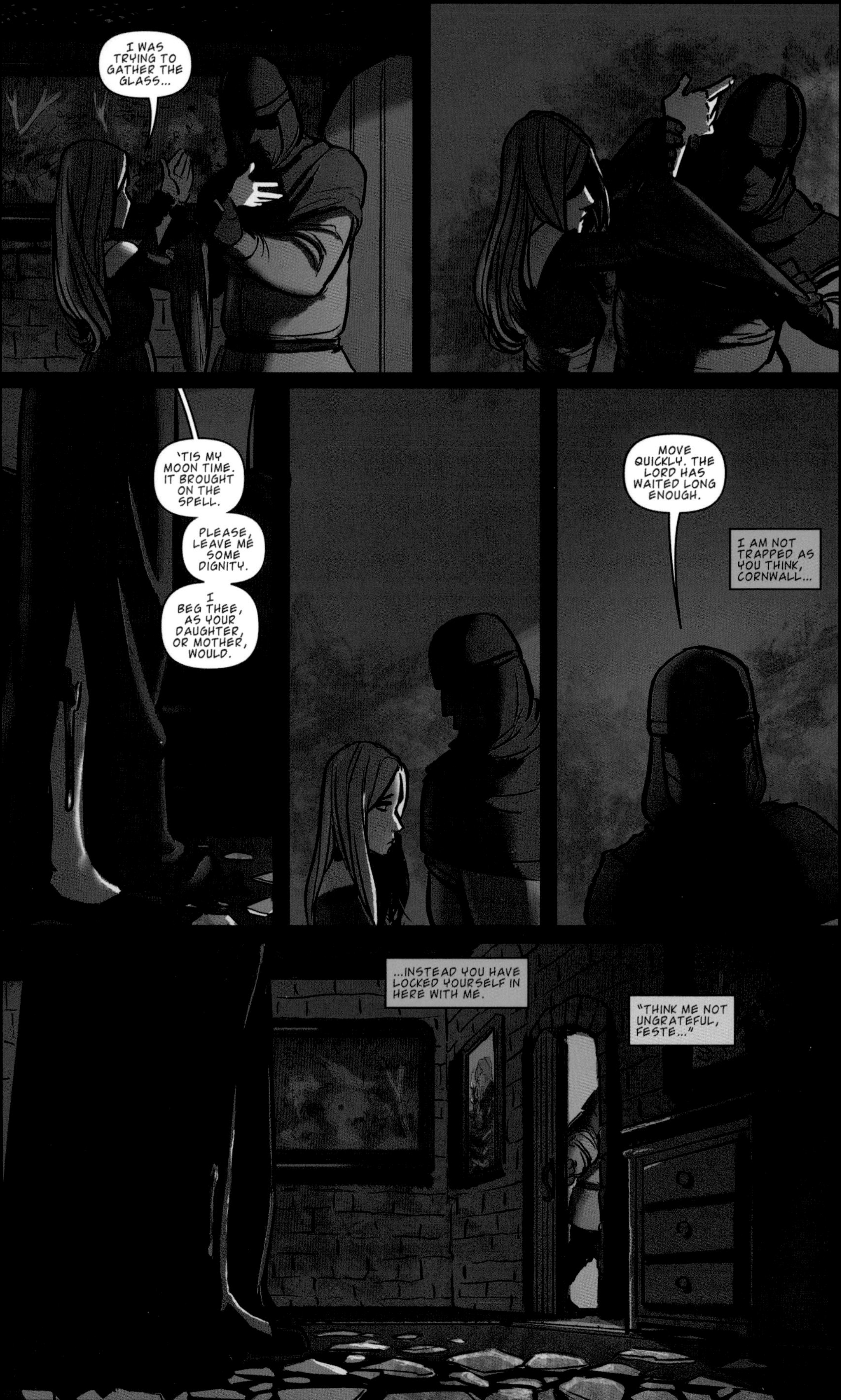
I WAS TRYING TO GATHER THE GLASS...
'TIS MY MOON TIME. IT BROUGHT ON THE SPELL.
PLEASE, LEAVE ME SOME DIGNITY.
I BEG THEE, AS YOUR DAUGHTER, OR MOTHER, WOULD.
MOVE QUICKLY. THE LORD HAS WAITED LONG ENOUGH.
I AM NOT TRAPPED AS YOU THINK, CORNWALL...
...INSTEAD YOU HAVE LOCKED YOURSELF IN HERE WITH ME.
"THINK ME NOT UNGRATEFUL, FESTE..."

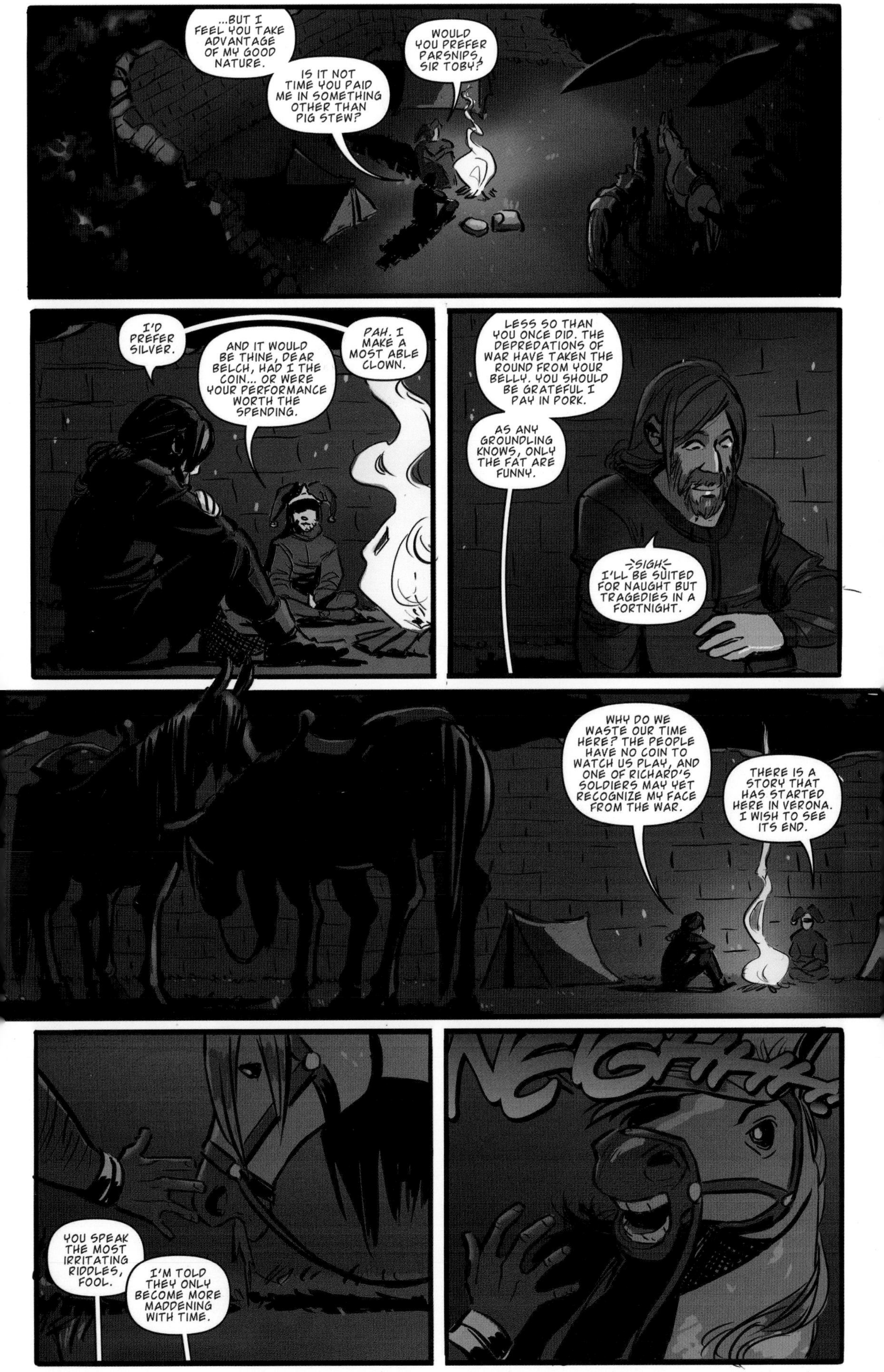
...BUT I FEEL YOU TAKE ADVANTAGE OF MY GOOD NATURE.
IS IT NOT TIME YOU PAID ME IN SOMETHING OTHER THAN PIG STEW?
WOULD YOU PREFER PARSNIPS, SIR TOBY?
I'D PREFER SILVER.
AND IT WOULD BE THINE, DEAR BELCH, HAD I THE COIN... OR WERE YOUR PERFORMANCE WORTH THE SPENDING.
PAH. I MAKE A MOST ABLE CLOWN.
LESS SO THAN YOU ONCE DID. THE DEPREDATIONS OF WAR HAVE TAKEN THE ROUND FROM YOUR BELLY. YOU SHOULD BE GRATEFUL I PAY IN PORK.
AS ANY GROUNDLING KNOWS, ONLY THE FAT ARE FUNNY.
SIGH
I'LL BE SUITED FOR NAUGHT BUT TRAGEDIES IN A FORTNIGHT.
WHY DO WE WASTE OUR TIME HERE? THE PEOPLE HAVE NO COIN TO WATCH US PLAY, AND ONE OF RICHARD'S SOLDIERS MAY YET RECOGNIZE MY FACE FROM THE WAR.
THERE IS A STORY THAT HAS STARTED HERE IN VERONA. I WISH TO SEE ITS END.
YOU SPEAK THE MOST IRRITATING RIDDLES, FOOL.
I'M TOLD THEY ONLY BECOME MORE MADDENING WITH TIME.
NEIGHHH

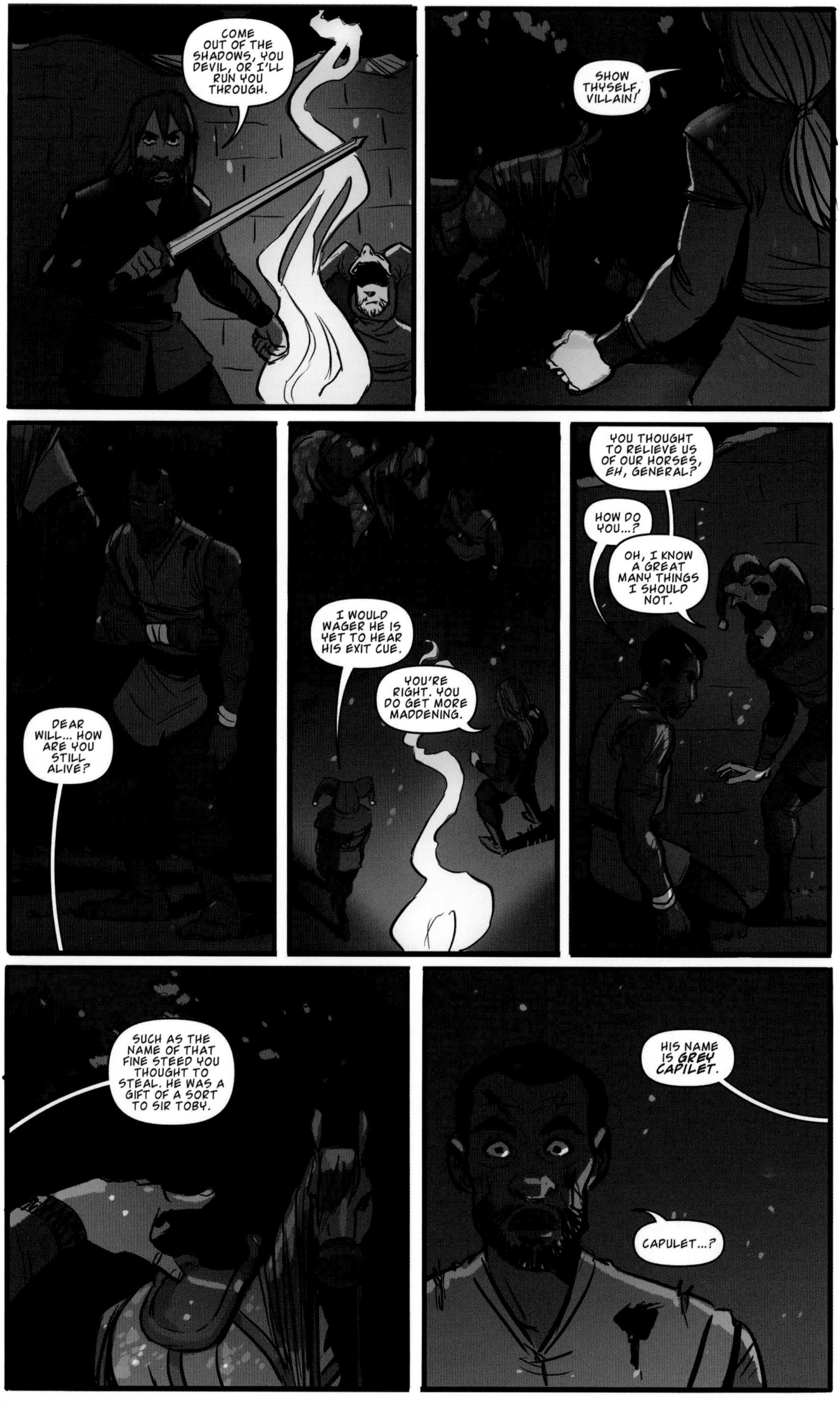
COME OUT OF THE SHADOWS, YOU DEVIL, OR I'LL RUN YOU THROUGH.
SHOW THYSELF, VILLAIN!
DEAR WILL... HOW ARE YOU STILL ALIVE?
I WOULD WAGER HE IS YET TO HEAR HIS EXIT CUE.
YOU'RE RIGHT. YOU DO GET MORE MADDENING.
YOU THOUGHT TO RELIEVE US OF OUR HORSES, EH, GENERAL?
HOW DO YOU...?
OH, I KNOW A GREAT MANY THINGS I SHOULD NOT.
SUCH AS THE NAME OF THAT FINE STEED YOU THOUGHT TO STEAL. HE WAS A GIFT OF A SORT TO SIR TOBY.
HIS NAME IS GREY CAPILET.
CAPULET...?

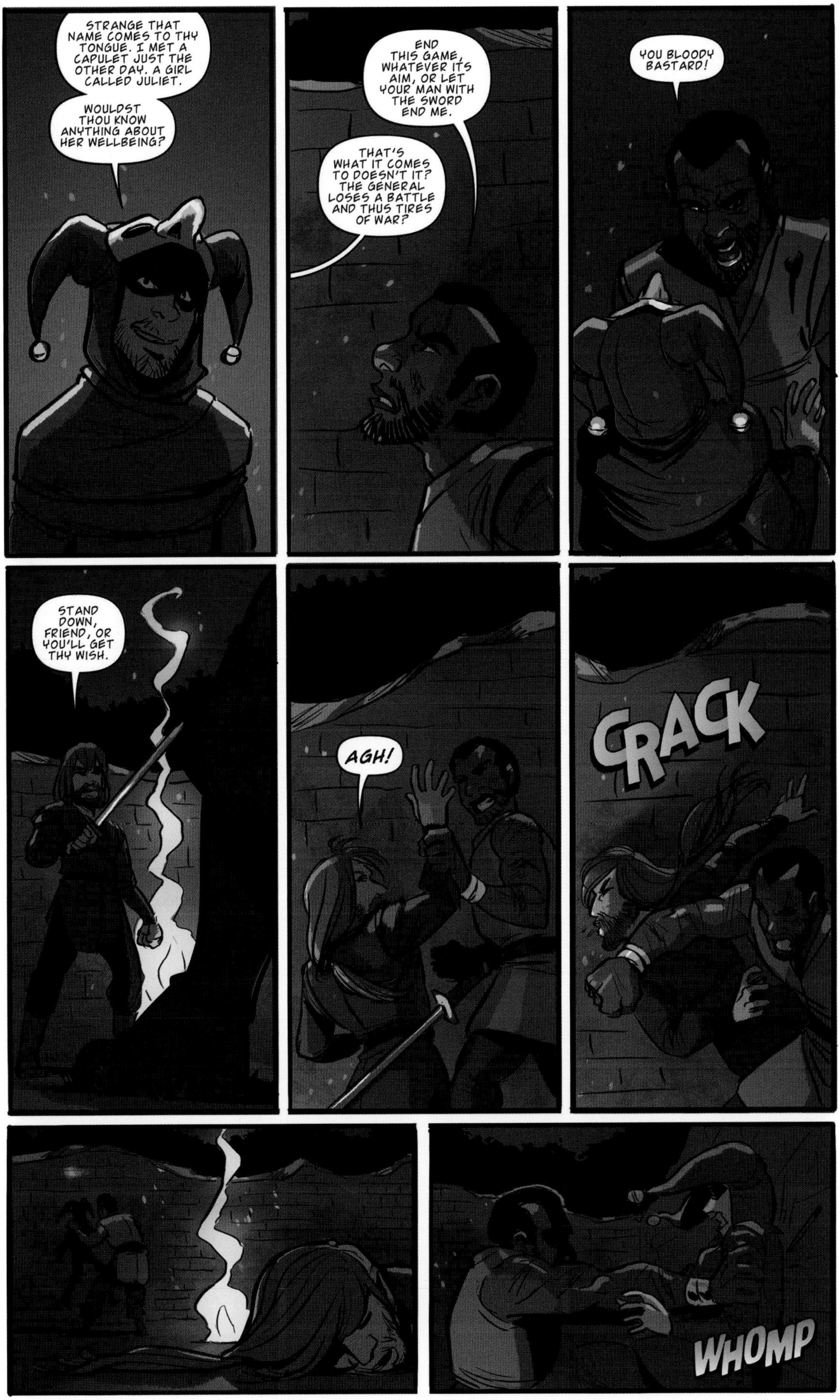
STRANGE THAT NAME COMES TO THY TONGUE. I MET A CAPULET JUST THE OTHER DAY. A GIRL CALLED JULIET.
WOULDST THOU KNOW ANYTHING ABOUT HER WELLBEING?
END THIS GAME, WHATEVER IT'S AIM, OR LET YOUR MAN WITH THE SWORD END ME.
THAT'S WHAT IT COMES TO DOESN'T IT? THE GENERAL LOSES A BATTLE AND THUS TIRES OF WAR?
YOU BLOODY BASTARD!
STAND DOWN, FRIEND, OR YOU'LL GET THY WISH.
AGH!
CRACK
WHOMP

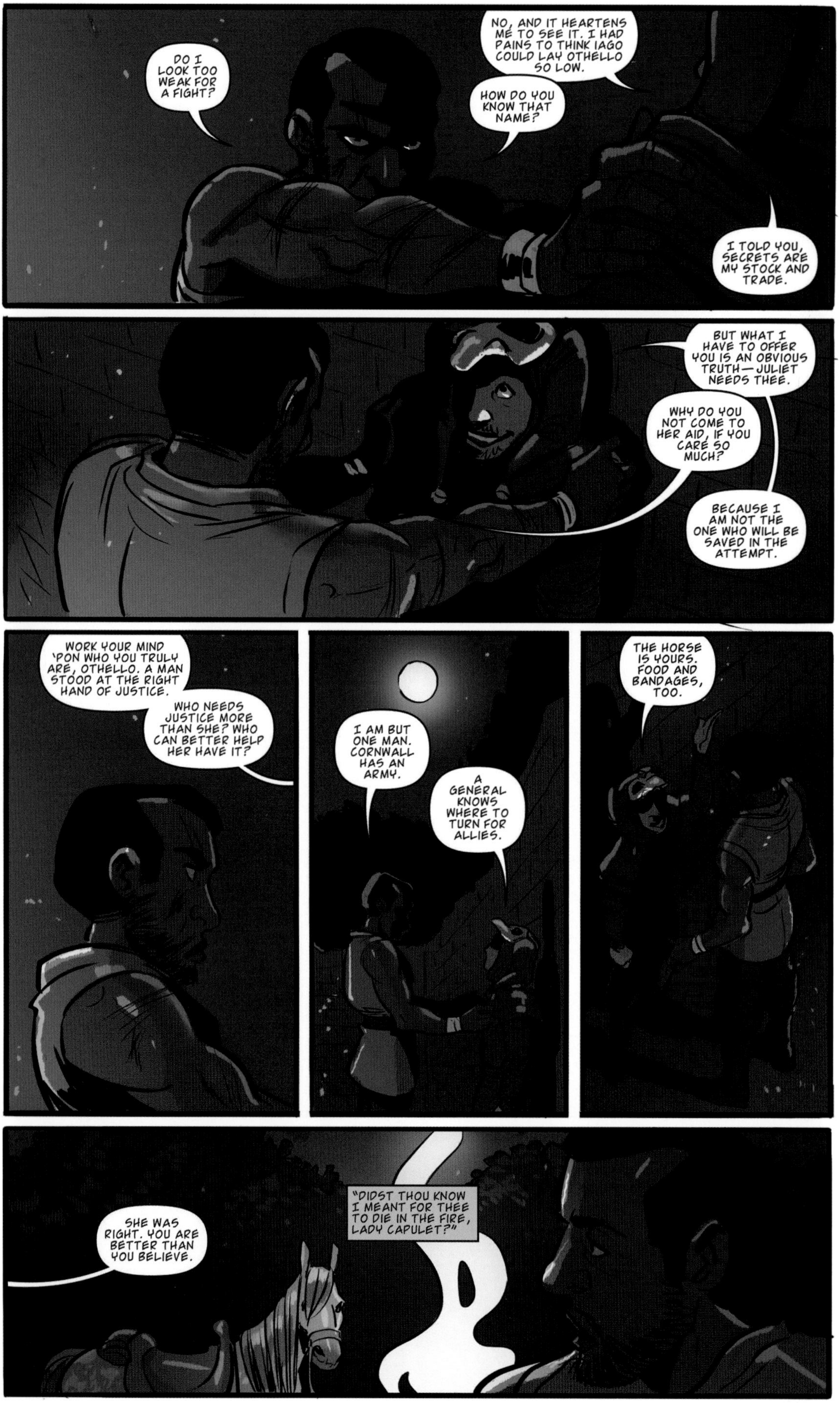
DO I LOOK TOO WEAK FOR A FIGHT?
NO, AND IT HEARTENS ME TO SEE IT. I HAD PAINS TO THINK IAGO COULD LAY OTHELLO SO LOW.
HOW DO YOU KNOW THAT NAME?
I TOLD YOU, SECRETS ARE MY STOCK AND TRADE.
BUT WHAT I HAVE TO OFFER YOU IS AN OBVIOUS TRUTH— JULIET NEEDS THEE.
WHY DO YOU NOT COME TO HER AID, IF YOU CARE SO MUCH?
BECAUSE I AM NOT THE ONE WHO WILL BE SAVED IN THE ATTEMPT.
WORK YOUR MIND 'PON WHO YOU TRULY ARE, OTHELLO. A MAN STOOD AT THE RIGHT HAND OF JUSTICE.
WHO NEEDS JUSTICE MORE THAN SHE? WHO CAN BETTER HELP HER HAVE IT?
I AM BUT ONE MAN. CORNWALL HAS AN ARMY.
A GENERAL KNOWS WHERE TO TURN FOR ALLIES.
THE HORSE IS YOURS. FOOD AND BANDAGES, TOO.
"DIDST THOU KNOW I MEANT FOR THEE TO DIE IN THE FIRE, LADY CAPULET?"
SHE WAS RIGHT. YOU ARE BETTER THAN YOU BELIEVE.

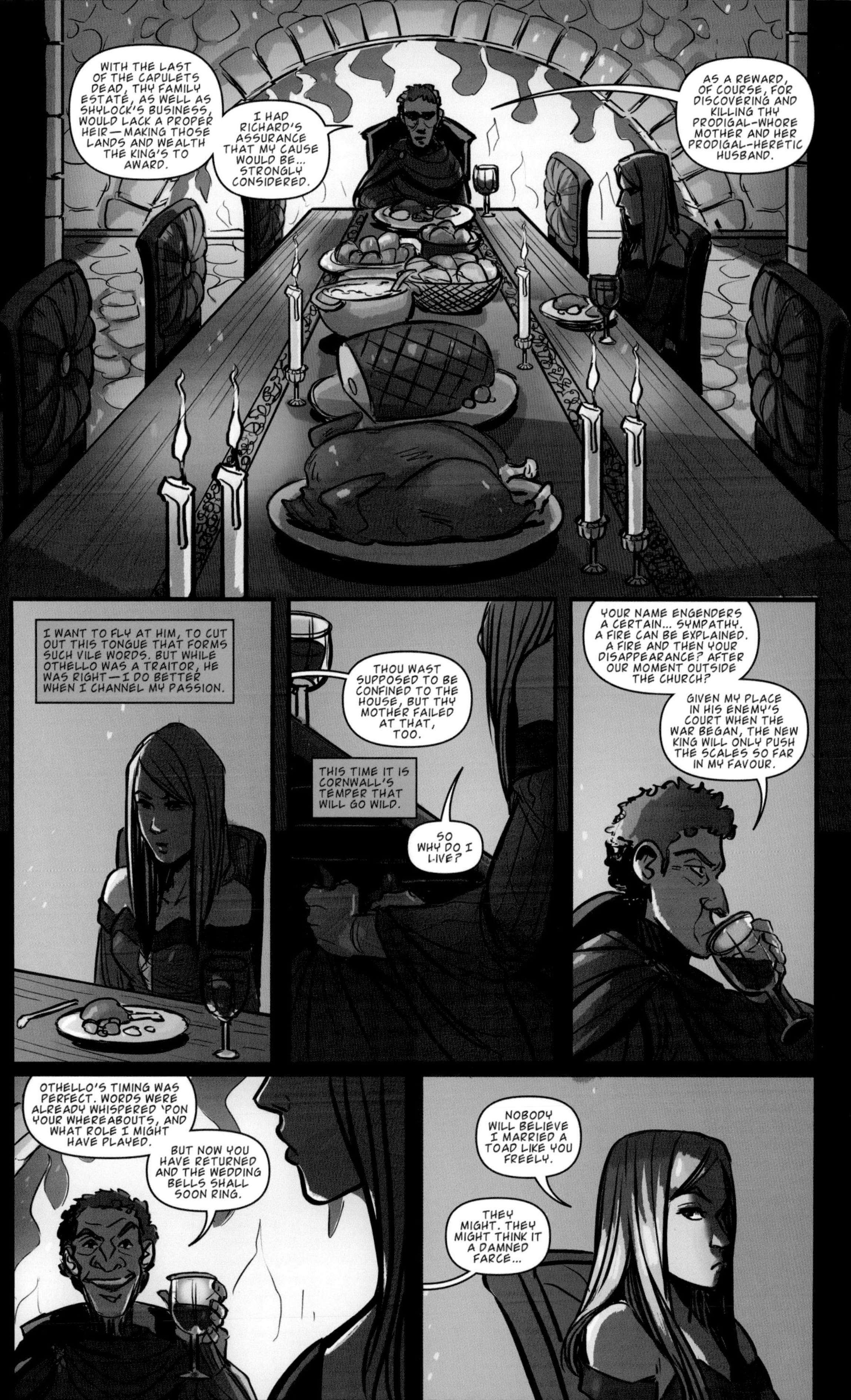

WITH THE LAST OF THE CAPULETS DEAD, THY FAMILY ESTATE, AS WELL AS SHYLOCK'S BUSINESS, WOULD LACK A PROPER HEIR—MAKING THOSE LANDS AND WEALTH THE KING'S TO AWARD.
I HAD RICHARD'S ASSURANCE THAT MY CAUSE WOULD BE... STRONGLY CONSIDERED.
AS A REWARD, OF COURSE, FOR DISCOVERING AND KILLING THY PRODIGAL-WHORE MOTHER AND HER PRODIGAL-HERETIC HUSBAND.
I WANT TO FLY AT HIM, TO CUT OUT THIS TONGUE THAT FORMS SUCH VILE WORDS. BUT WHILE OTHELLO WAS A TRAITOR, HE WAS RIGHT—I DO BETTER WHEN I CHANNEL MY PASSION.
THOU WAST SUPPOSED TO BE CONFINED TO THE HOUSE, BUT THY MOTHER FAILED AT THAT, TOO.
THIS TIME IT IS CORNWALL'S TEMPER THAT WILL GO WILD.
SO WHY DO I LIVE?
YOUR NAME ENGENDERS A CERTAIN... SYMPATHY. A FIRE CAN BE EXPLAINED. A FIRE AND THEN YOUR DISAPPEARANCE? AFTER OUR MOMENT OUTSIDE THE CHURCH?
GIVEN MY PLACE IN HIS ENEMY'S COURT WHEN THE WAR BEGAN, THE NEW KING WILL ONLY PUSH THE SCALES SO FAR IN MY FAVOUR.
OTHELLO'S TIMING WAS PERFECT. WORDS WERE ALREADY WHISPERED 'PON YOUR WHEREABOUTS, AND WHAT ROLE I MIGHT HAVE PLAYED.
BUT NOW YOU HAVE RETURNED AND THE WEDDING BELLS SHALL SOON RING.
NOBODY WILL BELIEVE I MARRIED A TOAD LIKE YOU FREELY.
THEY MIGHT. THEY MIGHT THINK IT A DAMNED FARCE...

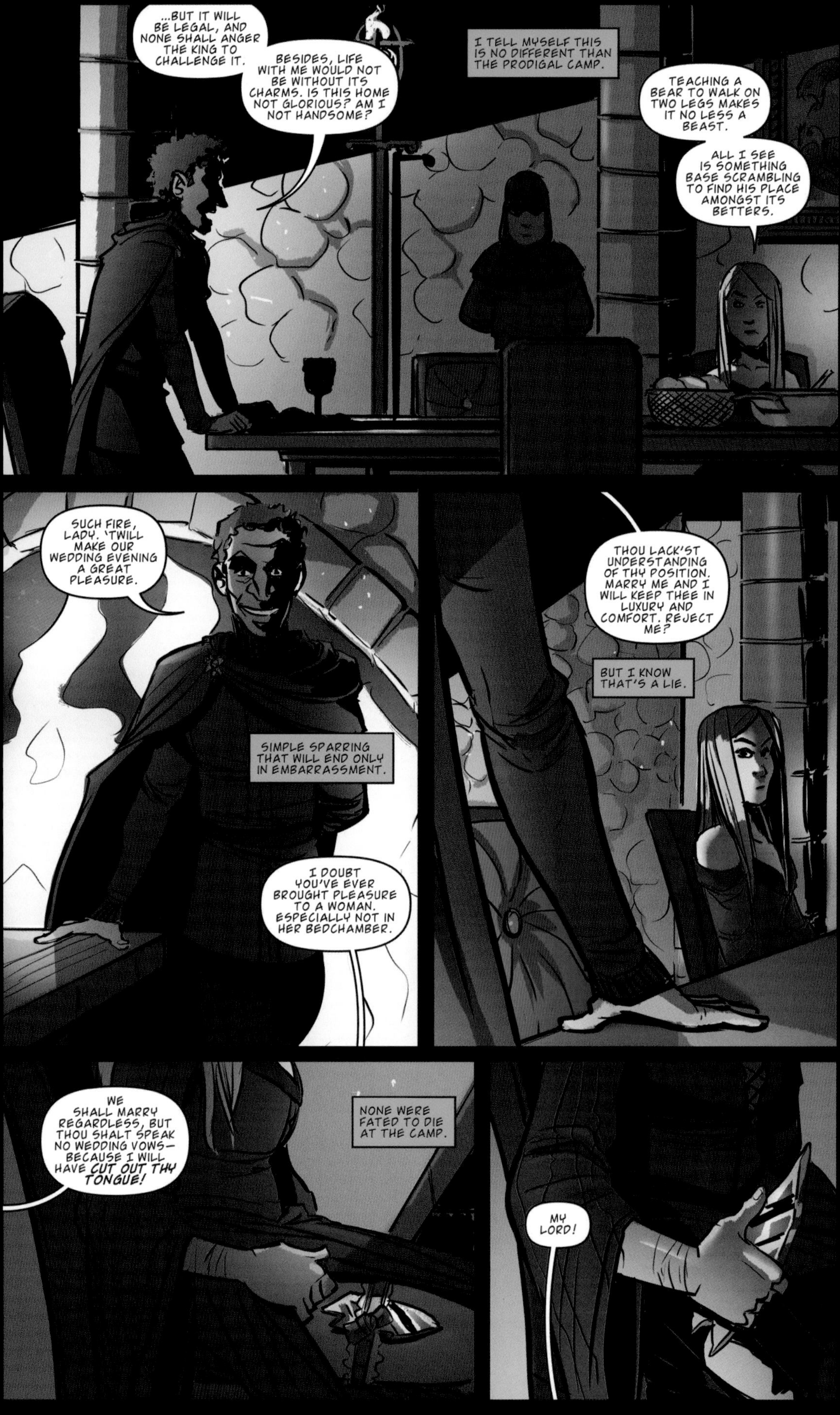
...BUT IT WILL BE LEGAL, AND NONE SHALL ANGER THE KING TO CHALLENGE IT.
BESIDES, LIFE WITH ME WOULD NOT BE WITHOUT ITS CHARMS. IS THIS HOME NOT GLORIOUS? AM I NOT HANDSOME?
I TELL MYSELF THIS IS NO DIFFERENT THAN THE PRODIGAL CAMP.
TEACHING A BEAR TO WALK ON TWO LEGS MAKES IT NO LESS A BEAST.
ALL I SEE IS SOMETHING BASE SCRAMBLING TO FIND HIS PLACE AMONGST ITS BETTERS.
SUCH FIRE, LADY. 'TWILL MAKE OUR WEDDING EVENING A GREAT PLEASURE.
SIMPLE SPARRING THAT WILL END ONLY IN EMBARRASSMENT.
I DOUBT YOU'VE EVER BROUGHT PLEASURE TO A WOMAN. ESPECIALLY NOT IN HER BEDCHAMBER.
THOU LACK'ST UNDERSTANDING OF THY POSITION. MARRY ME AND I WILL KEEP THEE IN LUXURY AND COMFORT. REJECT ME?
BUT I KNOW THAT'S A LIE.
WE SHALL MARRY REGARDLESS, BUT THOU SHALT SPEAK NO WEDDING VOWS— BECAUSE I WILL HAVE CUT OUT THY TONGUE!
NONE WERE FATED TO DIE AT THE CAMP.
MY LORD!

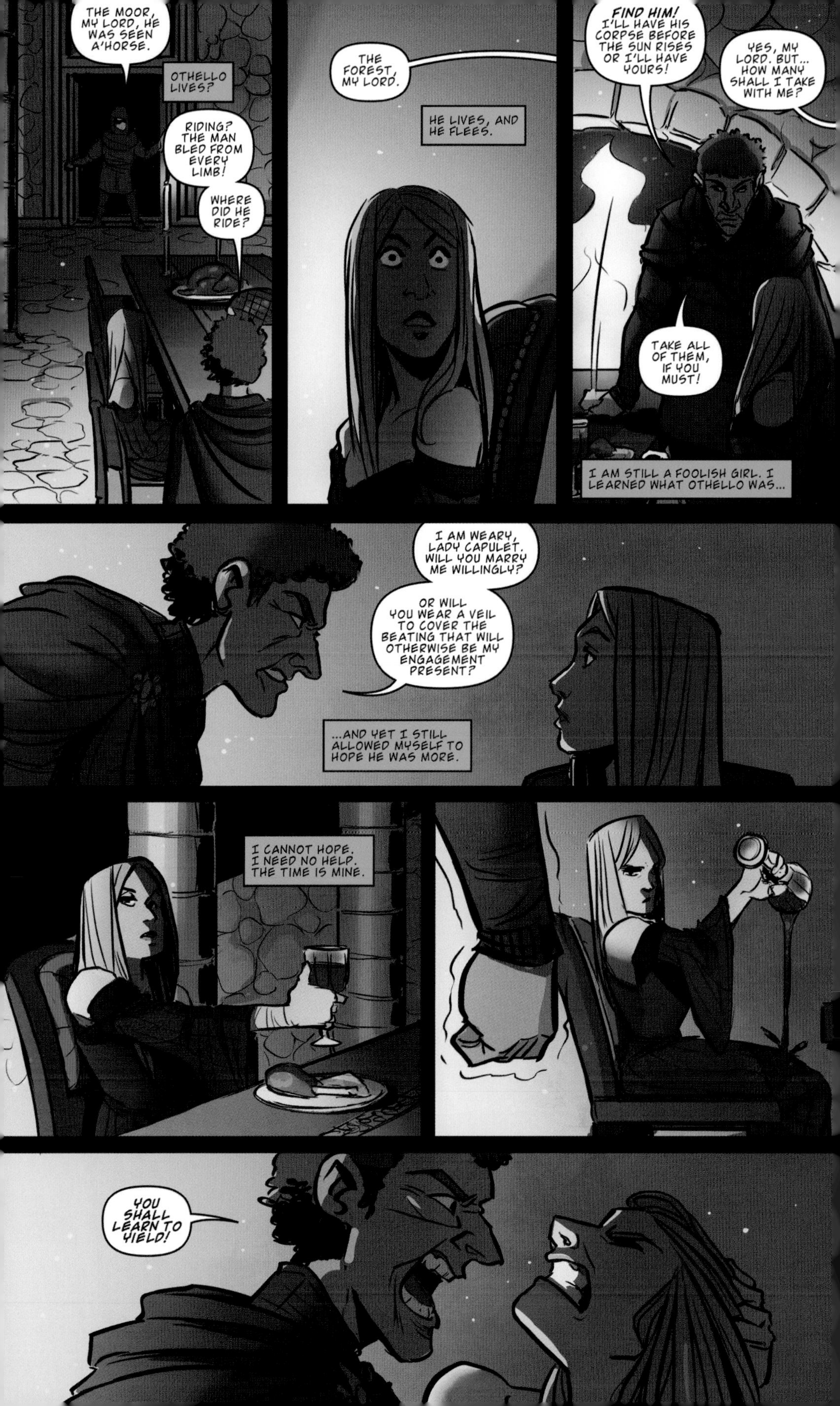
THE MOOR, MY LORD, HE WAS SEEN A'HORSE.
OTHELLO LIVES?
RIDING? THE MAN BLED FROM EVERY LIMB!
WHERE DID HE RIDE?
THE FOREST, MY LORD.
HE LIVES, AND HE FLEES.
FIND HIM! I'LL HAVE HIS CORPSE BEFORE THE SUN RISES OR I'LL HAVE YOURS!
YES, MY LORD. BUT... HOW MANY SHALL I TAKE WITH ME?
TAKE ALL OF THEM, IF YOU MUST!
I AM STILL A FOOLISH GIRL. I LEARNED WHAT OTHELLO WAS...
I AM WEARY, LADY CAPULET. WILL YOU MARRY ME WILLINGLY?
OR WILL YOU WEAR A VEIL TO COVER THE BEATING THAT WILL OTHERWISE BE MY ENGAGEMENT PRESENT?
...AND YET I STILL ALLOWED MYSELF TO HOPE HE WAS MORE.
I CANNOT HOPE. I NEED NO HELP. THE TIME IS MINE.
YOU SHALL LEARN TO YIELD!

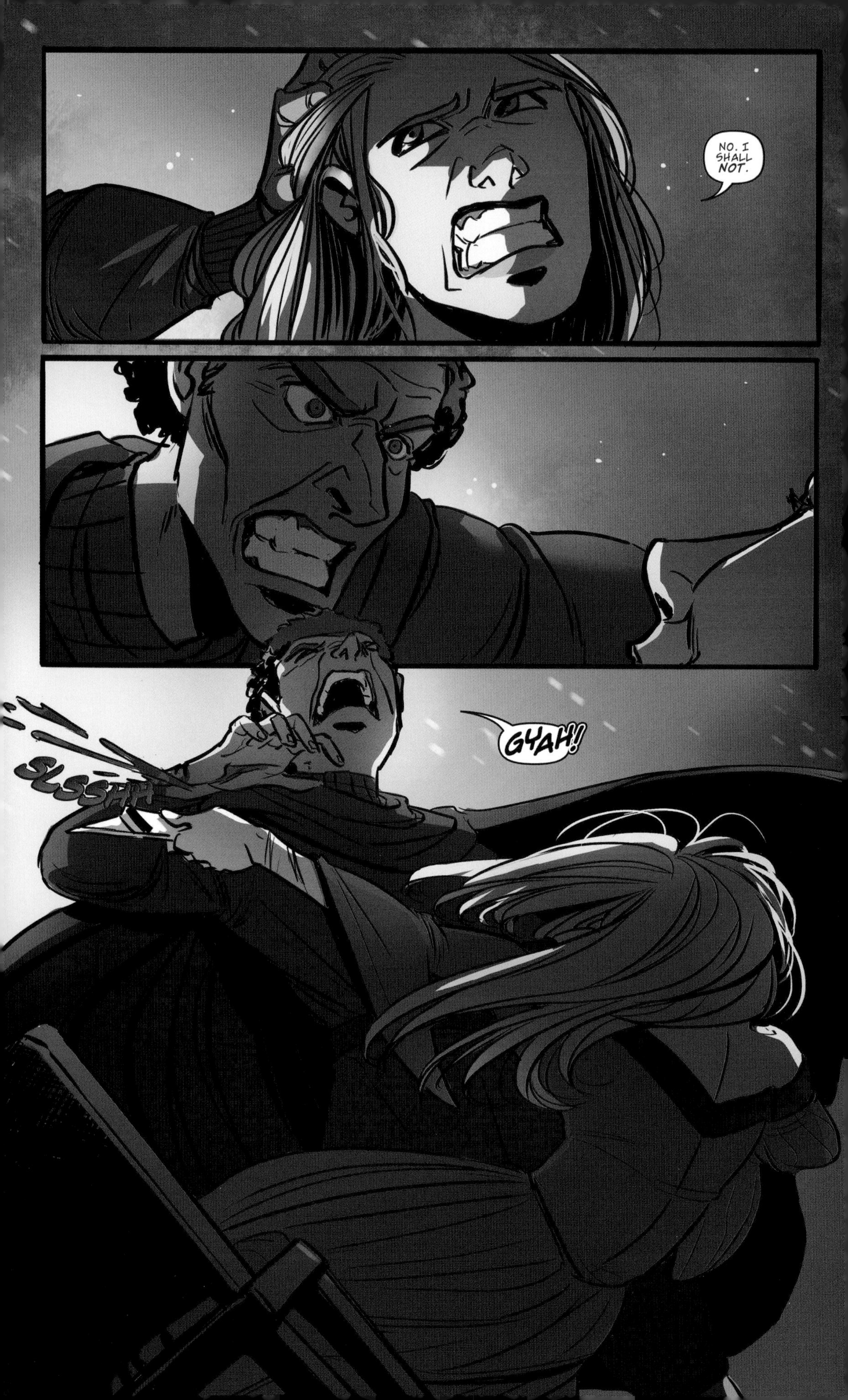
NO. I SHALL NOT.
GYAH!
SLSSHH

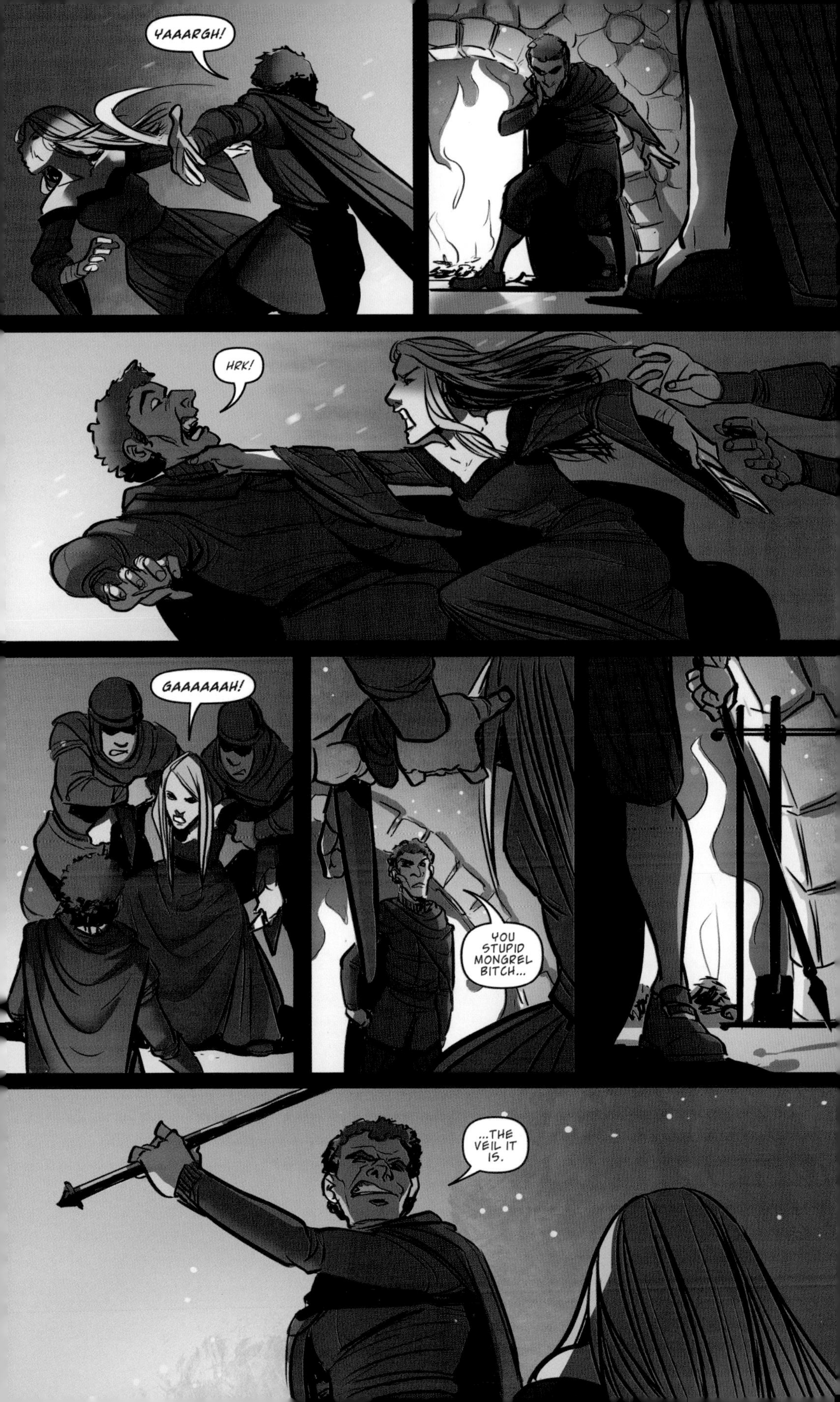
YAAARGH!
HRK!
GAAAAAAH!
YOU STUPID MONGREL BITCH...
...THE VEIL IT IS.

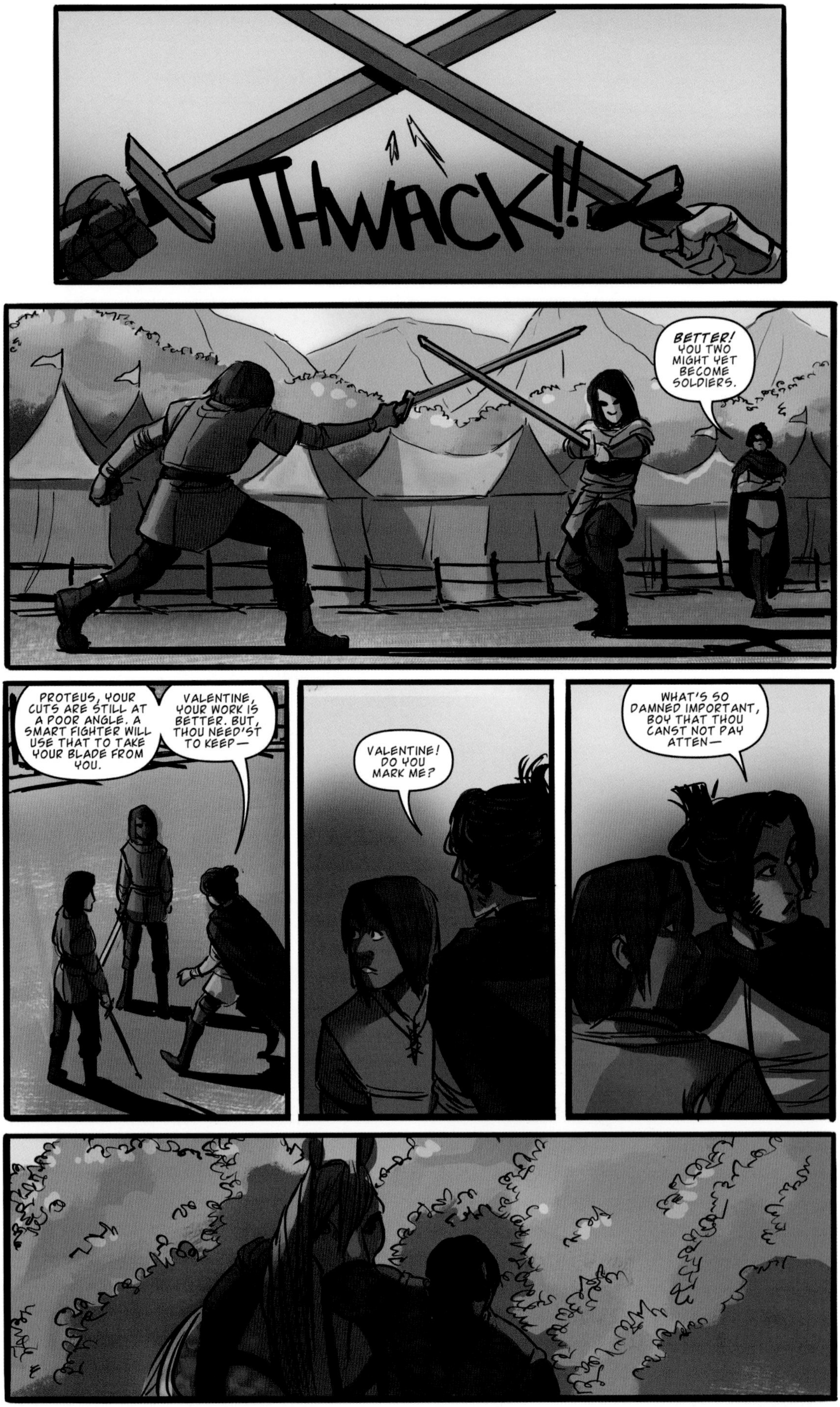
THWACK!!
BETTER! YOU TWO MIGHT YET BECOME SOLDIERS.
PROTEUS, YOUR CUTS ARE STILL AT A POOR ANGLE. A SMART FIGHTER WILL USE THAT TO TAKE YOUR BLADE FROM YOU.
VALENTINE, YOUR WORK IS BETTER. BUT, THOU NEED'ST TO KEEP—
VALENTINE! DO YOU MARK ME?
WHAT'S SO DAMNED IMPORTANT, BOY THAT THOU CANST NOT PAY ATTEN—

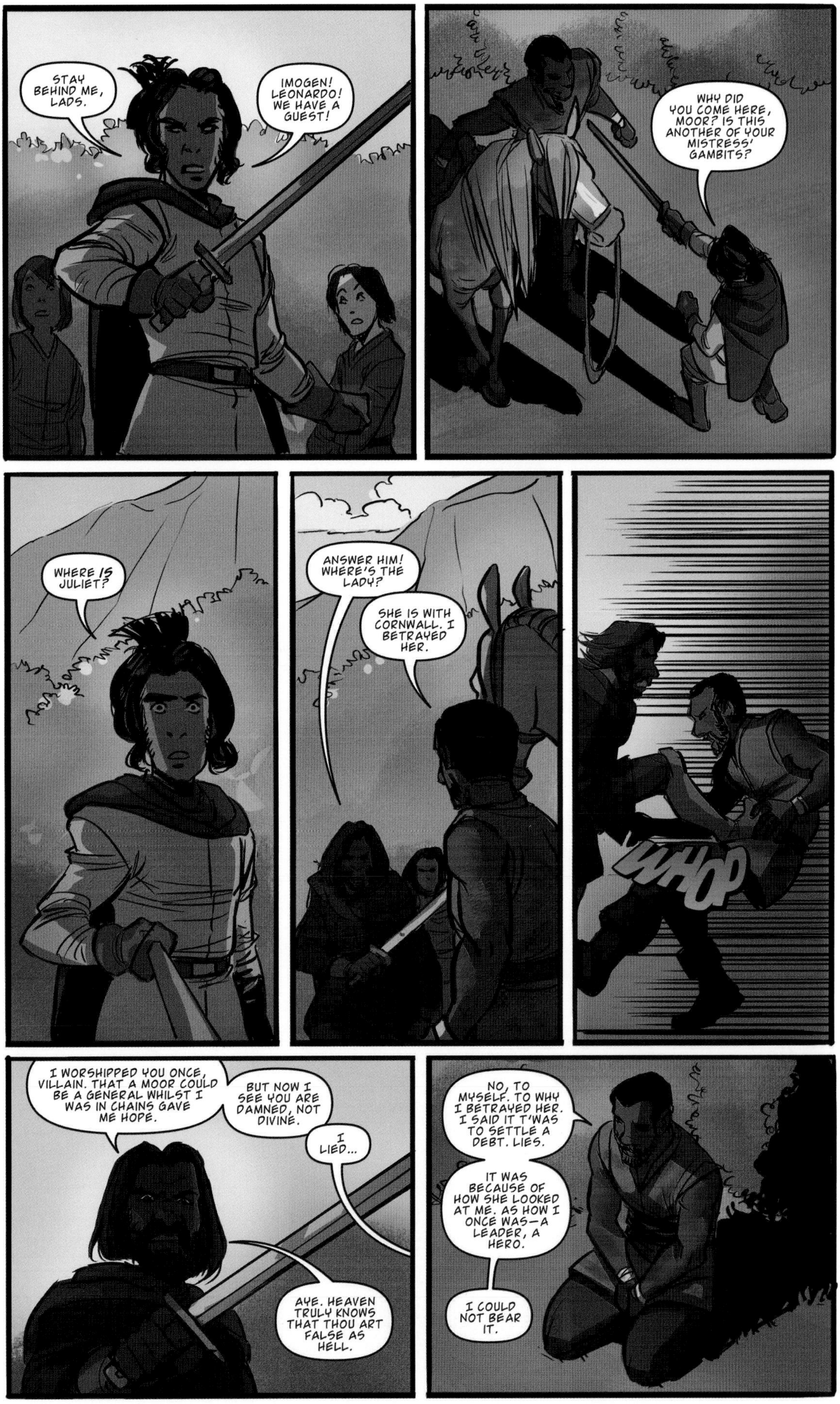
STAY BEHIND ME, LADS.
IMOGEN! LEONARDO! WE HAVE A GUEST!
WHY DID YOU COME HERE, MOOR? IS THIS ANOTHER OF YOUR MISTRESS' GAMBITS?
WHERE *IS* JULIET?
ANSWER HIM! WHERE'S THE LADY?
SHE IS WITH CORNWALL. I BETRAYED HER.
WHOP
I WORSHIPPED YOU ONCE, VILLAIN. THAT A MOOR COULD BE A GENERAL WHILST I WAS IN CHAINS GAVE ME HOPE.
BUT NOW I SEE YOU ARE DAMNED, NOT DIVINE.
I LIED...
AYE. HEAVEN TRULY KNOWS THAT THOU ART FALSE AS HELL.
NO, TO MYSELF. TO WHY I BETRAYED HER. I SAID IT T'WAS TO SETTLE A DEBT. LIES.
IT WAS BECAUSE OF HOW SHE LOOKED AT ME. AS HOW I ONCE WAS—A LEADER, A HERO.
I COULD NOT BEAR IT.

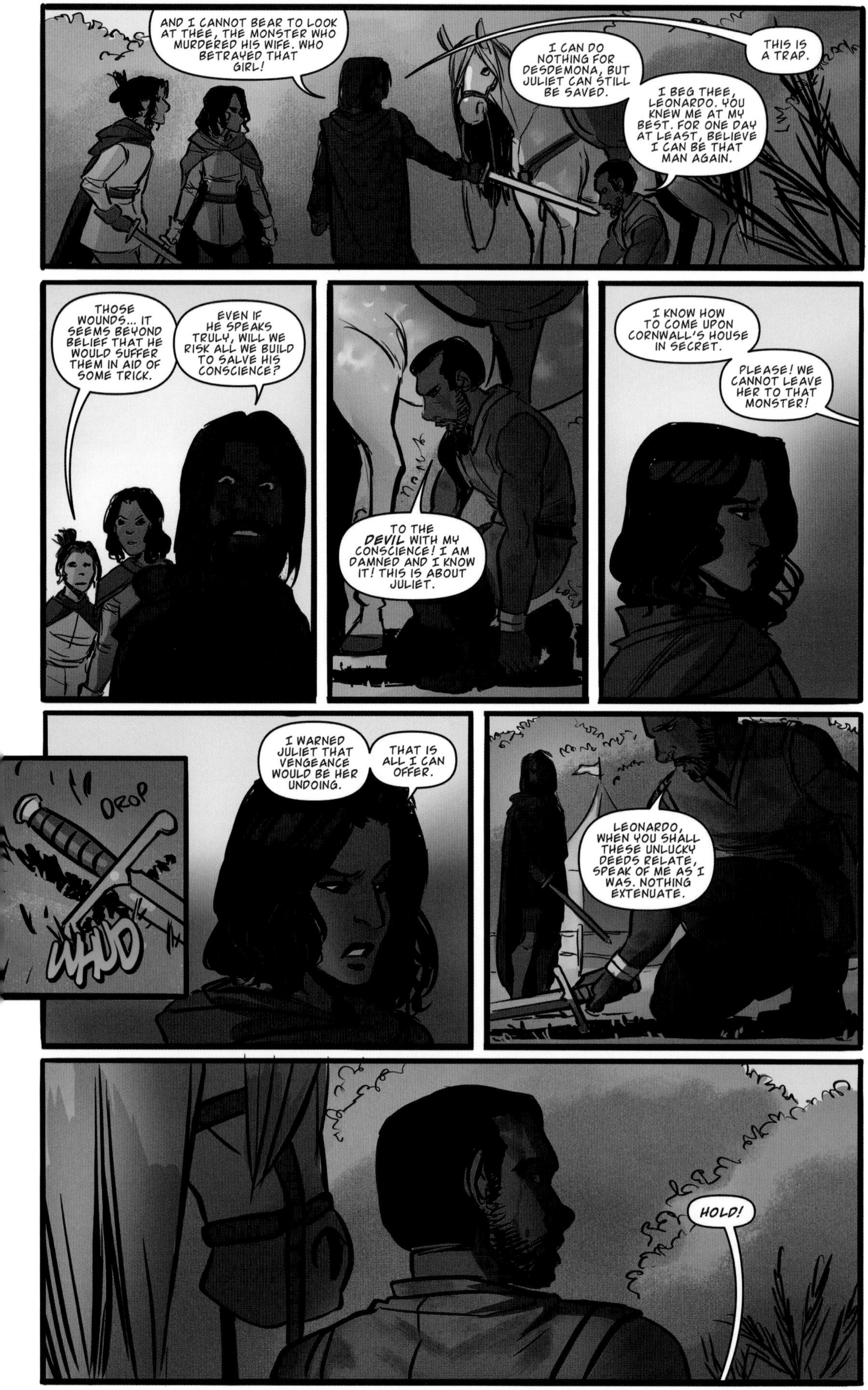
AND I CANNOT BEAR TO LOOK AT THEE, THE MONSTER WHO MURDERED HIS WIFE. WHO BETRAYED THAT GIRL!
I CAN DO NOTHING FOR DESDEMONA, BUT JULIET CAN STILL BE SAVED.
THIS IS A TRAP.
I BEG THEE, LEONARDO. YOU KNEW ME AT MY BEST. FOR ONE DAY AT LEAST, BELIEVE I CAN BE THAT MAN AGAIN.
THOSE WOUNDS... IT SEEMS BEYOND BELIEF THAT HE WOULD SUFFER THEM IN AID OF SOME TRICK.
EVEN IF HE SPEAKS TRULY, WILL WE RISK ALL WE BUILD TO SALVE HIS CONSCIENCE?
TO THE DEVIL WITH MY CONSCIENCE! I AM DAMNED AND I KNOW IT! THIS IS ABOUT JULIET.
I KNOW HOW TO COME UPON CORNWALL'S HOUSE IN SECRET.
PLEASE! WE CANNOT LEAVE HER TO THAT MONSTER!
DROP
WHUD
I WARNED JULIET THAT VENGEANCE WOULD BE HER UNDOING.
THAT IS ALL I CAN OFFER.
LEONARDO, WHEN YOU SHALL THESE UNLUCKY DEEDS RELATE, SPEAK OF ME AS I WAS. NOTHING EXTENUATE.
HOLD!

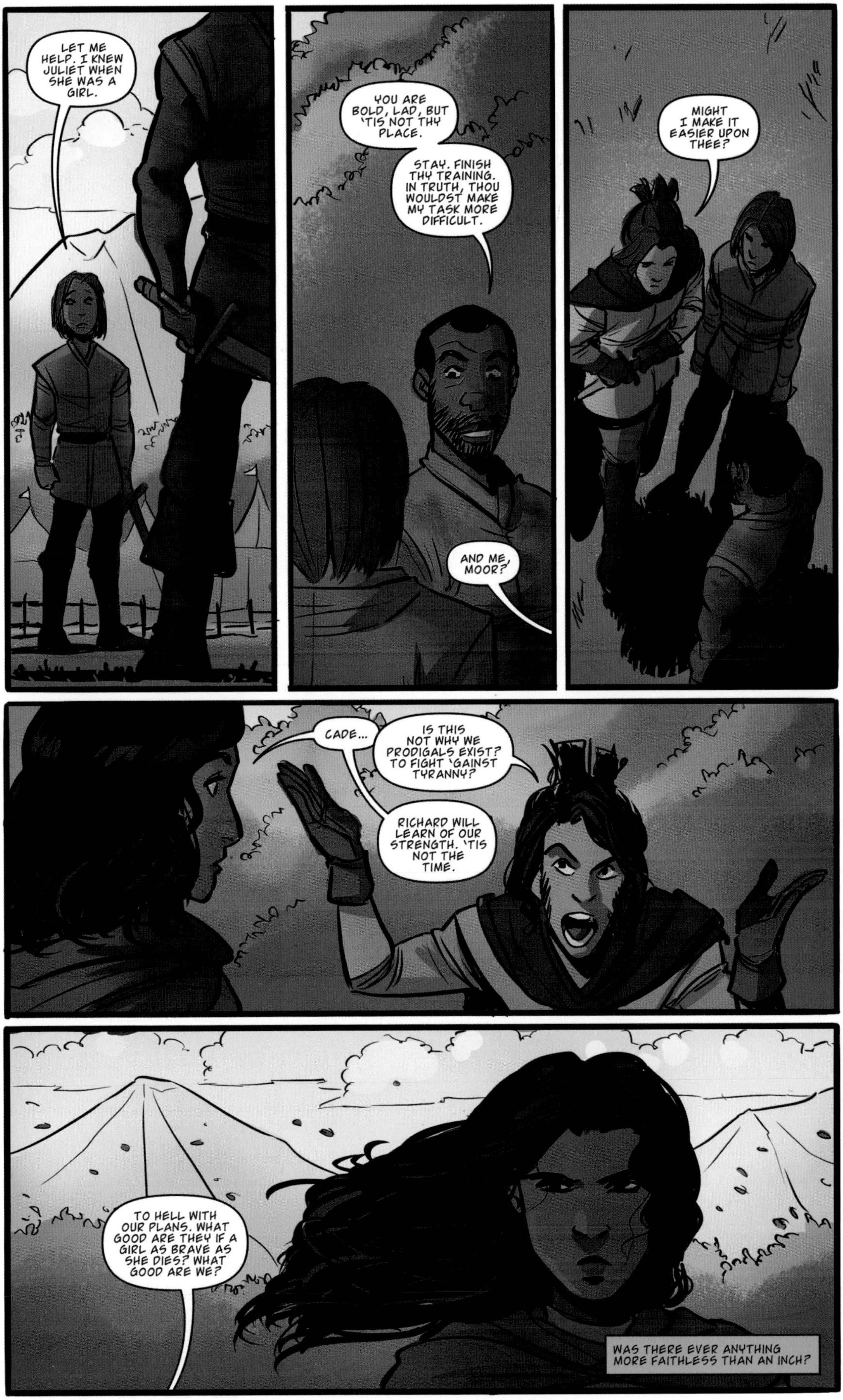
LET ME HELP. I KNEW JULIET WHEN SHE WAS A GIRL.
YOU ARE BOLD, LAD, BUT 'TIS NOT THY PLACE.
STAY. FINISH THY TRAINING. IN TRUTH, THOU WOULDST MAKE MY TASK MORE DIFFICULT.
AND ME, MOOR?
MIGHT I MAKE IT EASIER UPON THEE?
CADE...
IS THIS NOT WHY WE PRODIGALS EXIST? TO FIGHT 'GAINST TYRANNY?
RICHARD WILL LEARN OF OUR STRENGTH. 'TIS NOT THE TIME.
TO HELL WITH OUR PLANS. WHAT GOOD ARE THEY IF A GIRL AS BRAVE AS SHE DIES? WHAT GOOD ARE WE?
WAS THERE EVER ANYTHING MORE FAITHLESS THAN AN INCH?

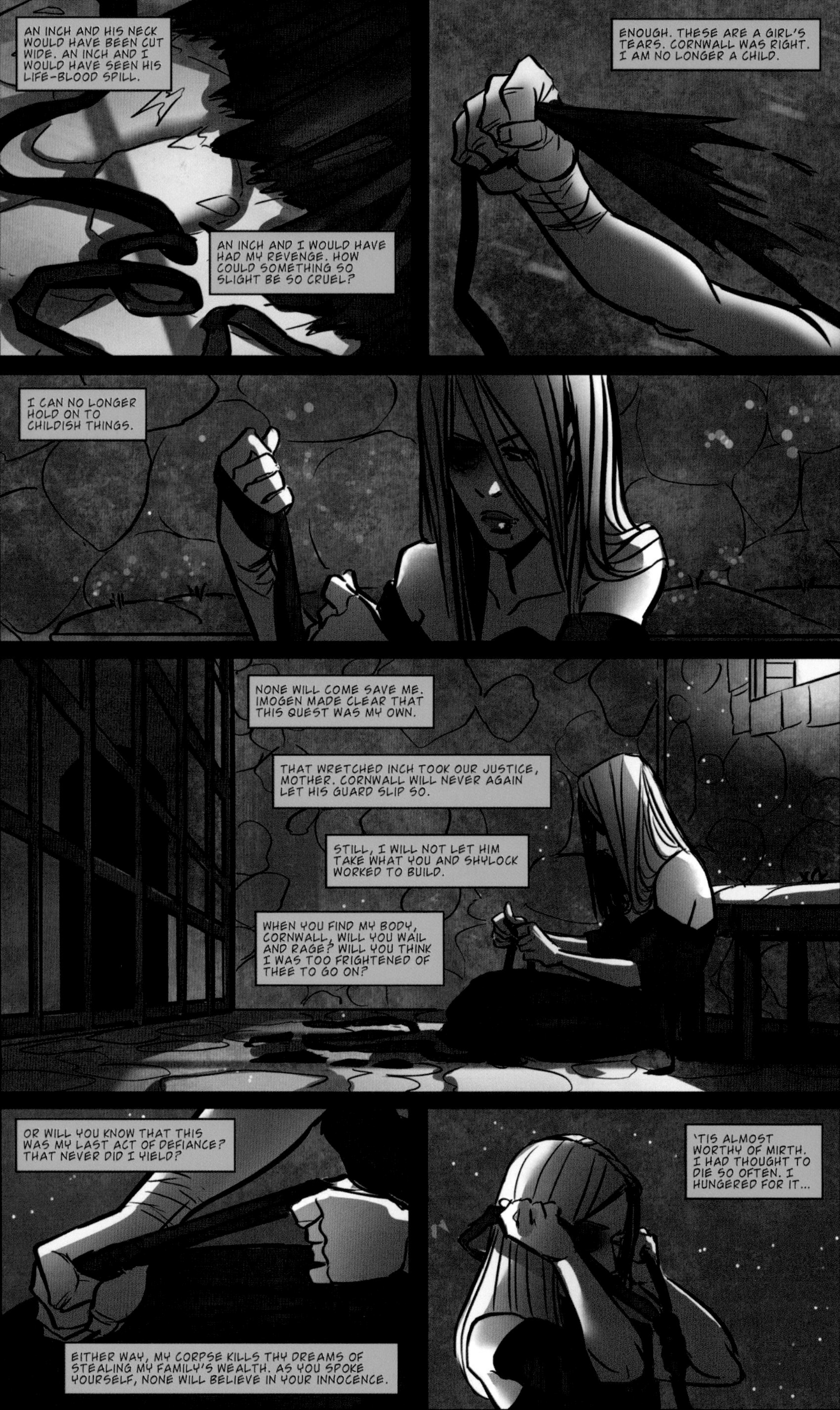
AN INCH AND HIS NECK WOULD HAVE BEEN CUT WIDE. AN INCH AND I WOULD HAVE SEEN HIS LIFE-BLOOD SPILL.
AN INCH AND I WOULD HAVE HAD MY REVENGE. HOW COULD SOMETHING SO SLIGHT BE SO CRUEL?
ENOUGH. THESE ARE A GIRL'S TEARS. CORNWALL WAS RIGHT. I AM NO LONGER A CHILD.
I CAN NO LONGER HOLD ON TO CHILDISH THINGS.
NONE WILL COME SAVE ME. IMOGEN MADE CLEAR THAT THIS QUEST WAS MY OWN.
THAT WRETCHED INCH TOOK OUR JUSTICE, MOTHER. CORNWALL WILL NEVER AGAIN LET HIS GUARD SLIP SO.
STILL, I WILL NOT LET HIM TAKE WHAT YOU AND SHYLOCK WORKED TO BUILD.
WHEN YOU FIND MY BODY, CORNWALL, WILL YOU WAIL AND RAGE? WILL YOU THINK I WAS TOO FRIGHTENED OF THEE TO GO ON?
OR WILL YOU KNOW THAT THIS WAS MY LAST ACT OF DEFIANCE? THAT NEVER DID I YIELD?
EITHER WAY, MY CORPSE KILLS THY DREAMS OF STEALING MY FAMILY'S WEALTH. AS YOU SPOKE YOURSELF, NONE WILL BELIEVE IN YOUR INNOCENCE.
'TIS ALMOST WORTHY OF MIRTH. I HAD THOUGHT TO DIE SO OFTEN. I HUNGERED FOR IT...

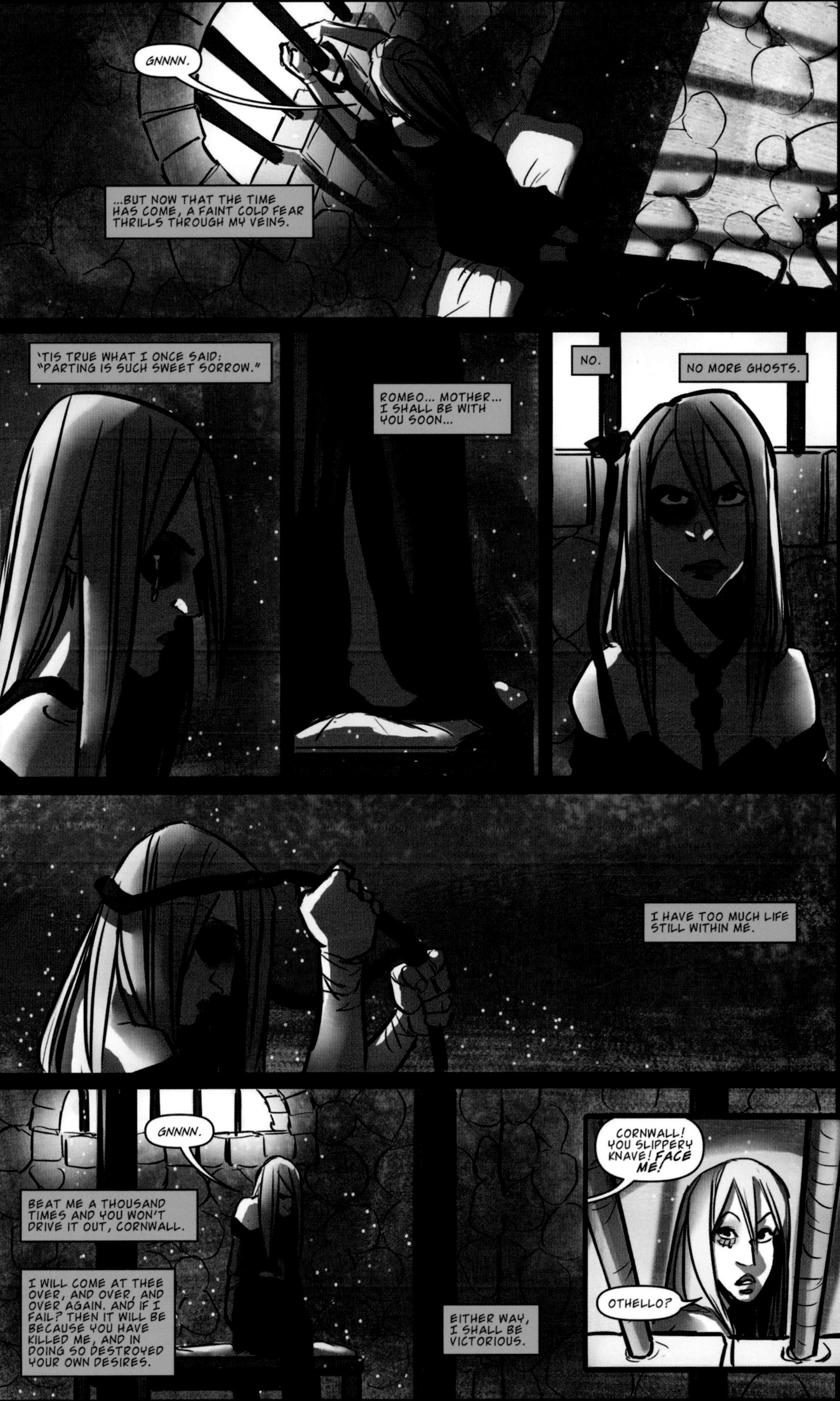
GNNNN.
...BUT NOW THAT THE TIME HAS COME, A FAINT COLD FEAR THRILLS THROUGH MY VEINS.
'TIS TRUE WHAT I ONCE SAID: "PARTING IS SUCH SWEET SORROW."
ROMEO... MOTHER... I SHALL BE WITH YOU SOON...
NO.
NO MORE GHOSTS.
I HAVE TOO MUCH LIFE STILL WITHIN ME.
GNNNN.
BEAT ME A THOUSAND TIMES AND YOU WON'T DRIVE IT OUT, CORNWALL.
I WILL COME AT THEE OVER, AND OVER, AND OVER AGAIN. AND IF I FAIL? THEN IT WILL BE BECAUSE YOU HAVE KILLED ME, AND IN DOING SO DESTROYED YOUR OWN DESIRES.
EITHER WAY, I SHALL BE VICTORIOUS.
CORNWALL! YOU SLIPPERY KNAVE! FACE ME!
OTHELLO?

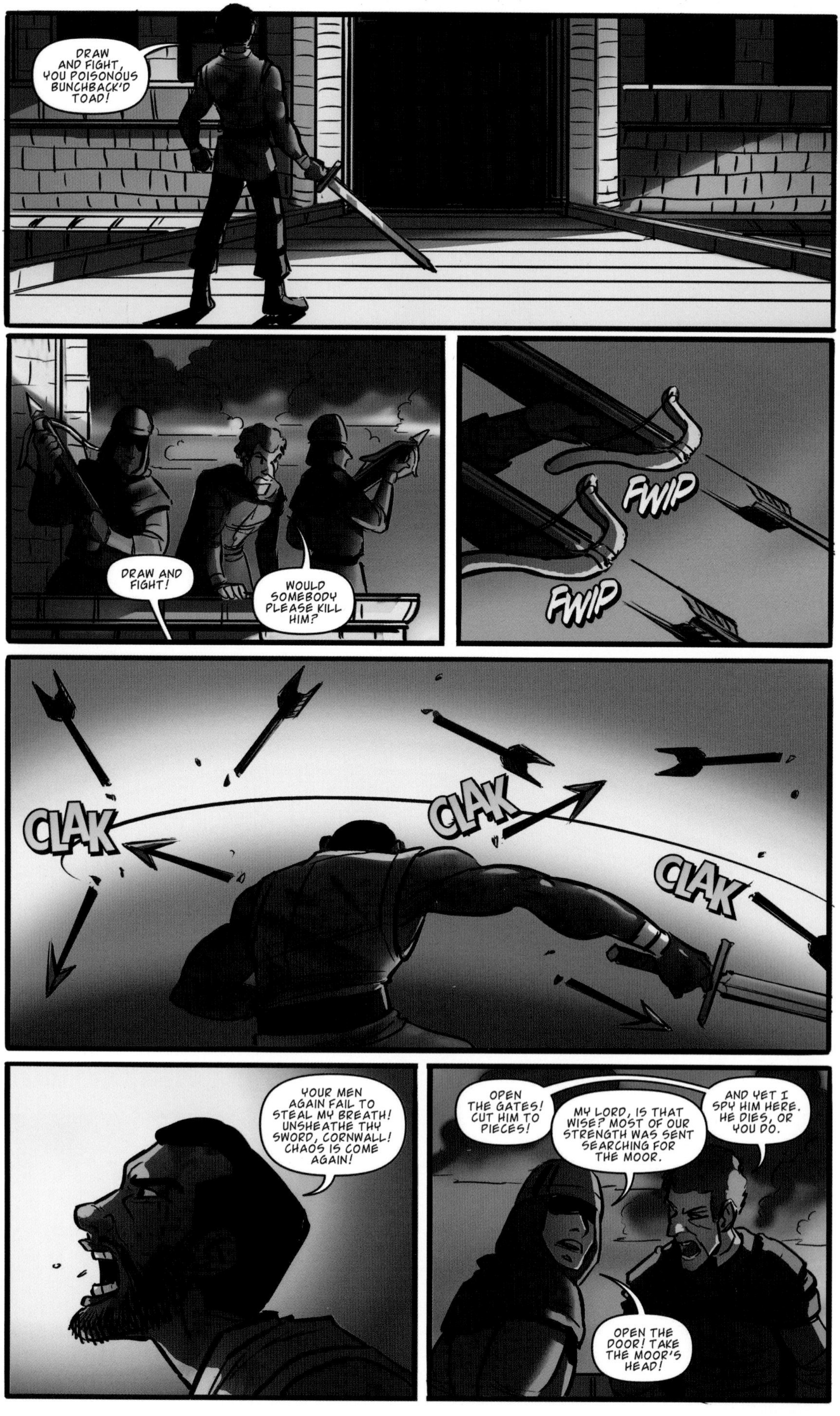
DRAW AND FIGHT, YOU POISONOUS BUNCHBACK'D TOAD!
DRAW AND FIGHT!
WOULD SOMEBODY PLEASE KILL HIM?
FWIP
FWIP
CLAK
CLAK
CLAK
YOUR MEN AGAIN FAIL TO STEAL MY BREATH! UNSHEATHE THY SWORD, CORNWALL! CHAOS IS COME AGAIN!
OPEN THE GATES! CUT HIM TO PIECES!
MY LORD, IS THAT WISE? MOST OF OUR STRENGTH WAS SENT SEARCHING FOR THE MOOR.
AND YET I SPY HIM HERE. HE DIES, OR YOU DO.
OPEN THE DOOR! TAKE THE MOOR'S HEAD!

CLOSE
THE GATE!
CLOSE
THE—

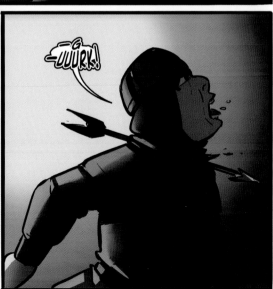

—G
UUURK!

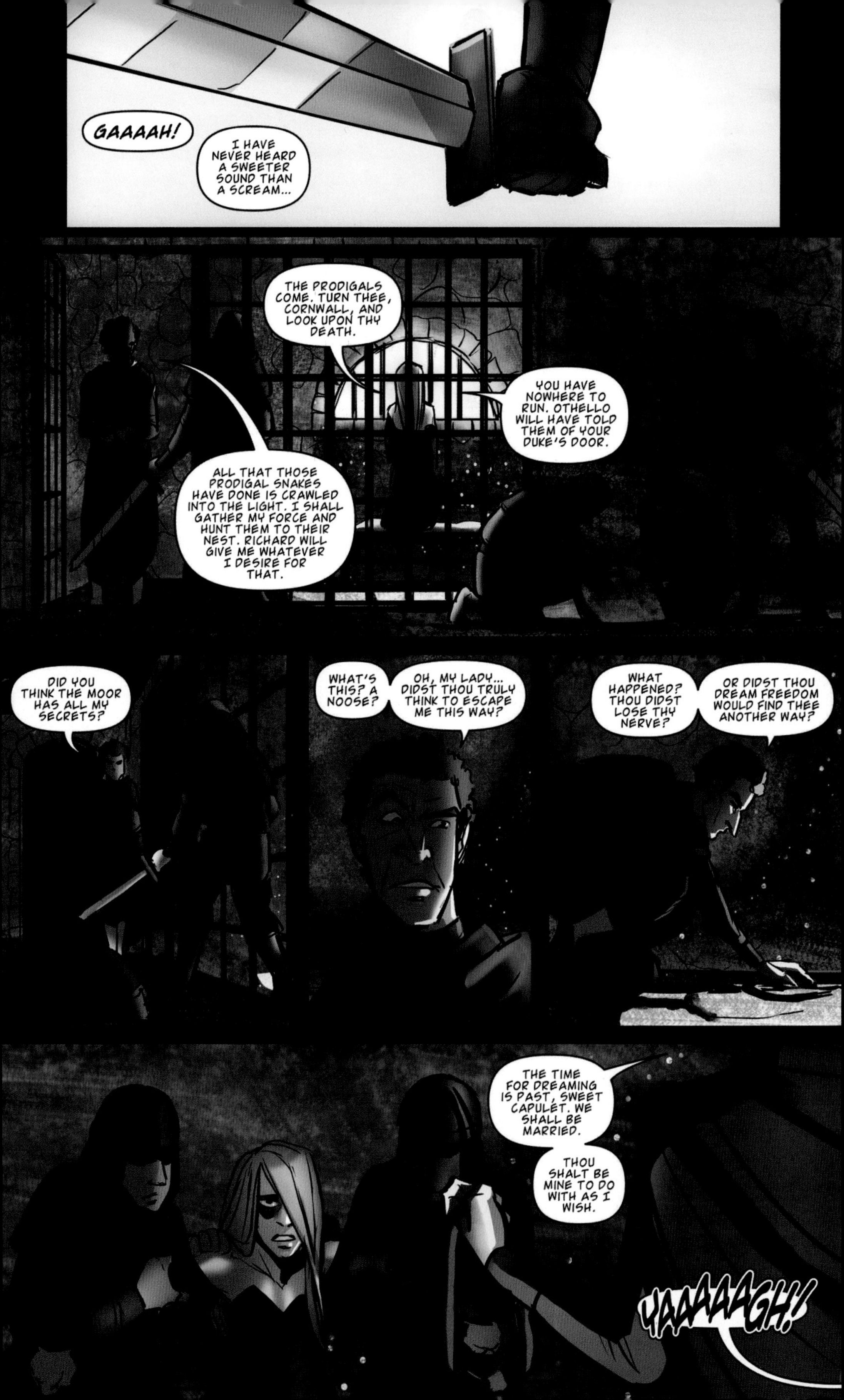

GAAAAH!
I HAVE NEVER HEARD A SWEETER SOUND THAN A SCREAM...
THE PRODIGALS COME. TURN THEE, CORNWALL, AND LOOK UPON THY DEATH.
ALL THAT THOSE PRODIGAL SNAKES HAVE DONE IS CRAWLED INTO THE LIGHT. I SHALL GATHER MY FORCE AND HUNT THEM TO THEIR NEST. RICHARD WILL GIVE ME WHATEVER I DESIRE FOR THAT.
YOU HAVE NOWHERE TO RUN. OTHELLO WILL HAVE TOLD THEM OF YOUR DUKE'S DOOR.
DID YOU THINK THE MOOR HAS ALL MY SECRETS?
WHAT'S THIS? A NOOSE?
OH, MY LADY... DIDST THOU TRULY THINK TO ESCAPE ME THIS WAY?
WHAT HAPPENED? THOU DIDST LOSE THY NERVE?
OR DIDST THOU DREAM FREEDOM WOULD FIND THEE ANOTHER WAY?
THE TIME FOR DREAMING IS PAST, SWEET CAPULET. WE SHALL BE MARRIED.
THOU SHALT BE MINE TO DO WITH AS I WISH.
YAAAAAGH!

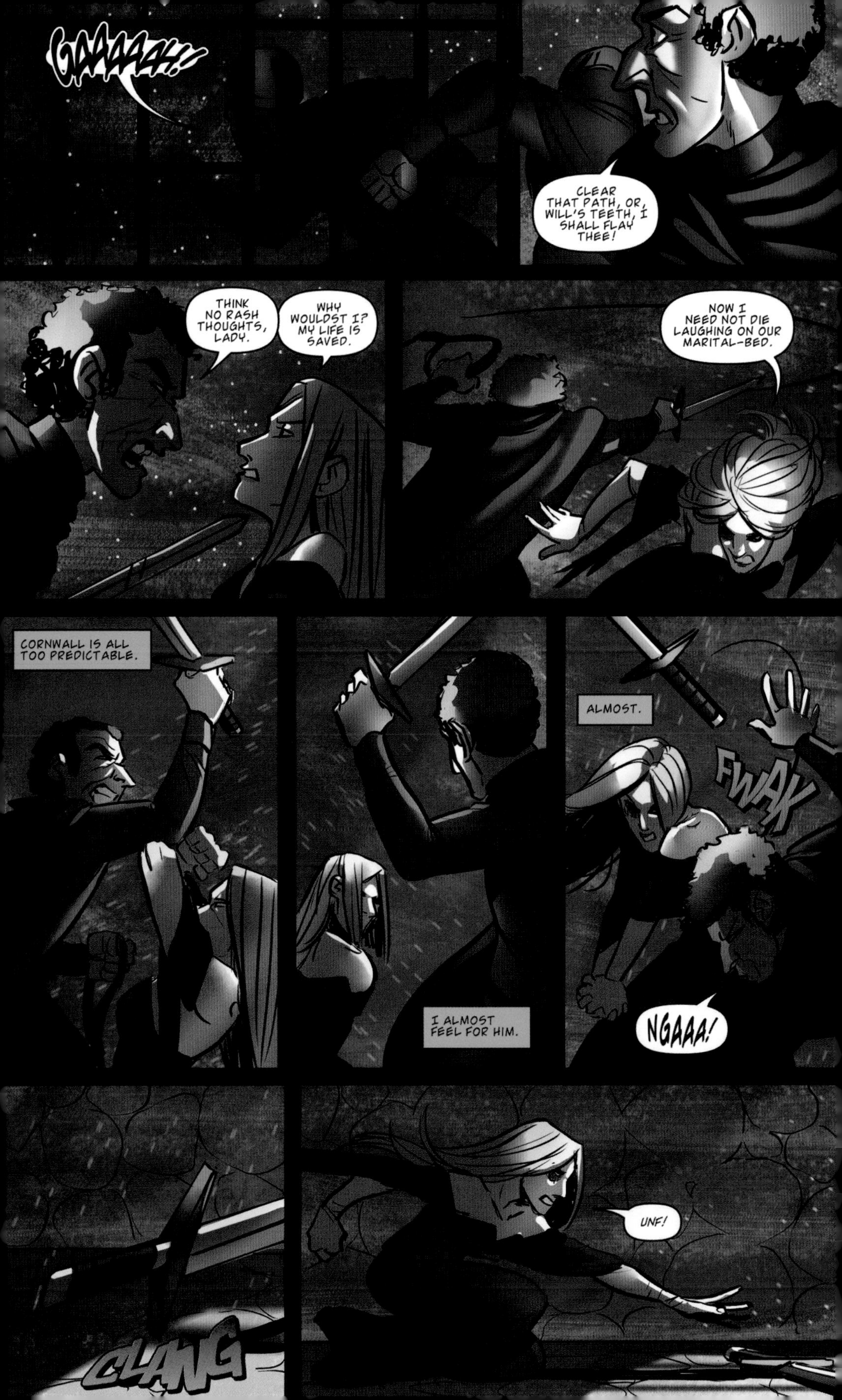
GAAAAAH!
CLEAR THAT PATH, OR, WILL'S TEETH, I SHALL FLAY THEE!
THINK NO RASH THOUGHTS, LADY.
WHY WOULDST I? MY LIFE IS SAVED.
NOW I NEED NOT DIE LAUGHING ON OUR MARITAL-BED.
CORNWALL IS ALL TOO PREDICTABLE.
I ALMOST FEEL FOR HIM.
ALMOST.
FWAK
NGAAA!
CLANG
UNF!

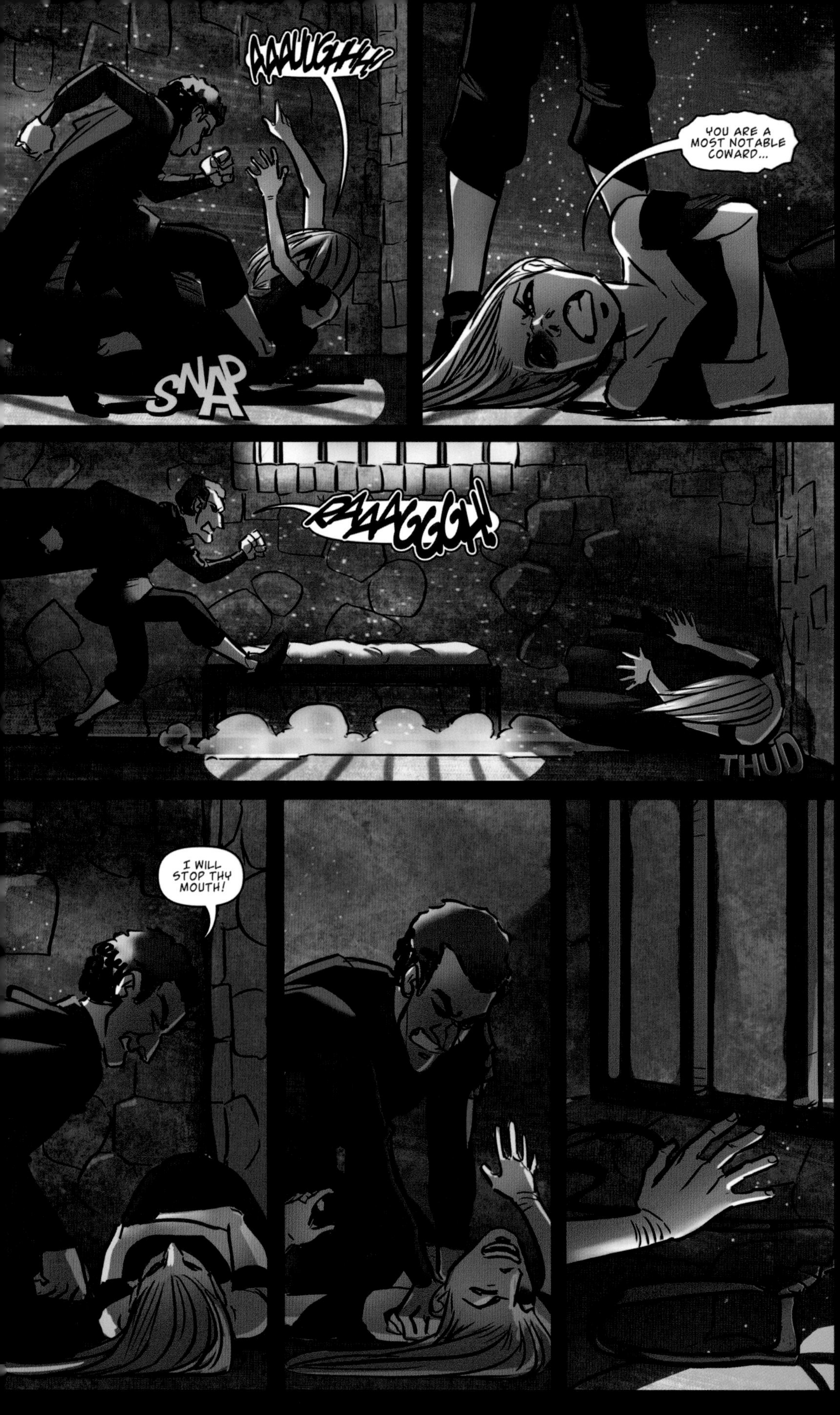
AAAUUGHHH!
SNAP
YOU ARE A MOST NOTABLE COWARD...
RAAAGGGH!
THUD
I WILL STOP THY MOUTH!

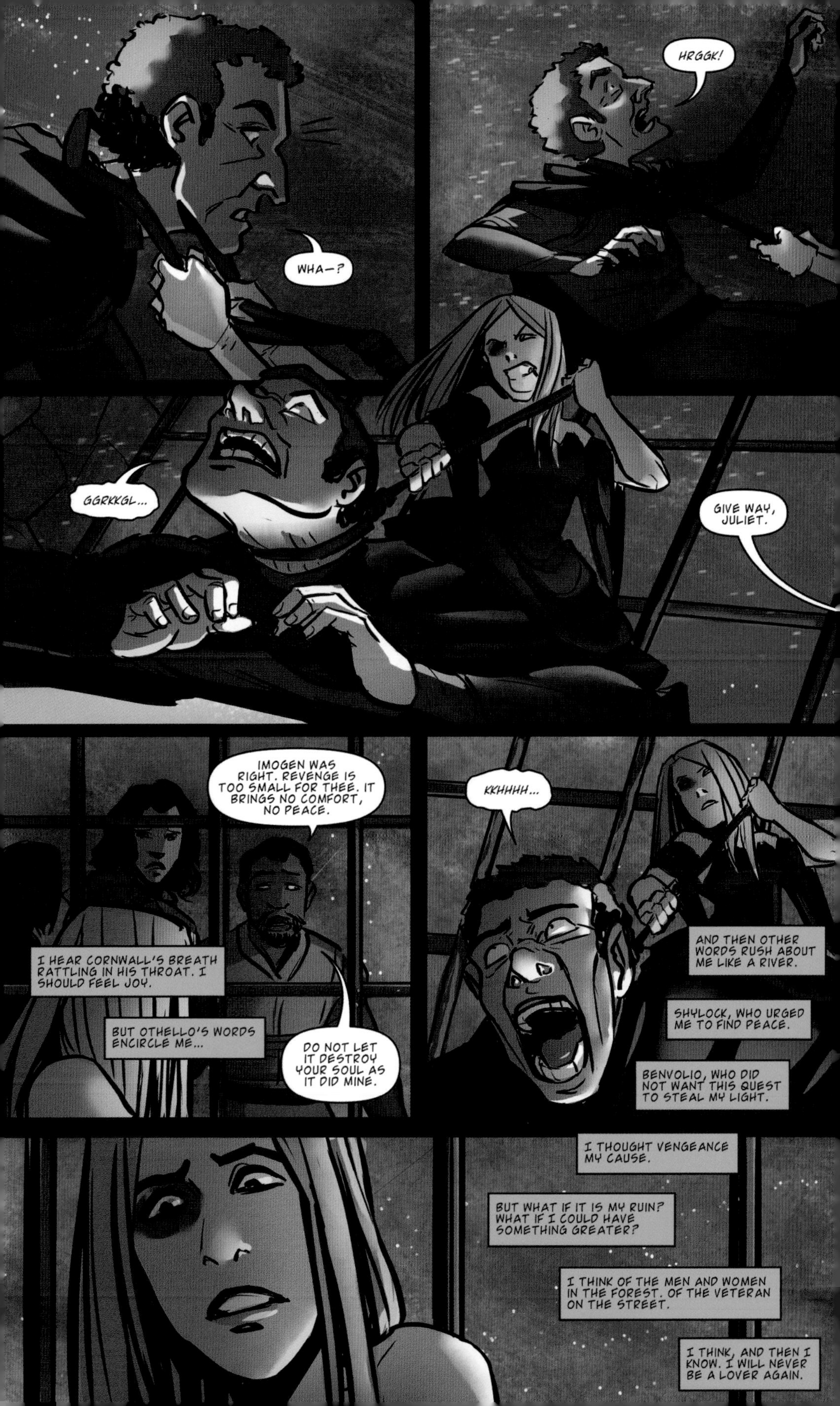
WHA—?
HRGGK!
GGRKKGL...
GIVE WAY, JULIET.
IMOGEN WAS RIGHT. REVENGE IS TOO SMALL FOR THEE. IT BRINGS NO COMFORT, NO PEACE.
I HEAR CORNWALL'S BREATH RATTLING IN HIS THROAT. I SHOULD FEEL JOY.
BUT OTHELLO'S WORDS ENCIRCLE ME...
DO NOT LET IT DESTROY YOUR SOUL AS IT DID MINE.
KKHHHH...
AND THEN OTHER WORDS RUSH ABOUT ME LIKE A RIVER.
SHYLOCK, WHO URGED ME TO FIND PEACE.
BENVOLIO, WHO DID NOT WANT THIS QUEST TO STEAL MY LIGHT.
I THOUGHT VENGEANCE MY CAUSE.
BUT WHAT IF IT IS MY RUIN? WHAT IF I COULD HAVE SOMETHING GREATER?
I THINK OF THE MEN AND WOMEN IN THE FOREST. OF THE VETERAN ON THE STREET.
I THINK, AND THEN I KNOW. I WILL NEVER BE A LOVER AGAIN.

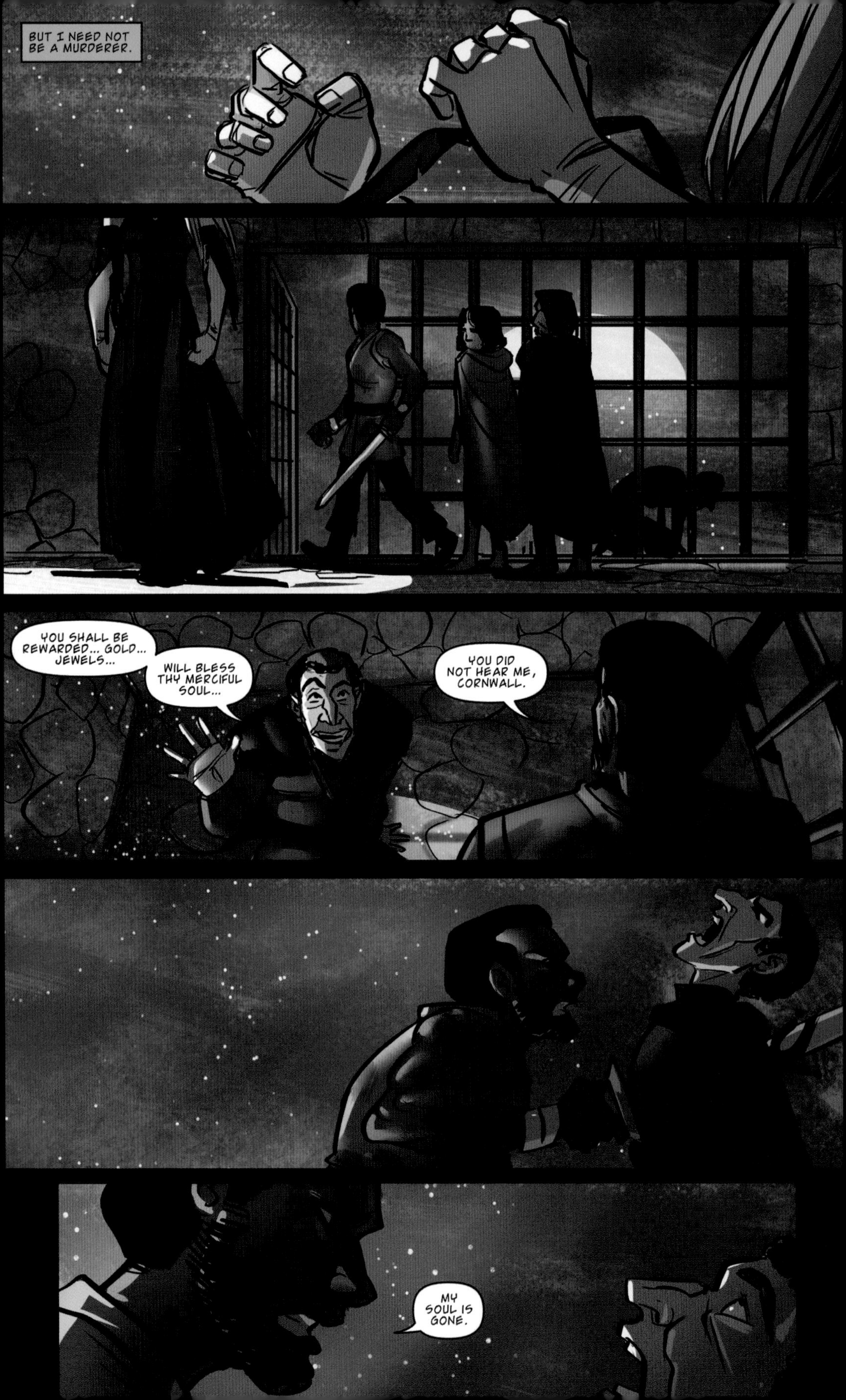
BUT I NEED NOT BE A MURDERER.
YOU SHALL BE REWARDED... GOLD... JEWELS...
WILL BLESS THY MERCIFUL SOUL...
YOU DID NOT HEAR ME, CORNWALL.
MY SOUL IS GONE.

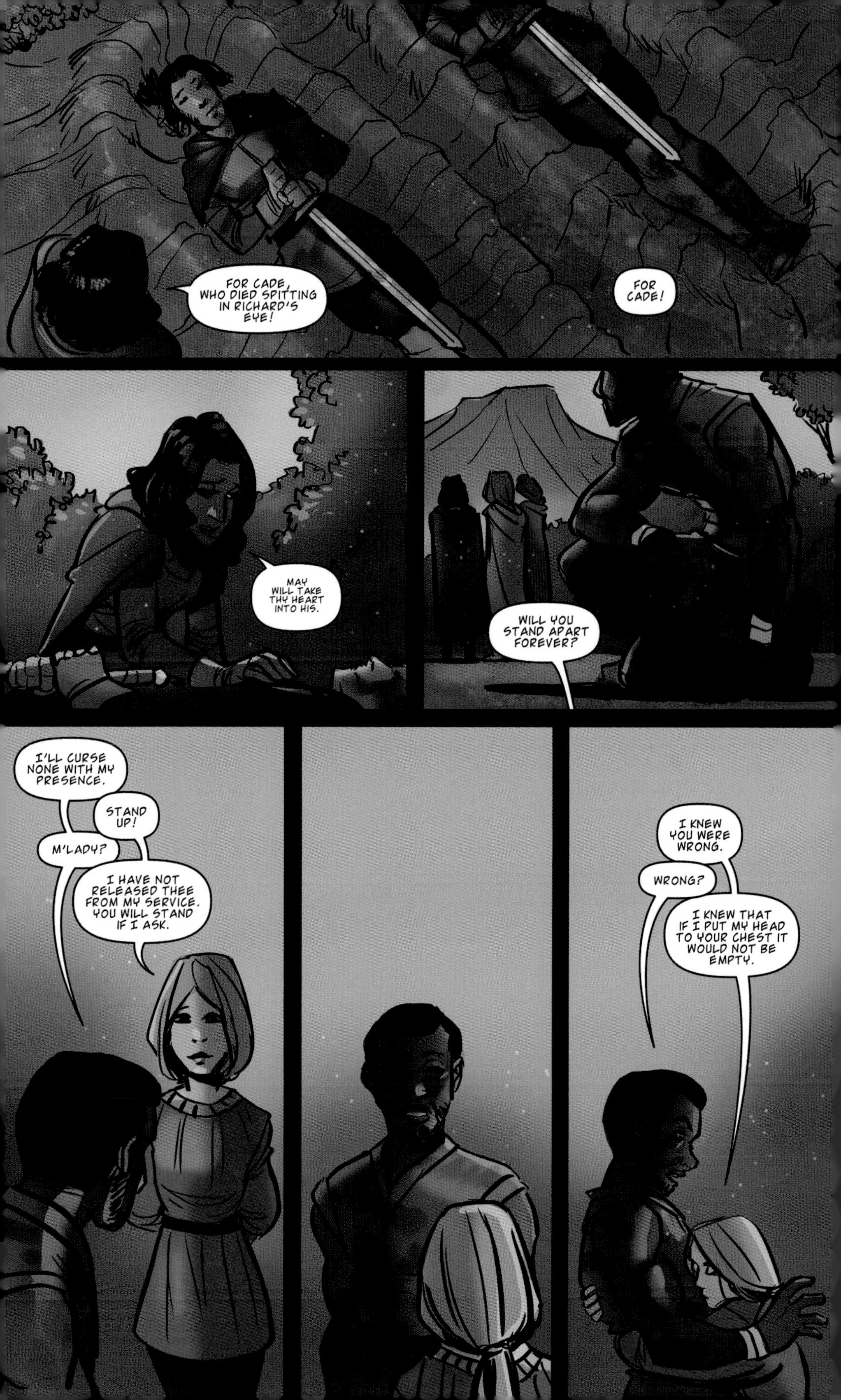

FOR CADE, WHO DIED SPITTING IN RICHARD'S EYE!
FOR CADE!
MAY WILL TAKE THY HEART INTO HIS.
WILL YOU STAND APART FOREVER?
I'LL CURSE NONE WITH MY PRESENCE.
STAND UP!
M'LADY?
I HAVE NOT RELEASED THEE FROM MY SERVICE. YOU WILL STAND IF I ASK.
I KNEW YOU WERE WRONG.
WRONG?
I KNEW THAT IF I PUT MY HEAD TO YOUR CHEST IT WOULD NOT BE EMPTY.

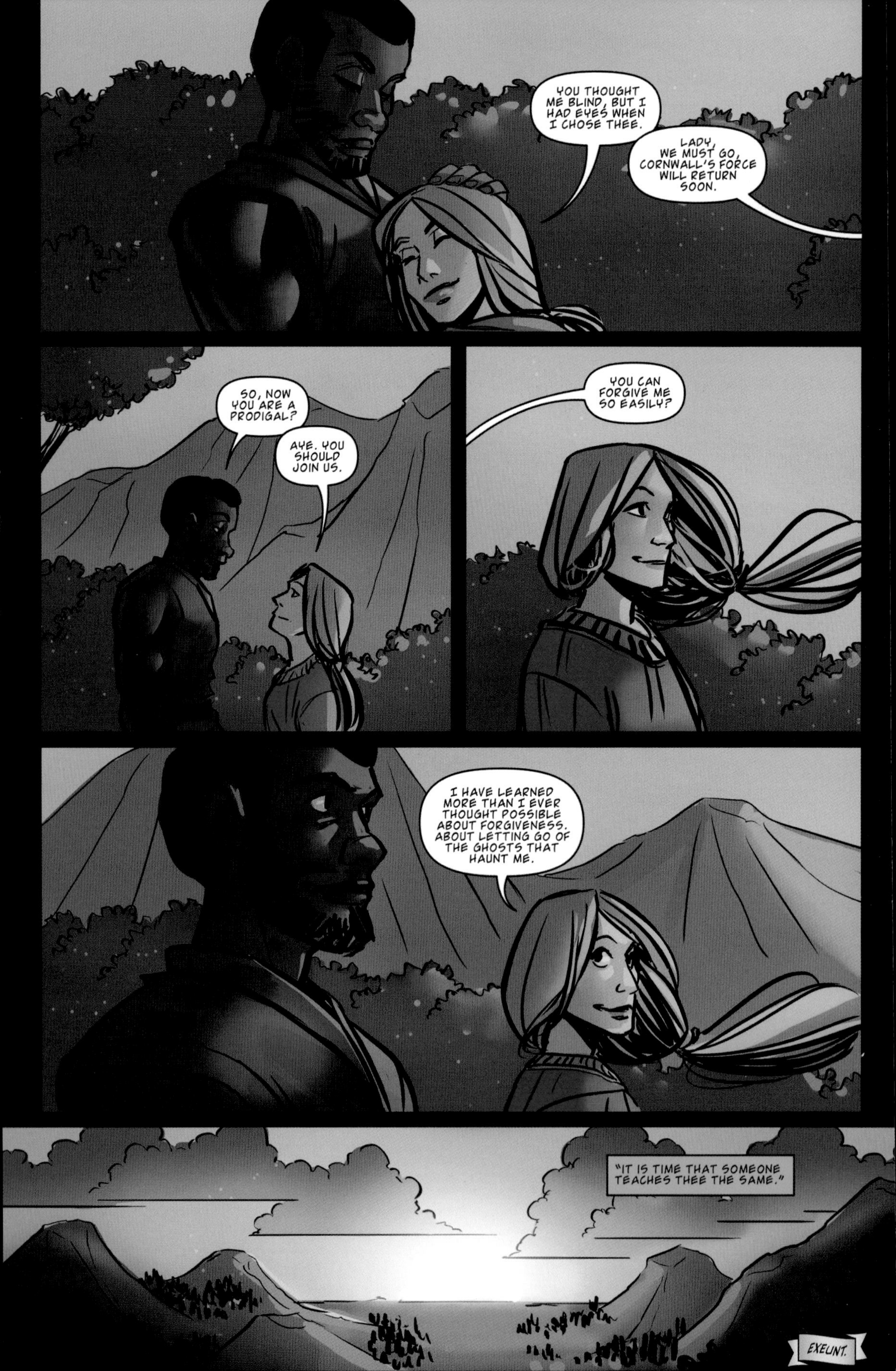
YOU THOUGHT ME BLIND, BUT I HAD EYES WHEN I CHOSE THEE.
LADY, WE MUST GO, CORNWALL'S FORCE WILL RETURN SOON.
SO, NOW YOU ARE A PRODIGAL?
AYE. YOU SHOULD JOIN US.
YOU CAN FORGIVE ME SO EASILY?
I HAVE LEARNED MORE THAN I EVER THOUGHT POSSIBLE ABOUT FORGIVENESS. ABOUT LETTING GO OF THE GHOSTS THAT HAUNT ME.
"IT IS TIME THAT SOMEONE TEACHES THEE THE SAME."
EXEUNT.

BONUS GALLERY

Featuring artwork from the series as well as the original story:

"12th Winter"

WRITTEN BY
Keith WTS Morris

ART & COLORS BY
Jason Loo
& Meghan Carter

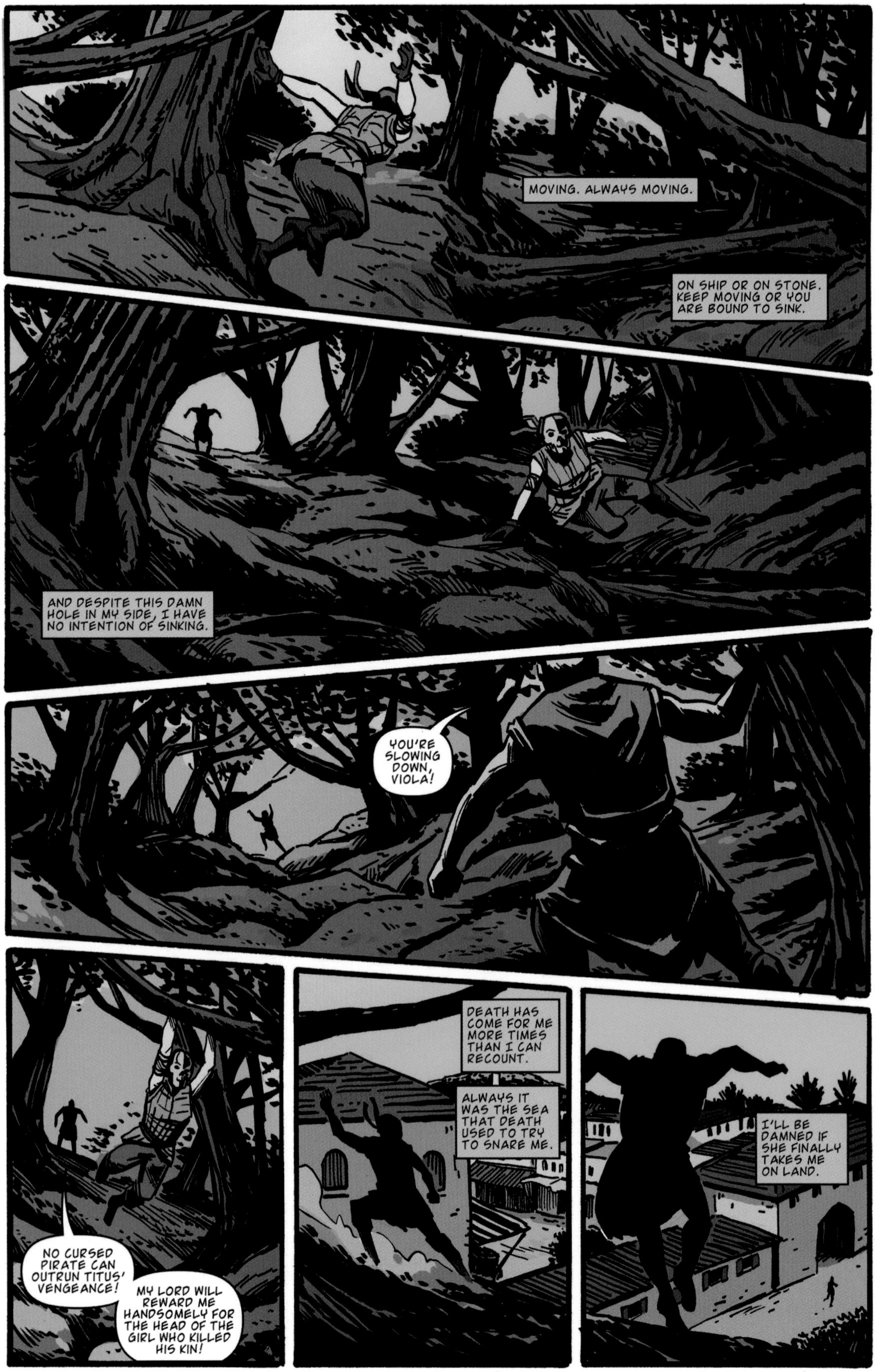
MOVING. ALWAYS MOVING.
ON SHIP OR ON STONE. KEEP MOVING OR YOU ARE BOUND TO SINK.
AND DESPITE THIS DAMN HOLE IN MY SIDE, I HAVE NO INTENTION OF SINKING.
YOU'RE SLOWING DOWN, VIOLA!
NO CURSED PIRATE CAN OUTRUN TITUS' VENGEANCE!
MY LORD WILL REWARD ME HANDSOMELY FOR THE HEAD OF THE GIRL WHO KILLED HIS KIN!
DEATH HAS COME FOR ME MORE TIMES THAN I CAN RECOUNT.
ALWAYS IT WAS THE SEA THAT DEATH USED TO TRY TO SNARE ME.
I'LL BE DAMNED IF SHE FINALLY TAKES ME ON LAND.

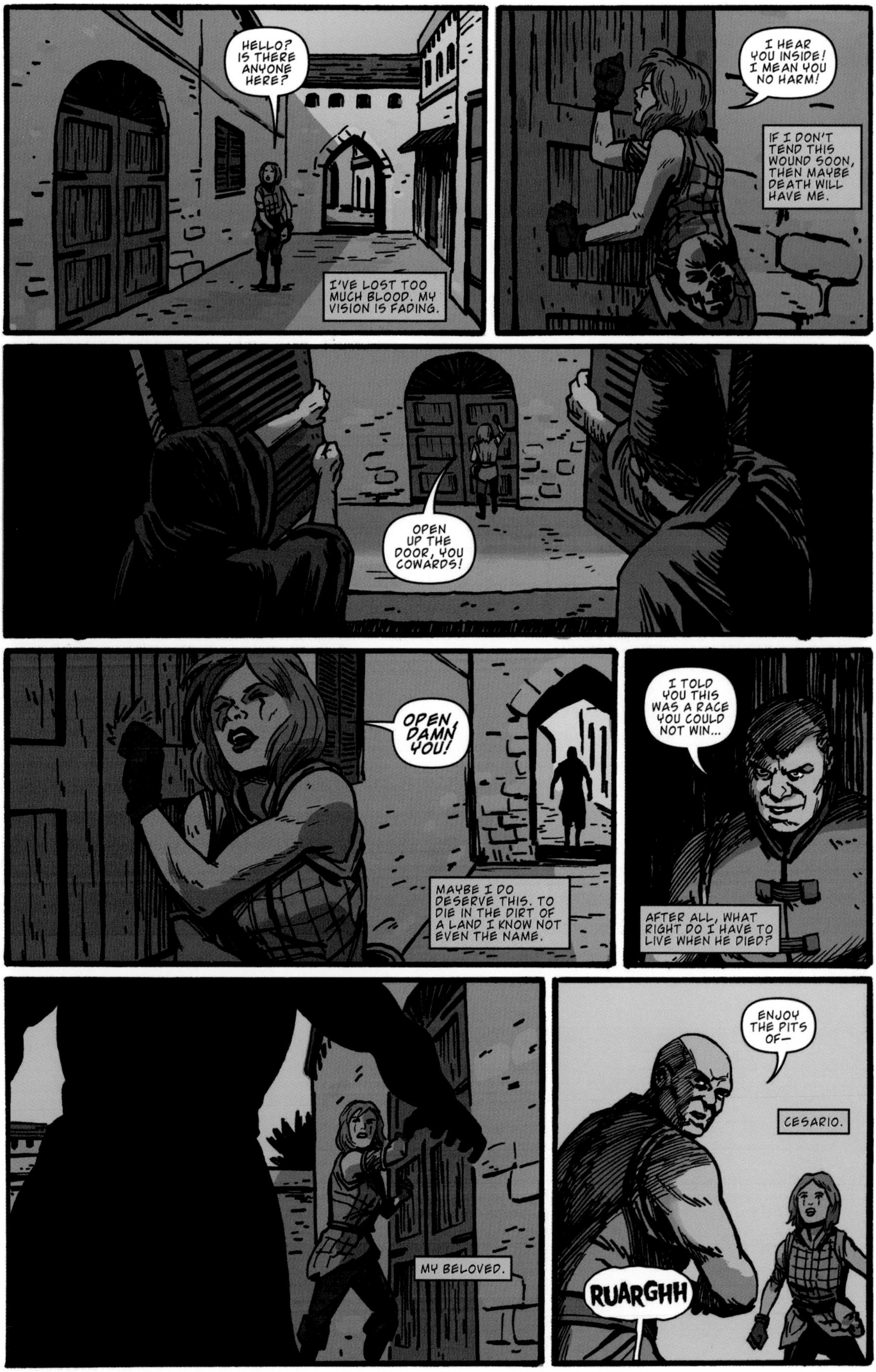
HELLO? IS THERE ANYONE HERE?
I'VE LOST TOO MUCH BLOOD. MY VISION IS FADING.
I HEAR YOU INSIDE! I MEAN YOU NO HARM!
IF I DON'T TEND THIS WOUND SOON, THEN MAYBE DEATH WILL HAVE ME.
OPEN UP THE DOOR, YOU COWARDS!
OPEN, DAMN YOU!
MAYBE I DO DESERVE THIS. TO DIE IN THE DIRT OF A LAND I KNOW NOT EVEN THE NAME.
I TOLD YOU THIS WAS A RACE YOU COULD NOT WIN...
AFTER ALL, WHAT RIGHT DO I HAVE TO LIVE WHEN HE DIED?
MY BELOVED.
ENJOY THE PITS OF—
CESARIO.
RUARGHH

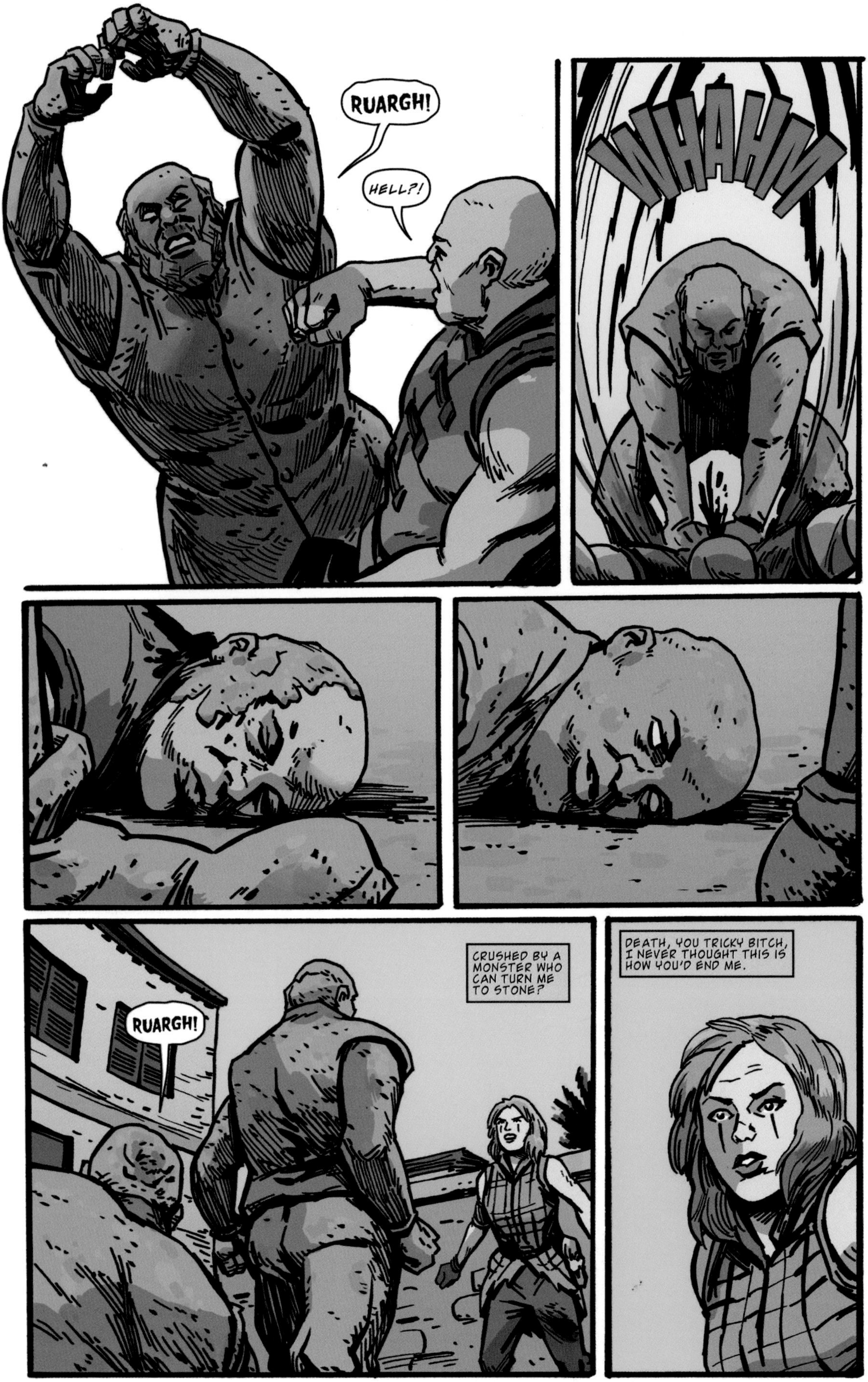
RUARGH!
HELL?!
WHAHM
RUARGH!
CRUSHED BY A MONSTER WHO CAN TURN ME TO STONE?
DEATH, YOU TRICKY BITCH, I NEVER THOUGHT THIS IS HOW YOU'D END ME.

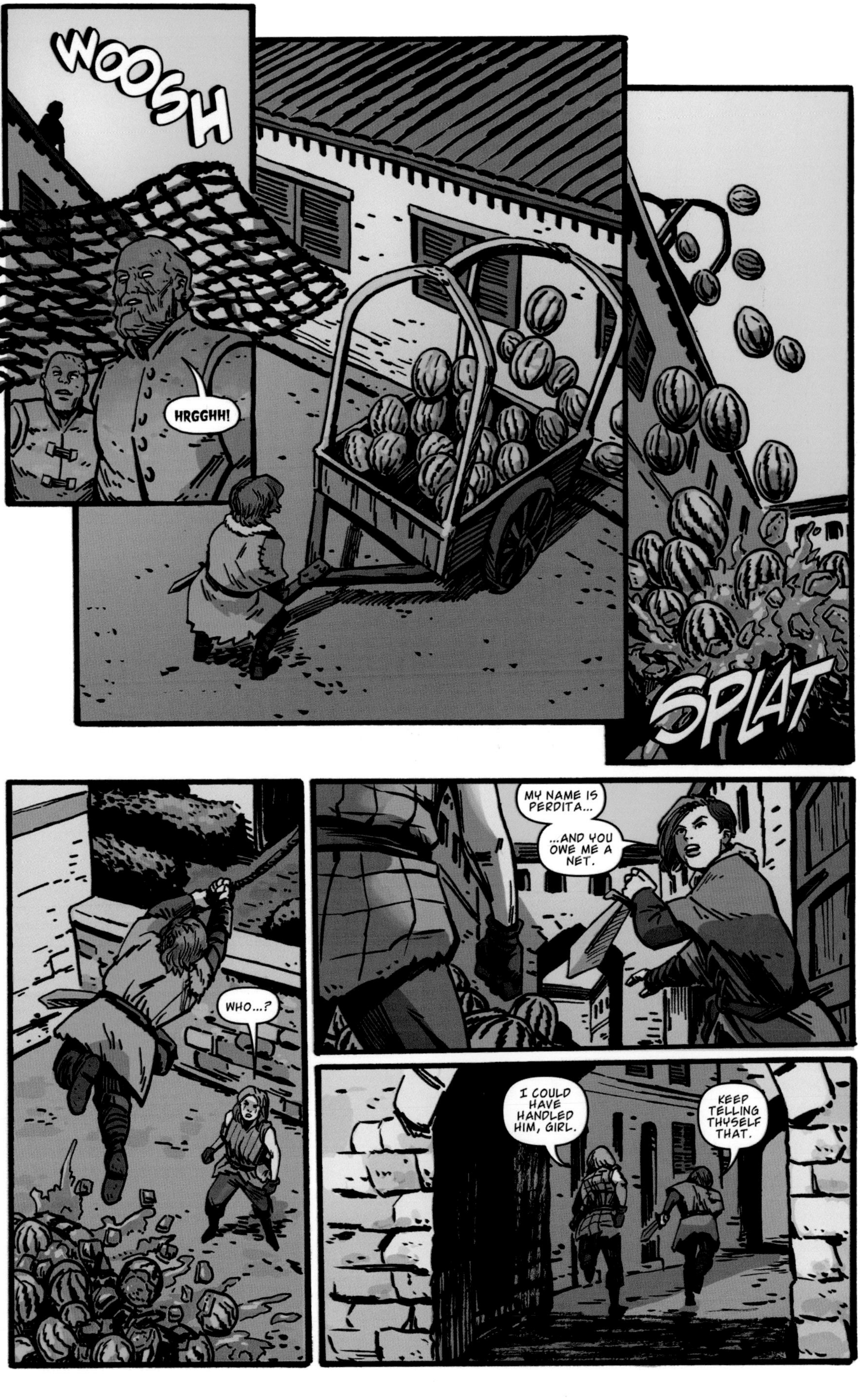
WOOSH
HRGGHH!
SPLAT
WHO...?
MY NAME IS PERDITA...
...AND YOU OWE ME A NET.
I COULD HAVE HANDLED HIM, GIRL.
KEEP TELLING THYSELF THAT.

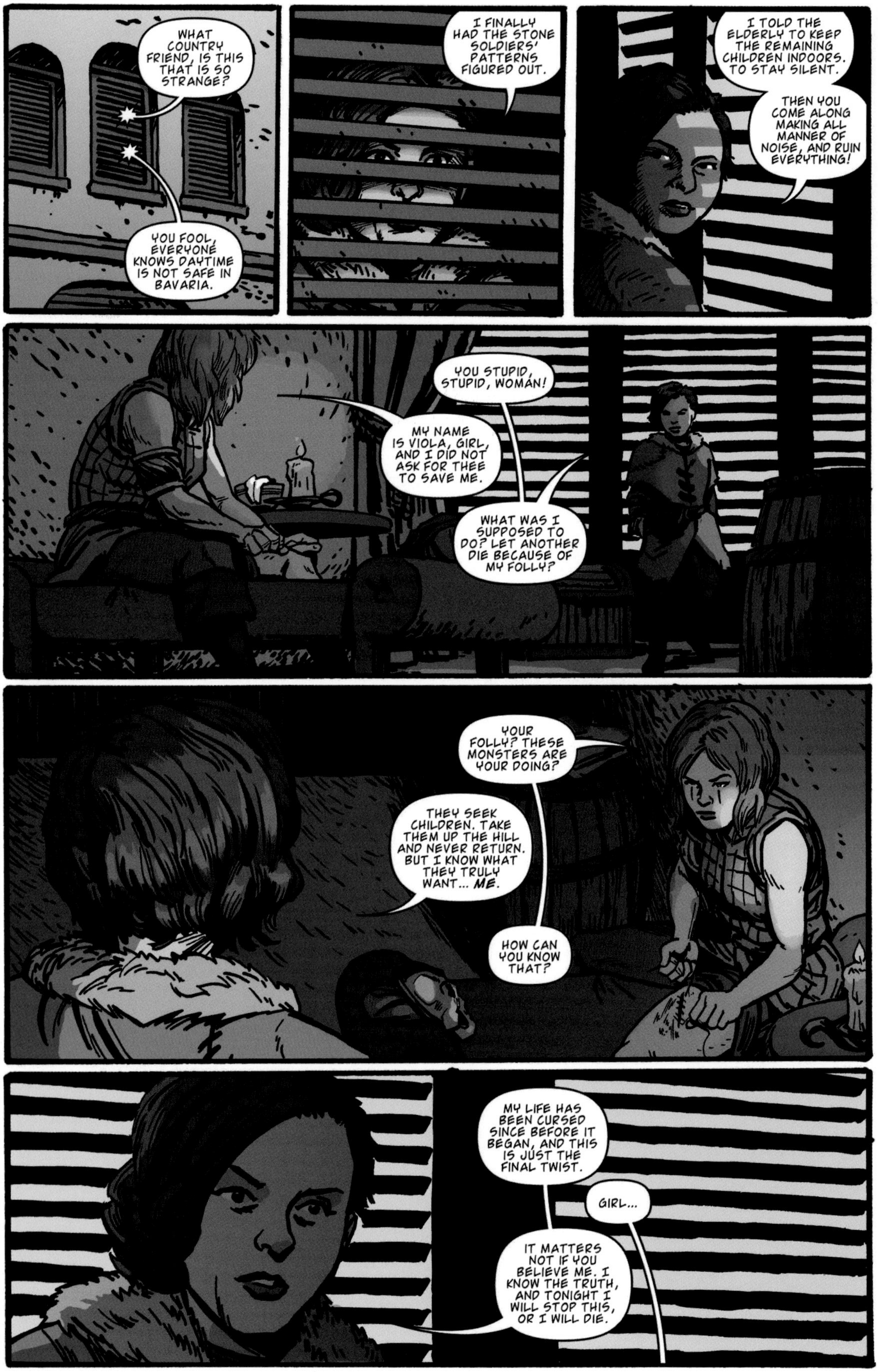
WHAT COUNTRY FRIEND, IS THIS THAT IS SO STRANGE?
YOU FOOL, EVERYONE KNOWS DAYTIME IS NOT SAFE IN BAVARIA.
I FINALLY HAD THE STONE SOLDIERS' PATTERNS FIGURED OUT.
I TOLD THE ELDERLY TO KEEP THE REMAINING CHILDREN INDOORS. TO STAY SILENT.
THEN YOU COME ALONG MAKING ALL MANNER OF NOISE, AND RUIN EVERYTHING!
YOU STUPID, STUPID, WOMAN!
MY NAME IS VIOLA, GIRL, AND I DID NOT ASK FOR THEE TO SAVE ME.
WHAT WAS I SUPPOSED TO DO? LET ANOTHER DIE BECAUSE OF MY FOLLY?
YOUR FOLLY? THESE MONSTERS ARE YOUR DOING?
THEY SEEK CHILDREN. TAKE THEM UP THE HILL AND NEVER RETURN. BUT I KNOW WHAT THEY TRULY WANT... *ME*.
HOW CAN YOU KNOW THAT?
MY LIFE HAS BEEN CURSED SINCE BEFORE IT BEGAN, AND THIS IS JUST THE FINAL TWIST.
GIRL...
IT MATTERS NOT IF YOU BELIEVE ME. I KNOW THE TRUTH, AND TONIGHT I WILL STOP THIS, OR I WILL DIE.

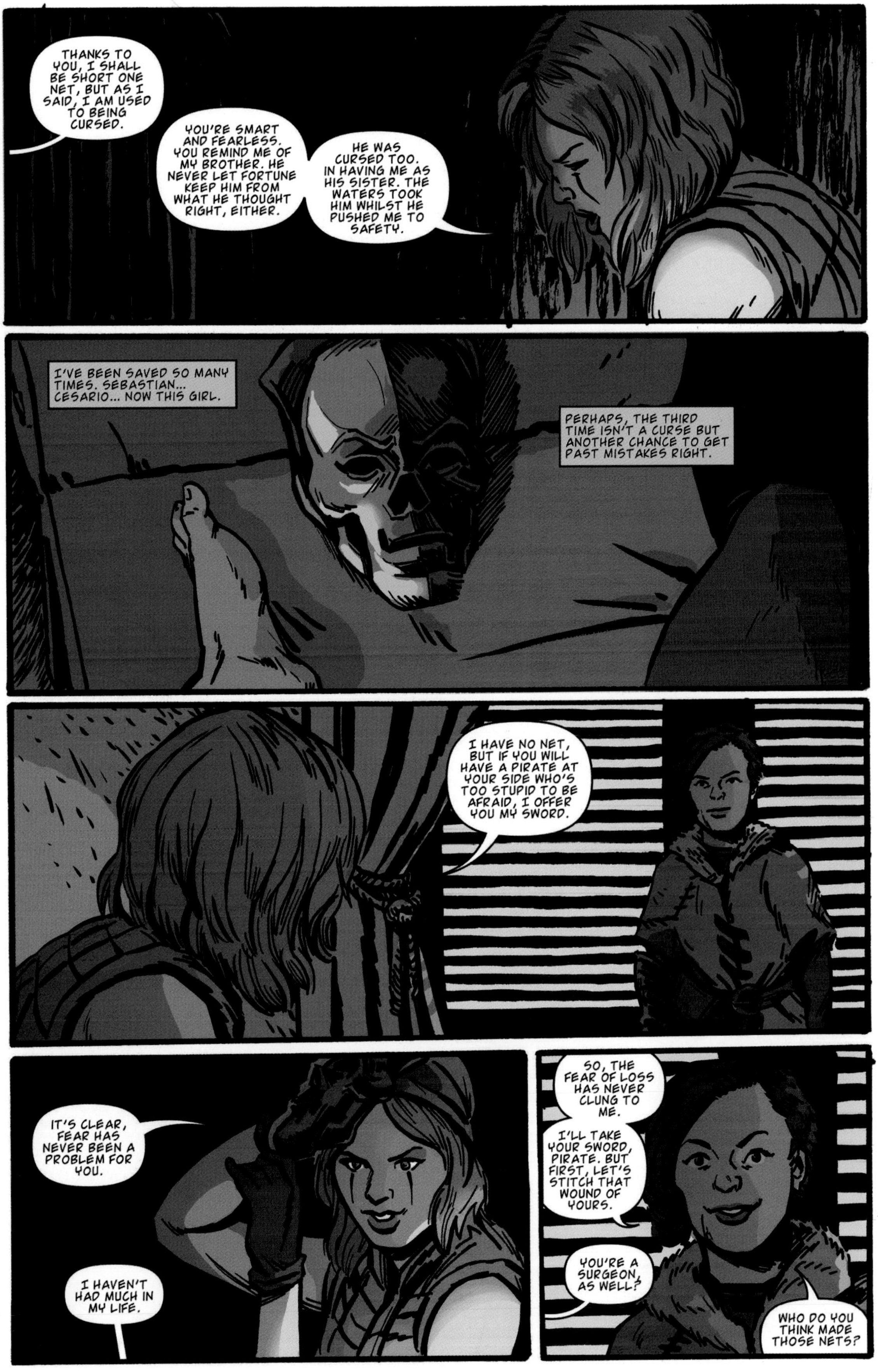
THANKS TO YOU, I SHALL BE SHORT ONE NET, BUT AS I SAID, I AM USED TO BEING CURSED.
YOU'RE SMART AND FEARLESS. YOU REMIND ME OF MY BROTHER. HE NEVER LET FORTUNE KEEP HIM FROM WHAT HE THOUGHT RIGHT, EITHER.
HE WAS CURSED TOO. IN HAVING ME AS HIS SISTER. THE WATERS TOOK HIM WHILST HE PUSHED ME TO SAFETY.
I'VE BEEN SAVED SO MANY TIMES. SEBASTIAN... CESARIO... NOW THIS GIRL.
PERHAPS, THE THIRD TIME ISN'T A CURSE BUT ANOTHER CHANCE TO GET PAST MISTAKES RIGHT.
I HAVE NO NET, BUT IF YOU WILL HAVE A PIRATE AT YOUR SIDE WHO'S TOO STUPID TO BE AFRAID, I OFFER YOU MY SWORD.
IT'S CLEAR, FEAR HAS NEVER BEEN A PROBLEM FOR YOU.
I HAVEN'T HAD MUCH IN MY LIFE.
SO, THE FEAR OF LOSS HAS NEVER CLUNG TO ME.
I'LL TAKE YOUR SWORD, PIRATE. BUT FIRST, LET'S STITCH THAT WOUND OF YOURS.
YOU'RE A SURGEON, AS WELL?
WHO DO YOU THINK MADE THOSE NETS?

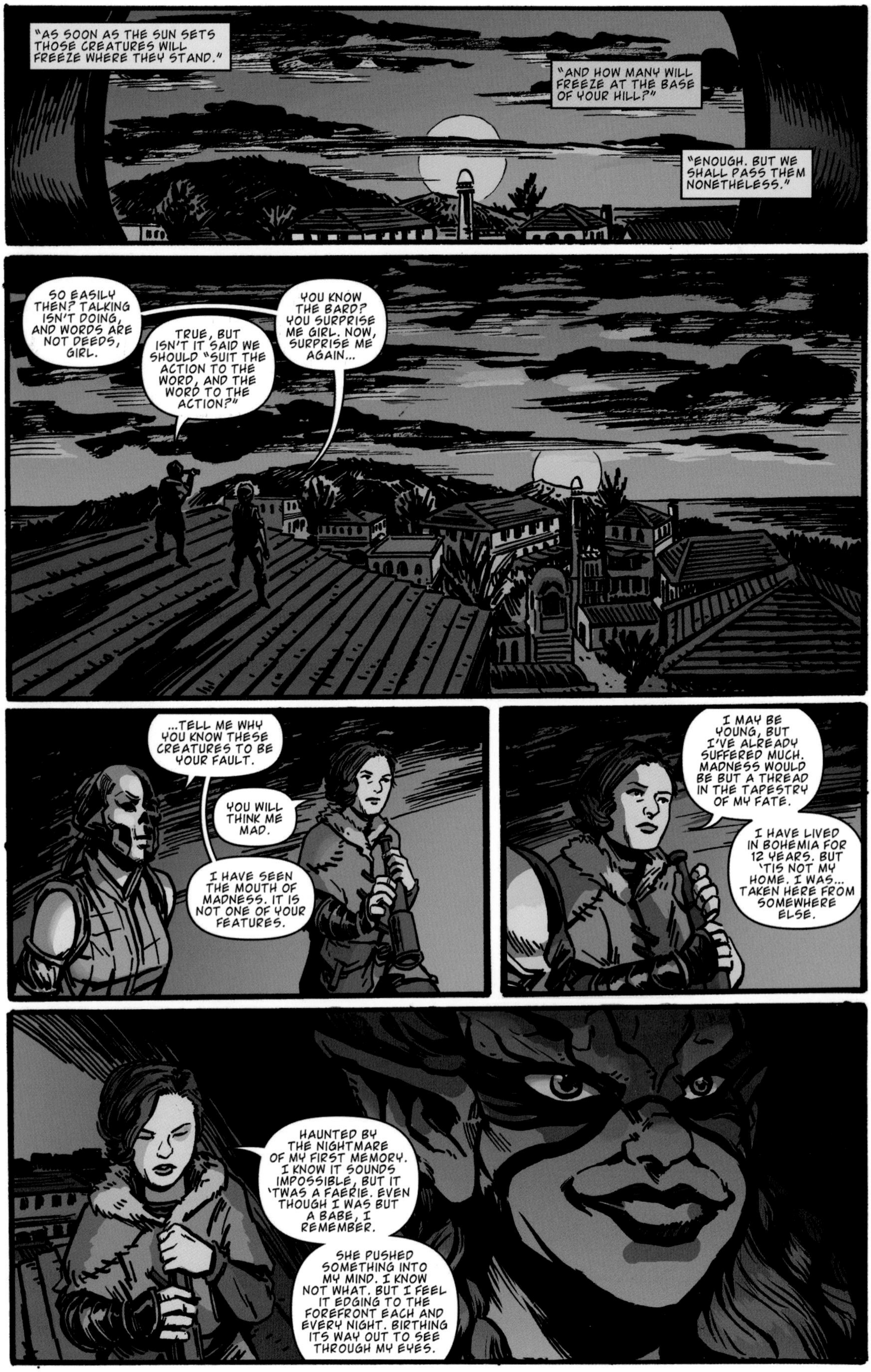
"AS SOON AS THE SUN SETS THOSE CREATURES WILL FREEZE WHERE THEY STAND."
"AND HOW MANY WILL FREEZE AT THE BASE OF YOUR HILL?"
"ENOUGH. BUT WE SHALL PASS THEM NONETHELESS."
SO EASILY THEN? TALKING ISN'T DOING, AND WORDS ARE NOT DEEDS, GIRL.
TRUE, BUT ISN'T IT SAID WE SHOULD "SUIT THE ACTION TO THE WORD, AND THE WORD TO THE ACTION?"
YOU KNOW THE BARD? YOU SURPRISE ME GIRL. NOW, SURPRISE ME AGAIN...
...TELL ME WHY YOU KNOW THESE CREATURES TO BE YOUR FAULT.
YOU WILL THINK ME MAD.
I HAVE SEEN THE MOUTH OF MADNESS. IT IS NOT ONE OF YOUR FEATURES.
I MAY BE YOUNG, BUT I'VE ALREADY SUFFERED MUCH. MADNESS WOULD BE BUT A THREAD IN THE TAPESTRY OF MY FATE.
I HAVE LIVED IN BOHEMIA FOR 12 YEARS. BUT 'TIS NOT MY HOME. I WAS... TAKEN HERE FROM SOMEWHERE ELSE.
HAUNTED BY THE NIGHTMARE OF MY FIRST MEMORY. I KNOW IT SOUNDS IMPOSSIBLE, BUT IT 'TWAS A FAERIE. EVEN THOUGH I WAS BUT A BABE, I REMEMBER.
SHE PUSHED SOMETHING INTO MY MIND. I KNOW NOT WHAT. BUT I FEEL IT EDGING TO THE FOREFRONT EACH AND EVERY NIGHT. BIRTHING ITS WAY OUT TO SEE THROUGH MY EYES.

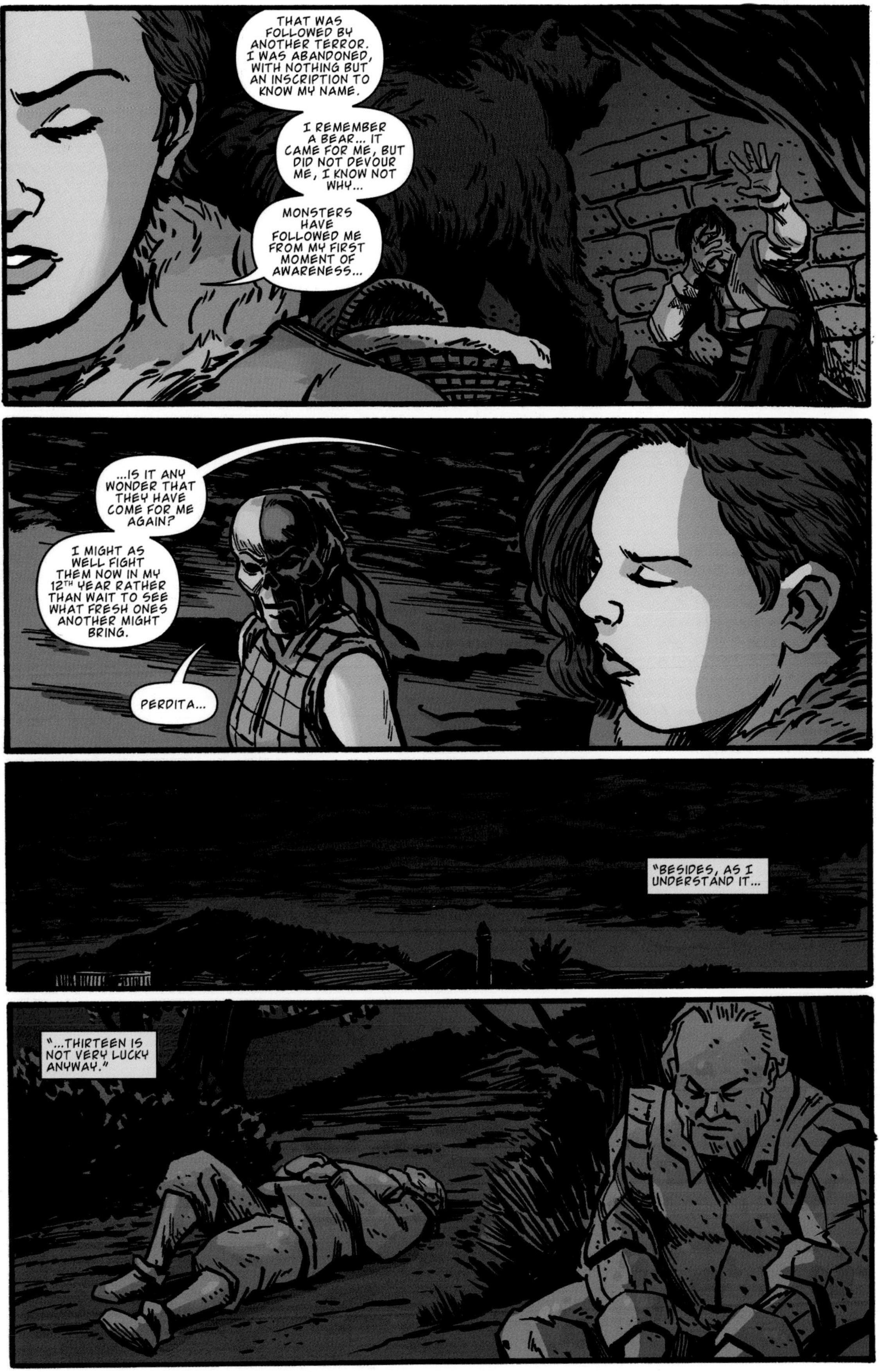
THAT WAS FOLLOWED BY ANOTHER TERROR. I WAS ABANDONED, WITH NOTHING BUT AN INSCRIPTION TO KNOW MY NAME.
I REMEMBER A BEAR... IT CAME FOR ME, BUT DID NOT DEVOUR ME, I KNOW NOT WHY...
MONSTERS HAVE FOLLOWED ME FROM MY FIRST MOMENT OF AWARENESS...
...IS IT ANY WONDER THAT THEY HAVE COME FOR ME AGAIN?
I MIGHT AS WELL FIGHT THEM NOW IN MY 12TH YEAR RATHER THAN WAIT TO SEE WHAT FRESH ONES ANOTHER MIGHT BRING.
PERDITA...
"BESIDES, AS I UNDERSTAND IT...
"...THIRTEEN IS NOT VERY LUCKY ANYWAY."

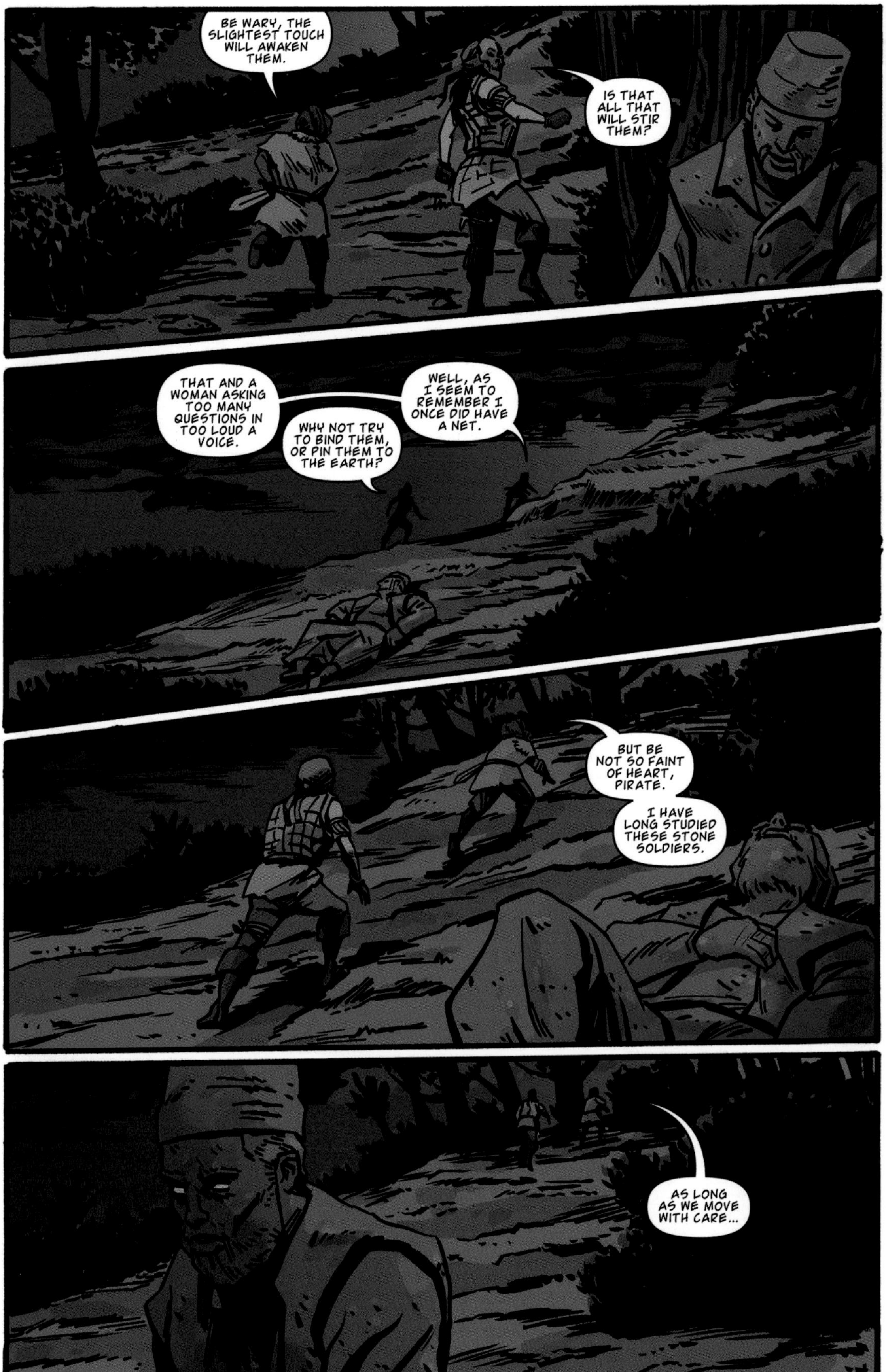
BE WARY, THE SLIGHTEST TOUCH WILL AWAKEN THEM.
IS THAT ALL THAT WILL STIR THEM?
THAT AND A WOMAN ASKING TOO MANY QUESTIONS IN TOO LOUD A VOICE.
WHY NOT TRY TO BIND THEM, OR PIN THEM TO THE EARTH?
WELL, AS I SEEM TO REMEMBER I ONCE DID HAVE A NET.
BUT BE NOT SO FAINT OF HEART, PIRATE.
I HAVE LONG STUDIED THESE STONE SOLDIERS.
AS LONG AS WE MOVE WITH CARE...

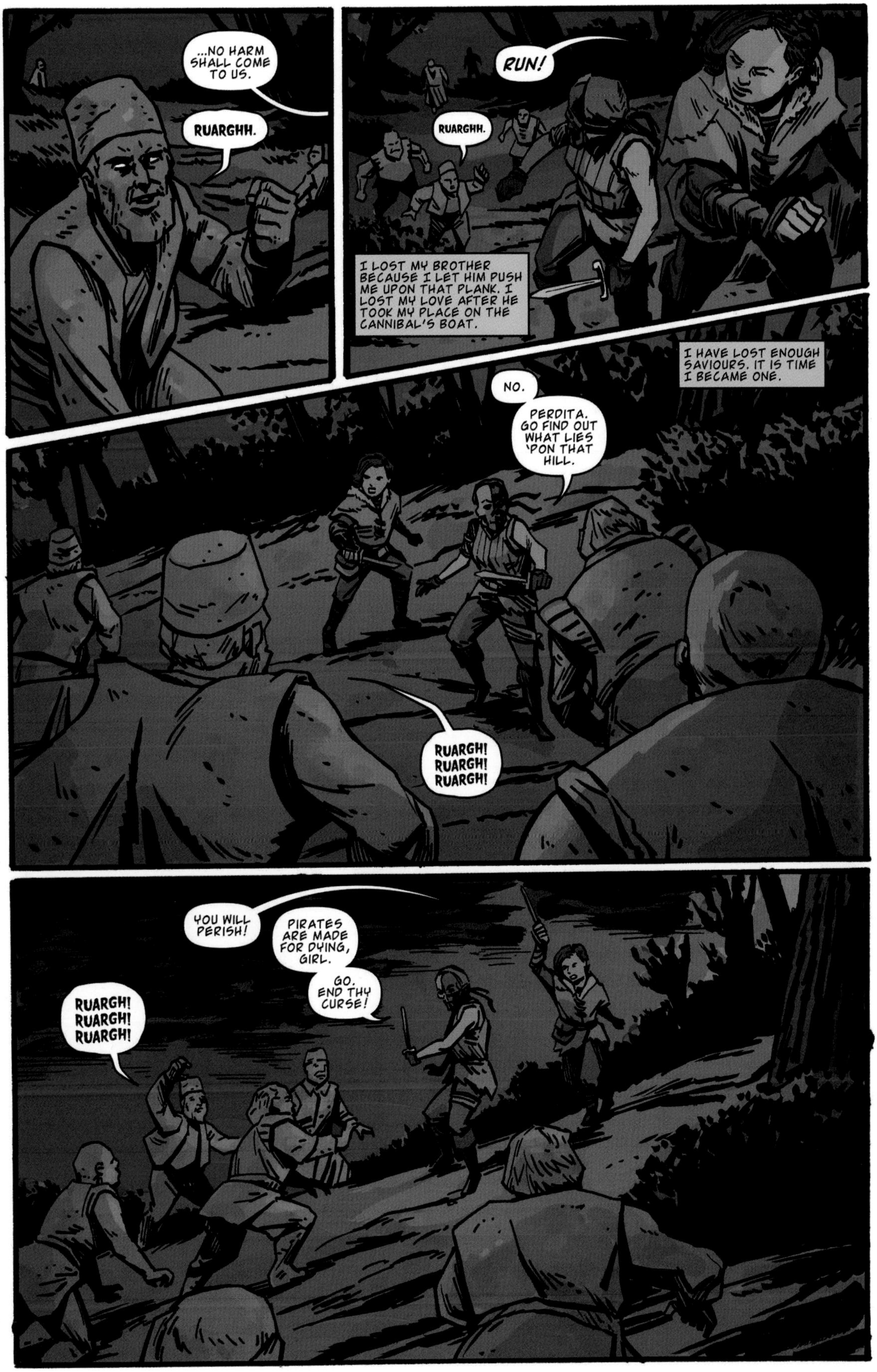
...NO HARM SHALL COME TO US.
RUARGHH.
RUN!
RUARGHH.
I LOST MY BROTHER BECAUSE I LET HIM PUSH ME UPON THAT PLANK. I LOST MY LOVE AFTER HE TOOK MY PLACE ON THE CANNIBAL'S BOAT.
I HAVE LOST ENOUGH SAVIOURS. IT IS TIME I BECAME ONE.
NO.
PERDITA. GO FIND OUT WHAT LIES 'PON THAT HILL.
RUARGH! RUARGH! RUARGH!
YOU WILL PERISH!
PIRATES ARE MADE FOR DYING, GIRL.
GO. END THY CURSE!
RUARGH! RUARGH! RUARGH!

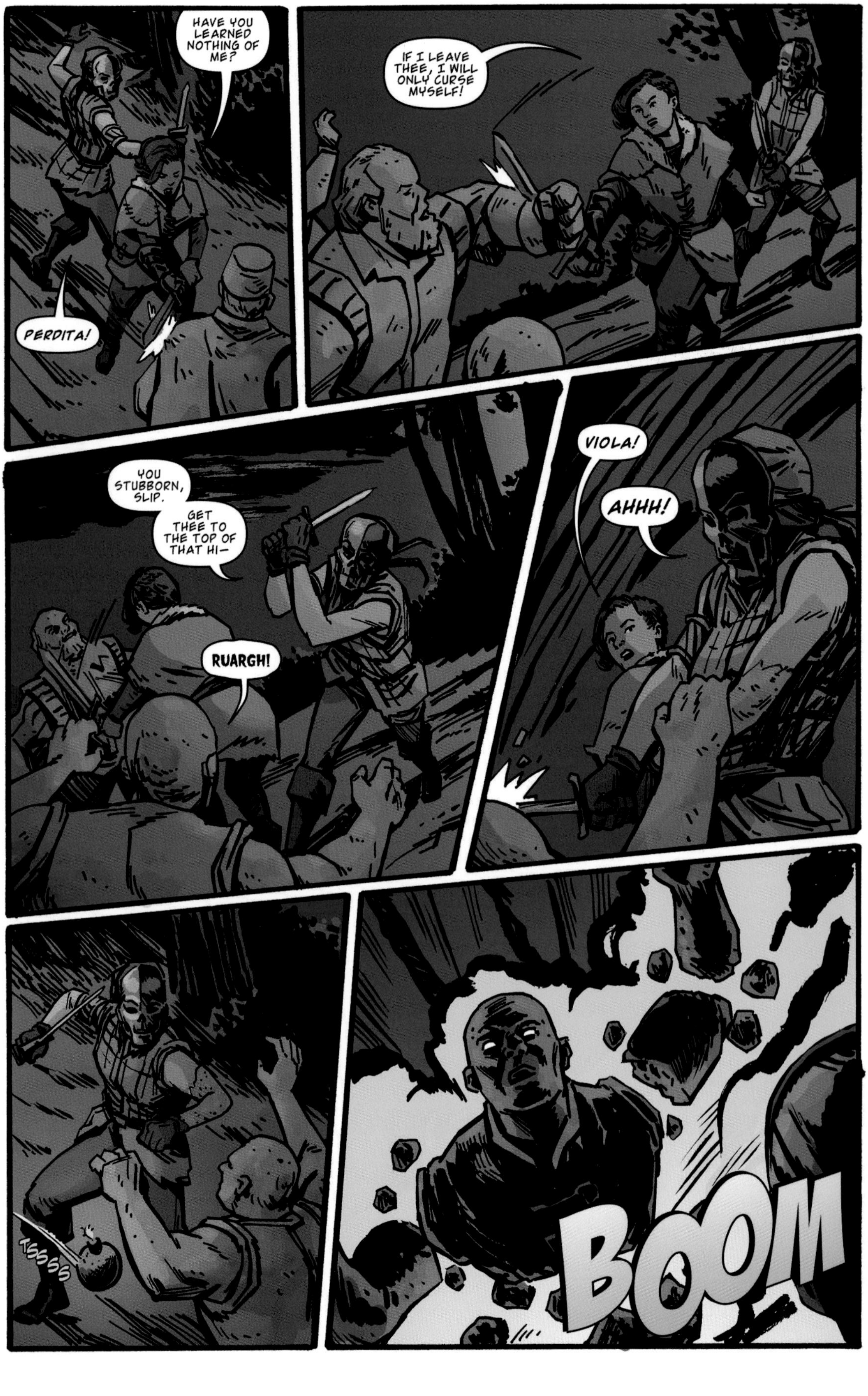
HAVE YOU LEARNED NOTHING OF ME?
PERDITA!
IF I LEAVE THEE, I WILL ONLY CURSE MYSELF!
YOU STUBBORN, SLIP.
GET THEE TO THE TOP OF THAT HI—
RUARGH!
VIOLA!
AHHH!
TSSSS
BOOM

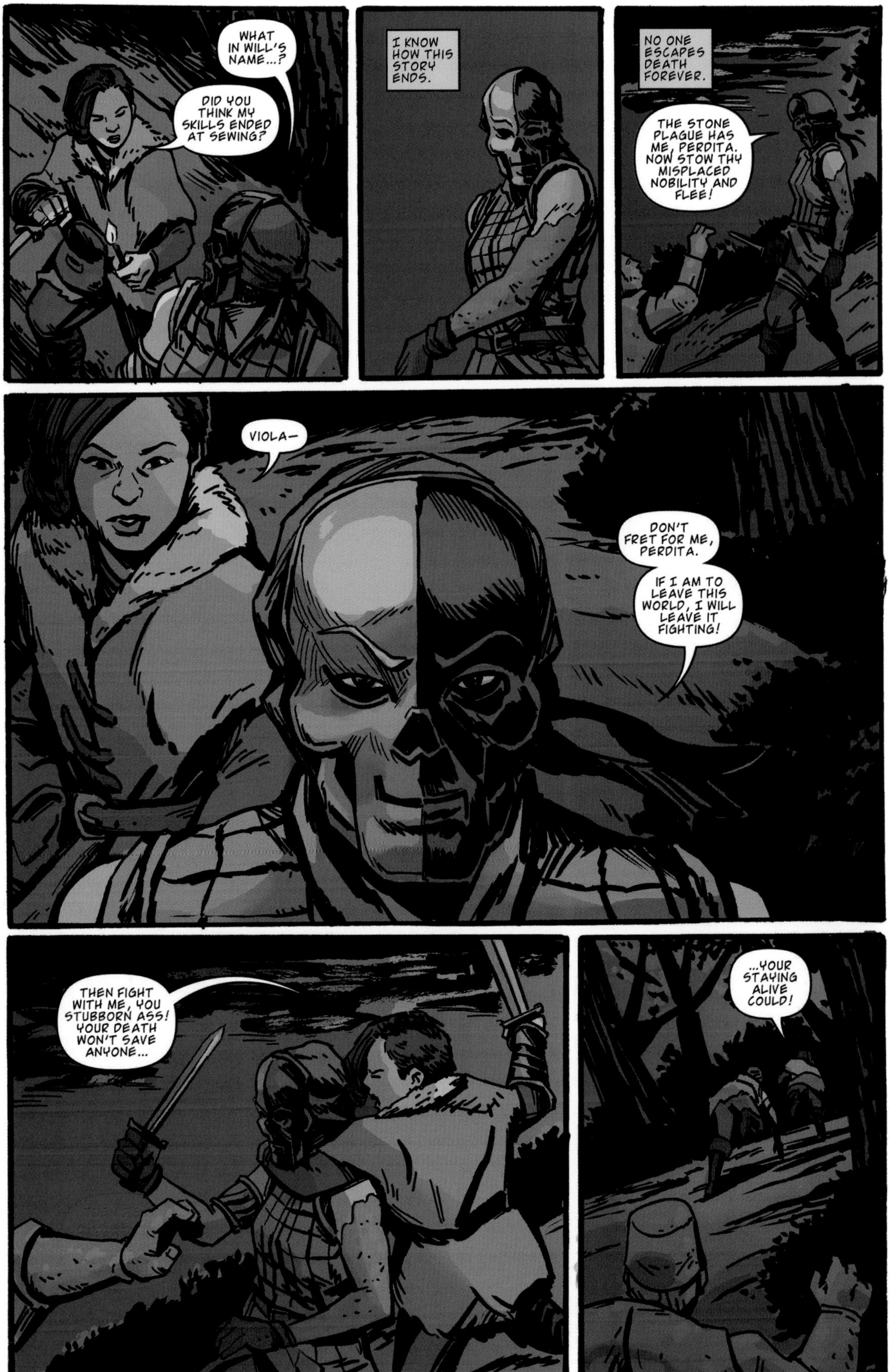

WHAT IN WILL'S NAME...?
DID YOU THINK MY SKILLS ENDED AT SEWING?
I KNOW HOW THIS STORY ENDS.
NO ONE ESCAPES DEATH FOREVER.
THE STONE PLAGUE HAS ME, PERDITA. NOW STOW THY MISPLACED NOBILITY AND FLEE!
VIOLA—
DON'T FRET FOR ME, PERDITA.
IF I AM TO LEAVE THIS WORLD, I WILL LEAVE IT FIGHTING!
THEN FIGHT WITH ME, YOU STUBBORN ASS! YOUR DEATH WON'T SAVE ANYONE...
...YOUR STAYING ALIVE COULD!

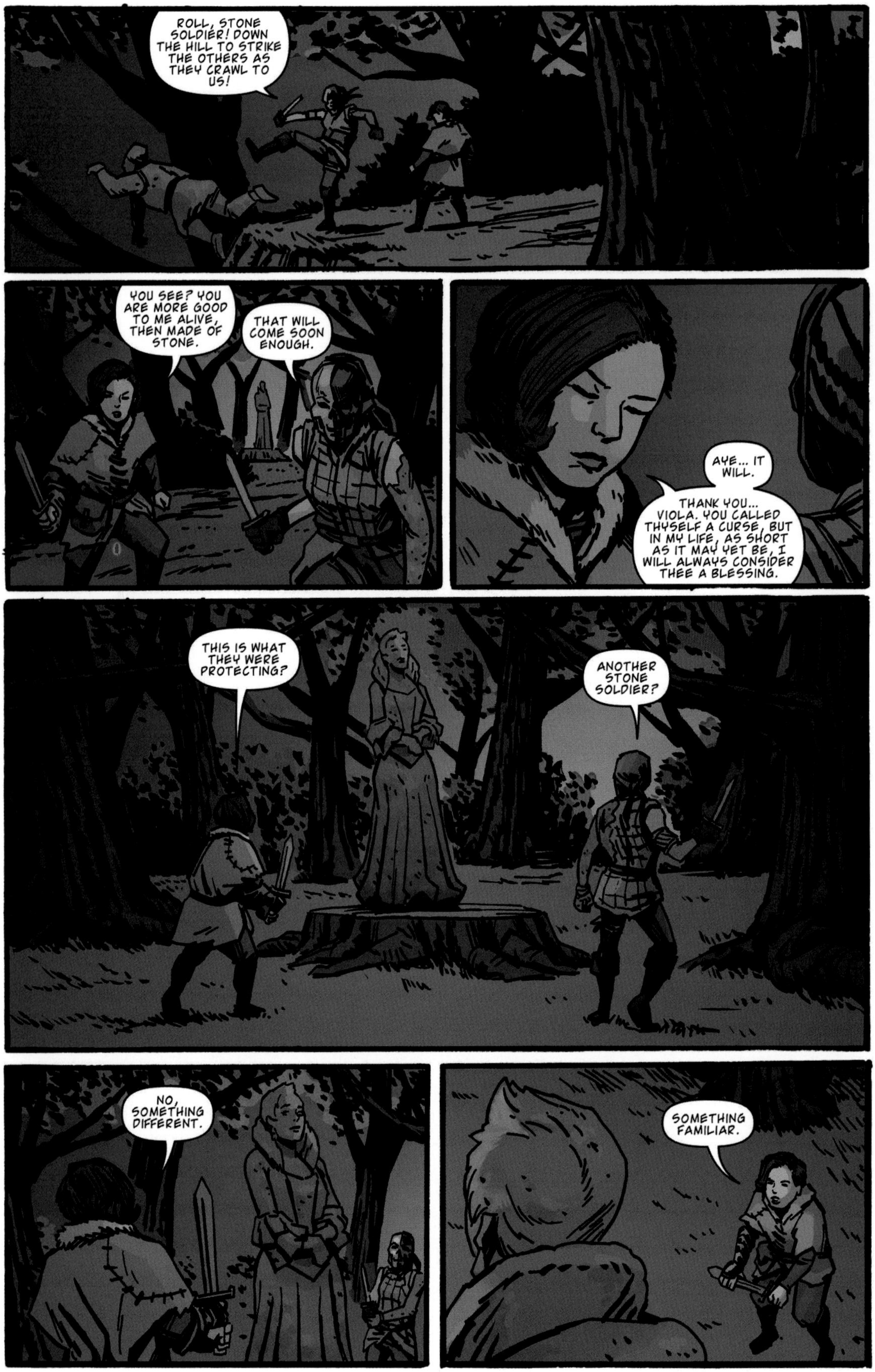
ROLL, STONE SOLDIER! DOWN THE HILL TO STRIKE THE OTHERS AS THEY CRAWL TO US!
YOU SEE? YOU ARE MORE GOOD TO ME ALIVE, THEN MADE OF STONE.
THAT WILL COME SOON ENOUGH.
AYE... IT WILL.
THANK YOU... VIOLA. YOU CALLED THYSELF A CURSE, BUT IN MY LIFE, AS SHORT AS IT MAY YET BE, I WILL ALWAYS CONSIDER THEE A BLESSING.
THIS IS WHAT THEY WERE PROTECTING?
ANOTHER STONE SOLDIER?
NO, SOMETHING DIFFERENT.
SOMETHING FAMILIAR.

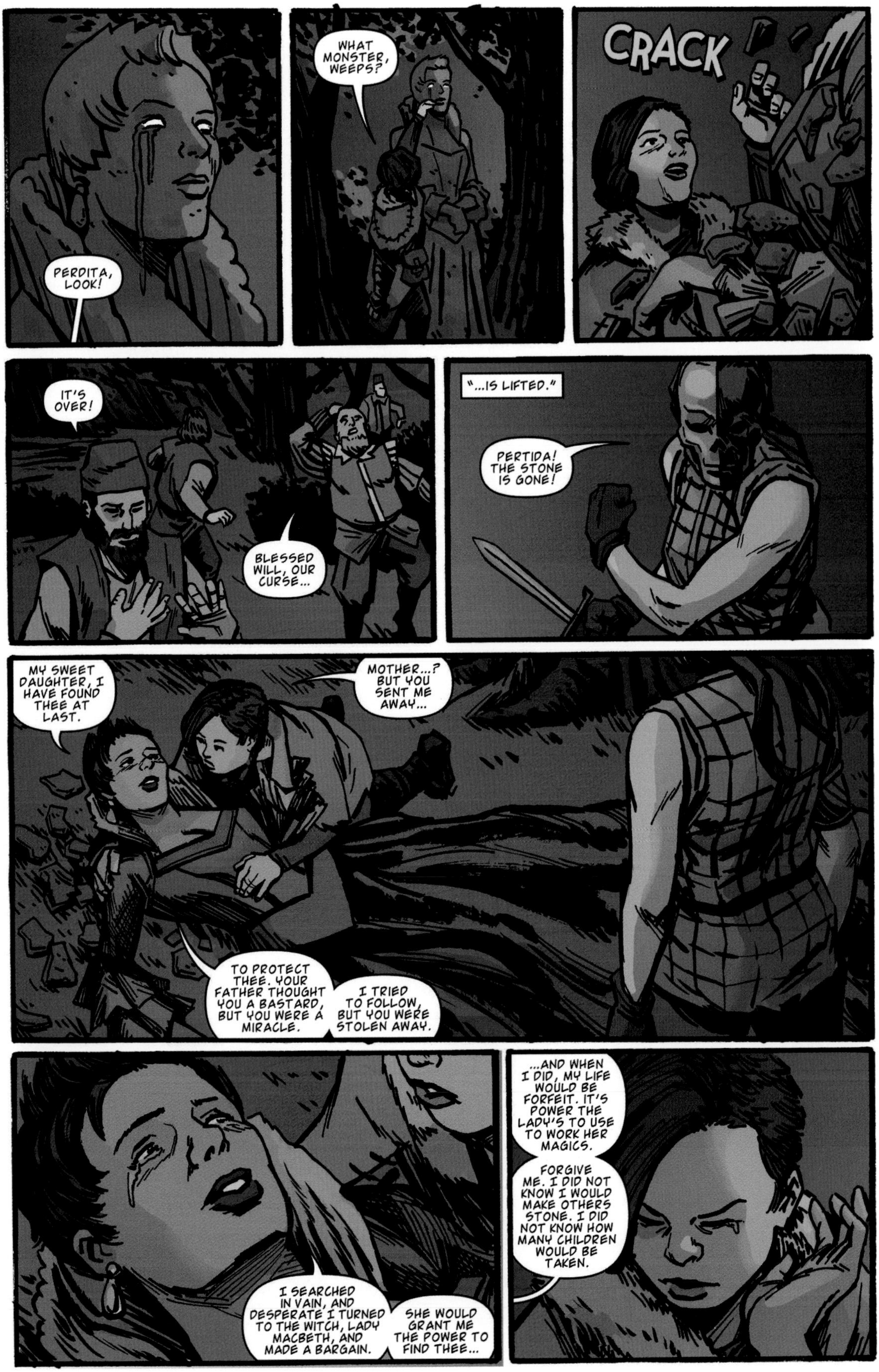
PERDITA, LOOK!
WHAT MONSTER, WEEPS?
CRACK
IT'S OVER!
BLESSED WILL, OUR CURSE...
"...IS LIFTED."
PERTIDA! THE STONE IS GONE!
MY SWEET DAUGHTER, I HAVE FOUND THEE AT LAST.
MOTHER...? BUT YOU SENT ME AWAY...
TO PROTECT THEE. YOUR FATHER THOUGHT YOU A BASTARD, BUT YOU WERE A MIRACLE.
I TRIED TO FOLLOW, BUT YOU WERE STOLEN AWAY.
I SEARCHED IN VAIN, AND DESPERATE I TURNED TO THE WITCH, LADY MACBETH, AND MADE A BARGAIN.
SHE WOULD GRANT ME THE POWER TO FIND THEE...
...AND WHEN I DID, MY LIFE WOULD BE FORFEIT. IT'S POWER THE LADY'S TO USE TO WORK HER MAGICS.
FORGIVE ME. I DID NOT KNOW I WOULD MAKE OTHERS STONE. I DID NOT KNOW HOW MANY CHILDREN WOULD BE TAKEN.

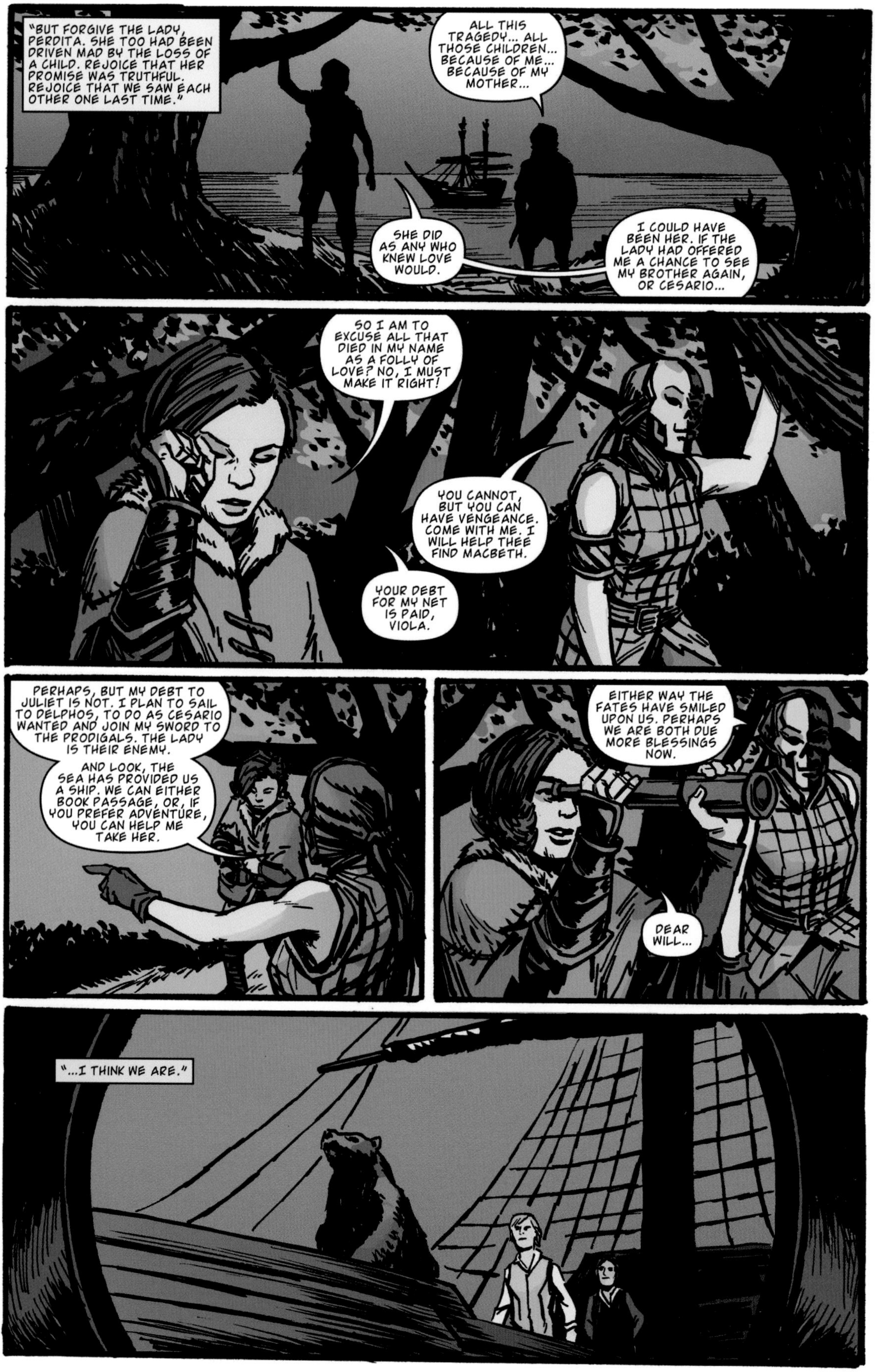
"BUT FORGIVE THE LADY, PERDITA. SHE TOO HAD BEEN DRIVEN MAD BY THE LOSS OF A CHILD. REJOICE THAT HER PROMISE WAS TRUTHFUL. REJOICE THAT WE SAW EACH OTHER ONE LAST TIME."
ALL THIS TRAGEDY... ALL THOSE CHILDREN... BECAUSE OF ME... BECAUSE OF MY MOTHER...
SHE DID AS ANY WHO KNEW LOVE WOULD.
I COULD HAVE BEEN HER. IF THE LADY HAD OFFERED ME A CHANCE TO SEE MY BROTHER AGAIN, OR CESARIO...
SO I AM TO EXCUSE ALL THAT DIED IN MY NAME AS A FOLLY OF LOVE? NO, I MUST MAKE IT RIGHT!
YOU CANNOT, BUT YOU CAN HAVE VENGEANCE. COME WITH ME. I WILL HELP THEE FIND MACBETH.
YOUR DEBT FOR MY NET IS PAID, VIOLA.
PERHAPS, BUT MY DEBT TO JULIET IS NOT. I PLAN TO SAIL TO DELPHOS, TO DO AS CESARIO WANTED AND JOIN MY SWORD TO THE PRODIGALS. THE LADY IS THEIR ENEMY.
AND LOOK, THE SEA HAS PROVIDED US A SHIP. WE CAN EITHER BOOK PASSAGE, OR, IF YOU PREFER ADVENTURE, YOU CAN HELP ME TAKE HER.
EITHER WAY THE FATES HAVE SMILED UPON US. PERHAPS WE ARE BOTH DUE MORE BLESSINGS NOW.
DEAR WILL...
"...I THINK WE ARE."

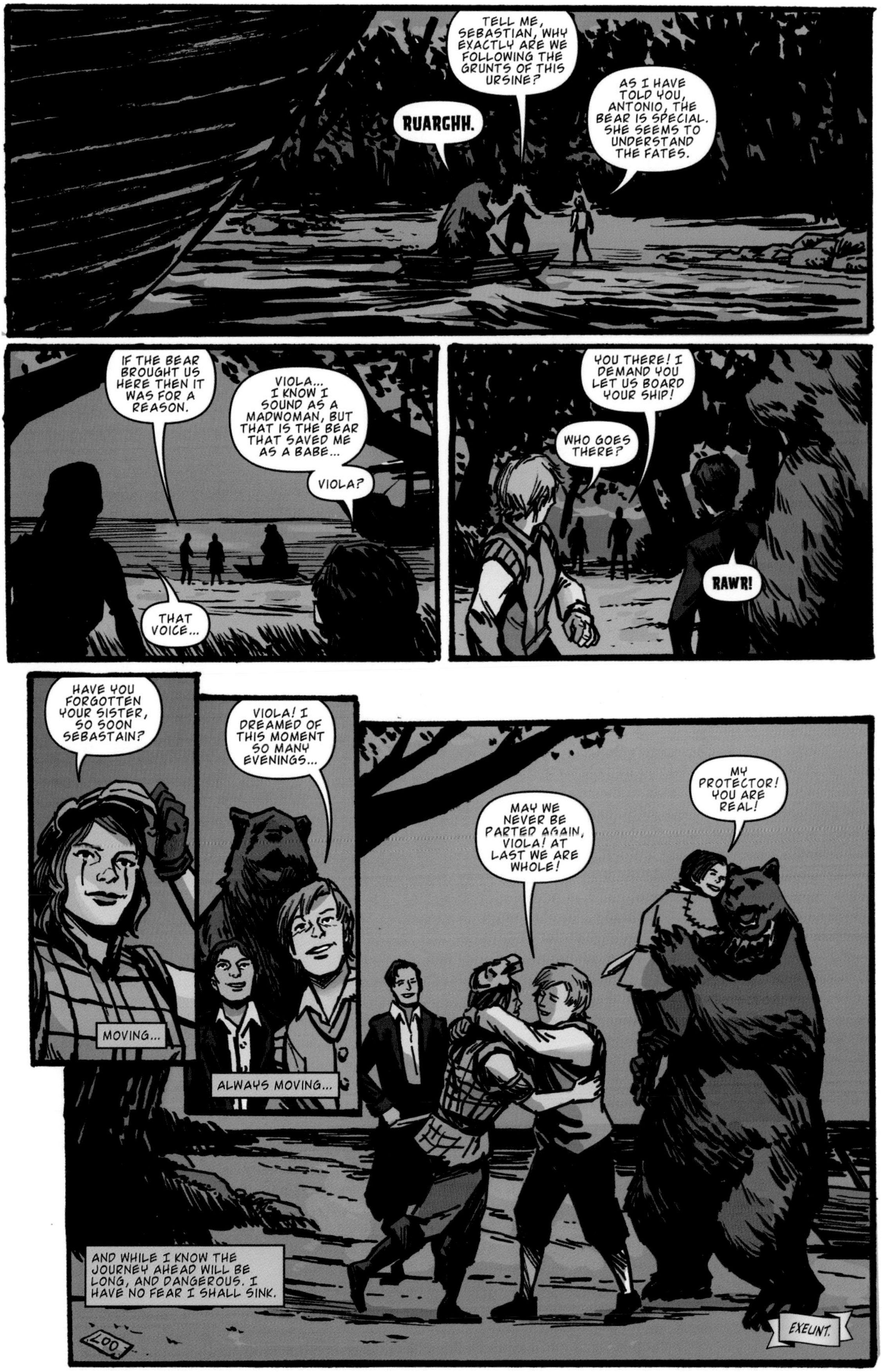
TELL ME, SEBASTIAN, WHY EXACTLY ARE WE FOLLOWING THE GRUNTS OF THIS URSINE?
RUARGHH.
AS I HAVE TOLD YOU, ANTONIO, THE BEAR IS SPECIAL. SHE SEEMS TO UNDERSTAND THE FATES.
IF THE BEAR BROUGHT US HERE THEN IT WAS FOR A REASON.
VIOLA... I KNOW I SOUND AS A MADWOMAN, BUT THAT IS THE BEAR THAT SAVED ME AS A BABE...
VIOLA?
THAT VOICE...
YOU THERE! I DEMAND YOU LET US BOARD YOUR SHIP!
WHO GOES THERE?
RAWR!
HAVE YOU FORGOTTEN YOUR SISTER, SO SOON SEBASTAIN?
MOVING...
VIOLA! I DREAMED OF THIS MOMENT SO MANY EVENINGS...
ALWAYS MOVING...
MAY WE NEVER BE PARTED AGAIN, VIOLA! AT LAST WE ARE WHOLE!
MY PROTECTOR! YOU ARE REAL!
AND WHILE I KNOW THE JOURNEY AHEAD WILL BE LONG, AND DANGEROUS. I HAVE NO FEAR I SHALL SINK.
EXEUNT.

Artwork by Simon Davis — Issue #2

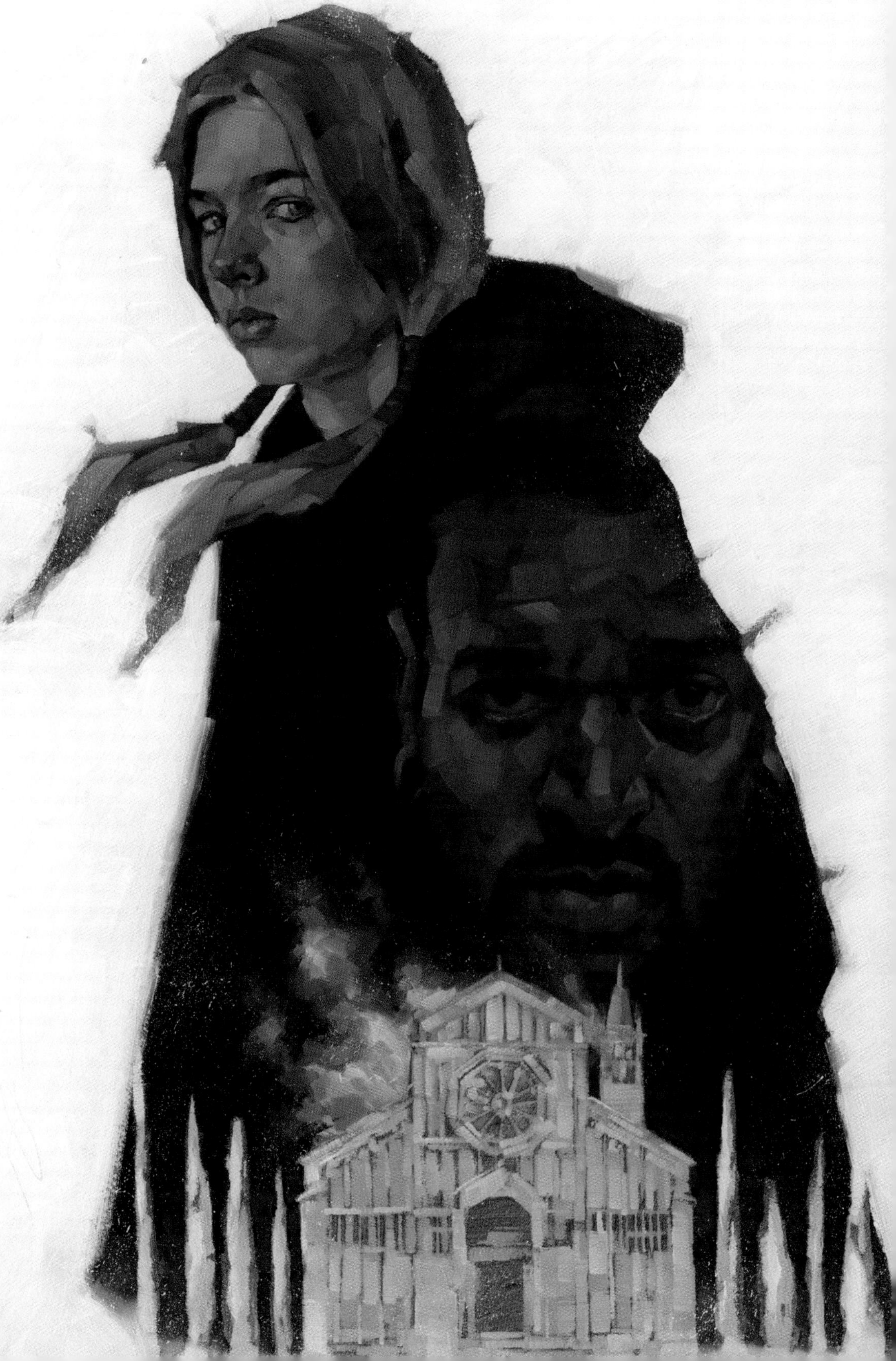

Artwork by Simon Davis — Issue #3

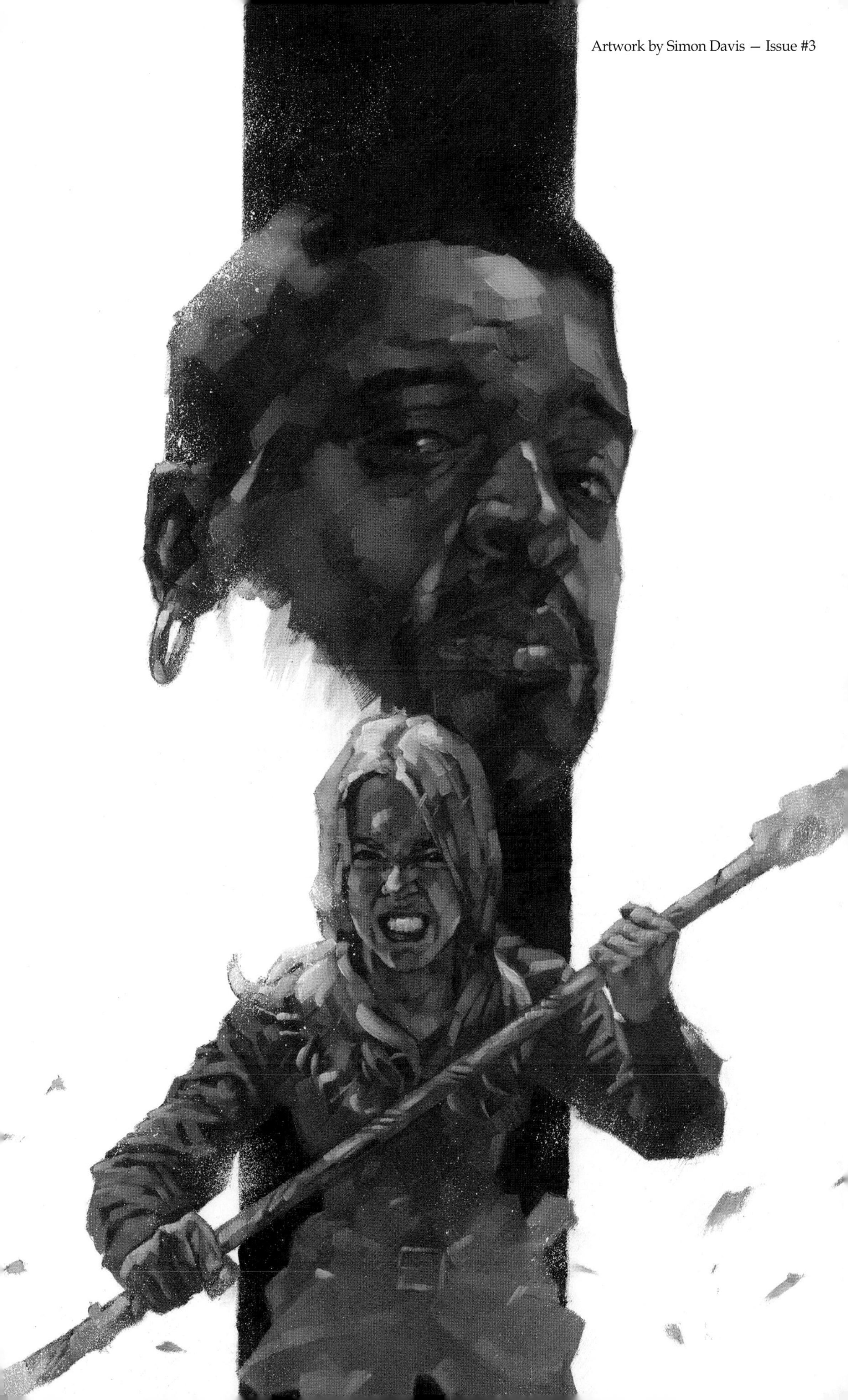

Artwork by Simon Davis — Issue #4

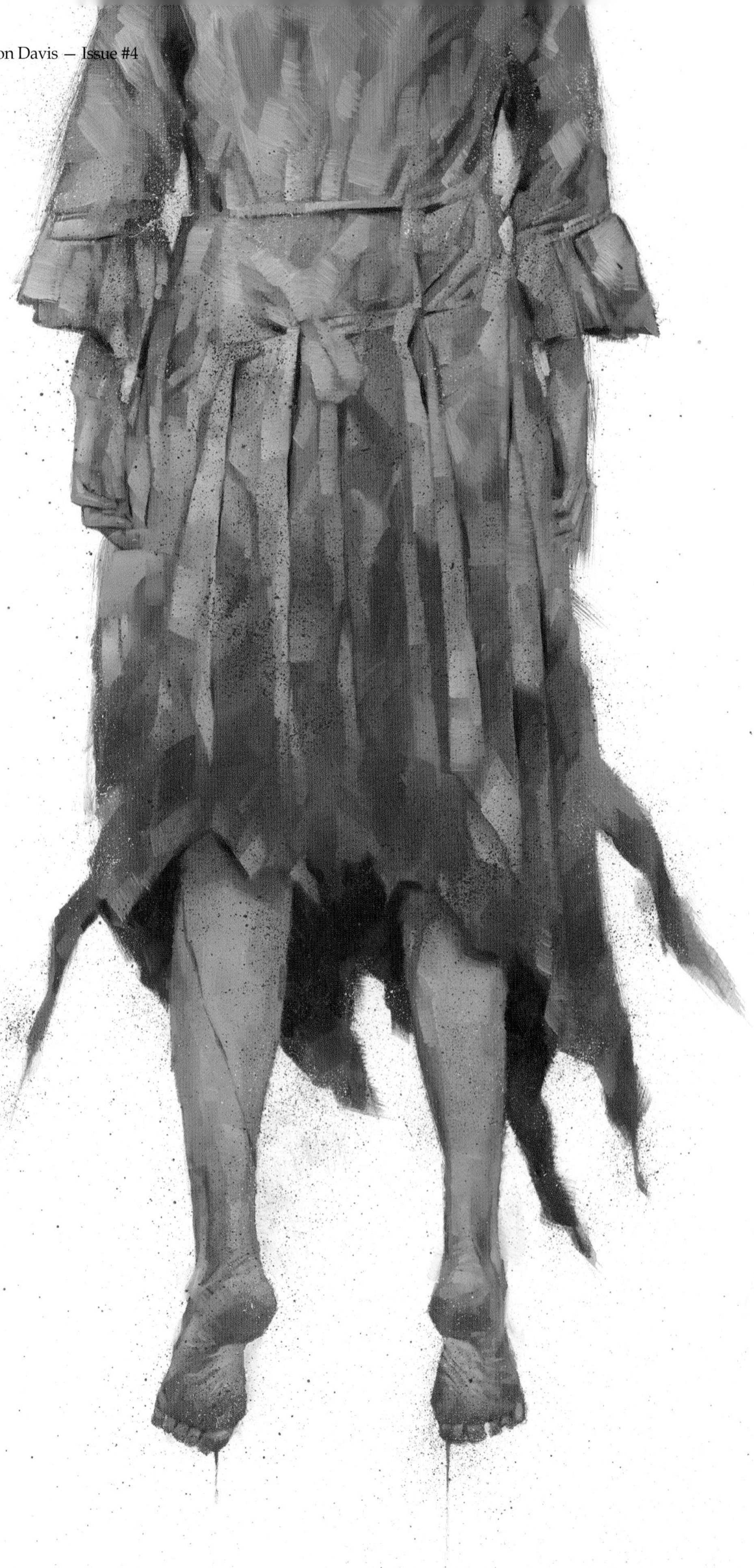

Artwork by Adam Gorham | Colors by Shari Chankahamma — Issue #1

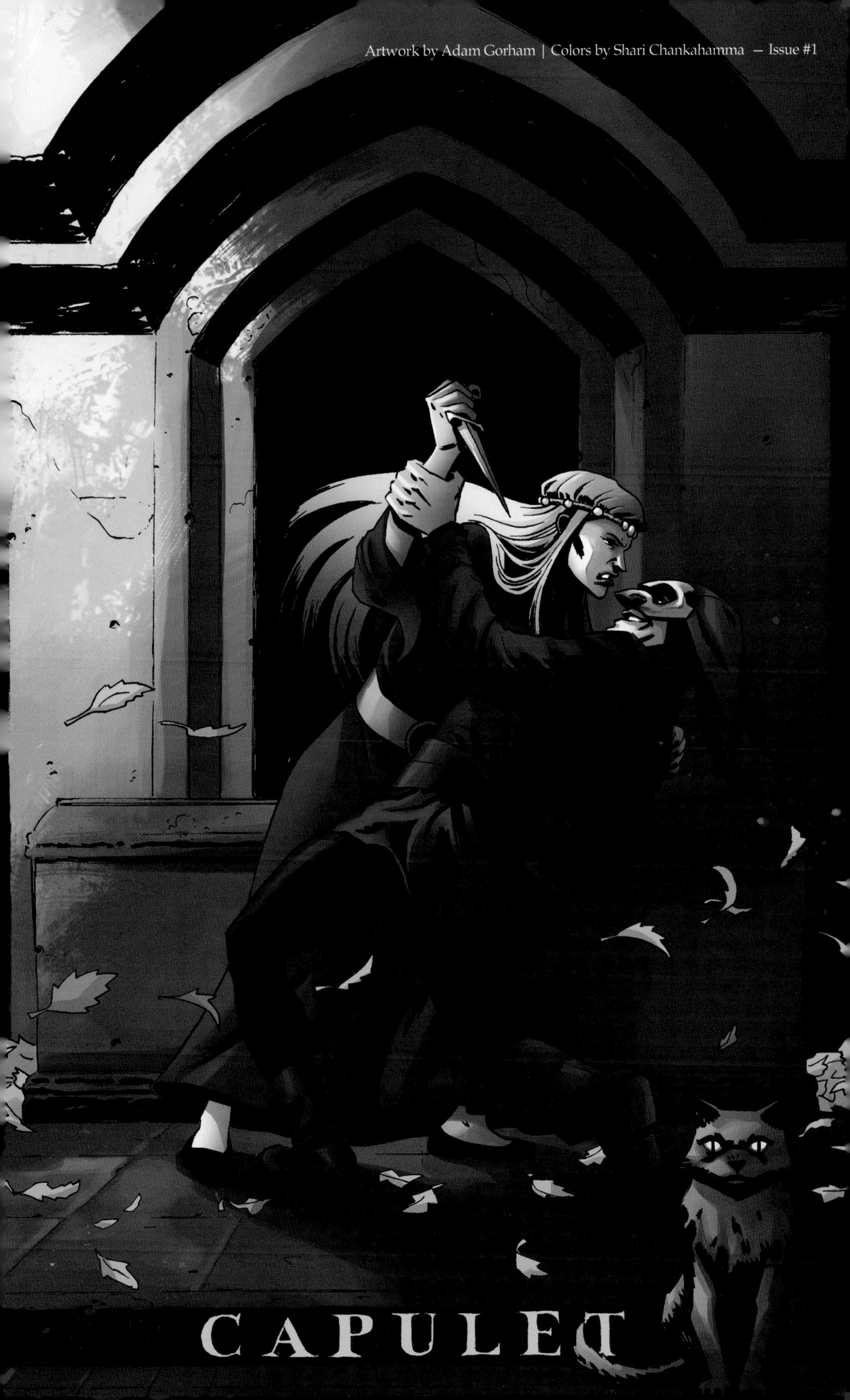
CAPULET

Artwork by Adam Gorham | Colors by Dee Cunniffe — Issue #2

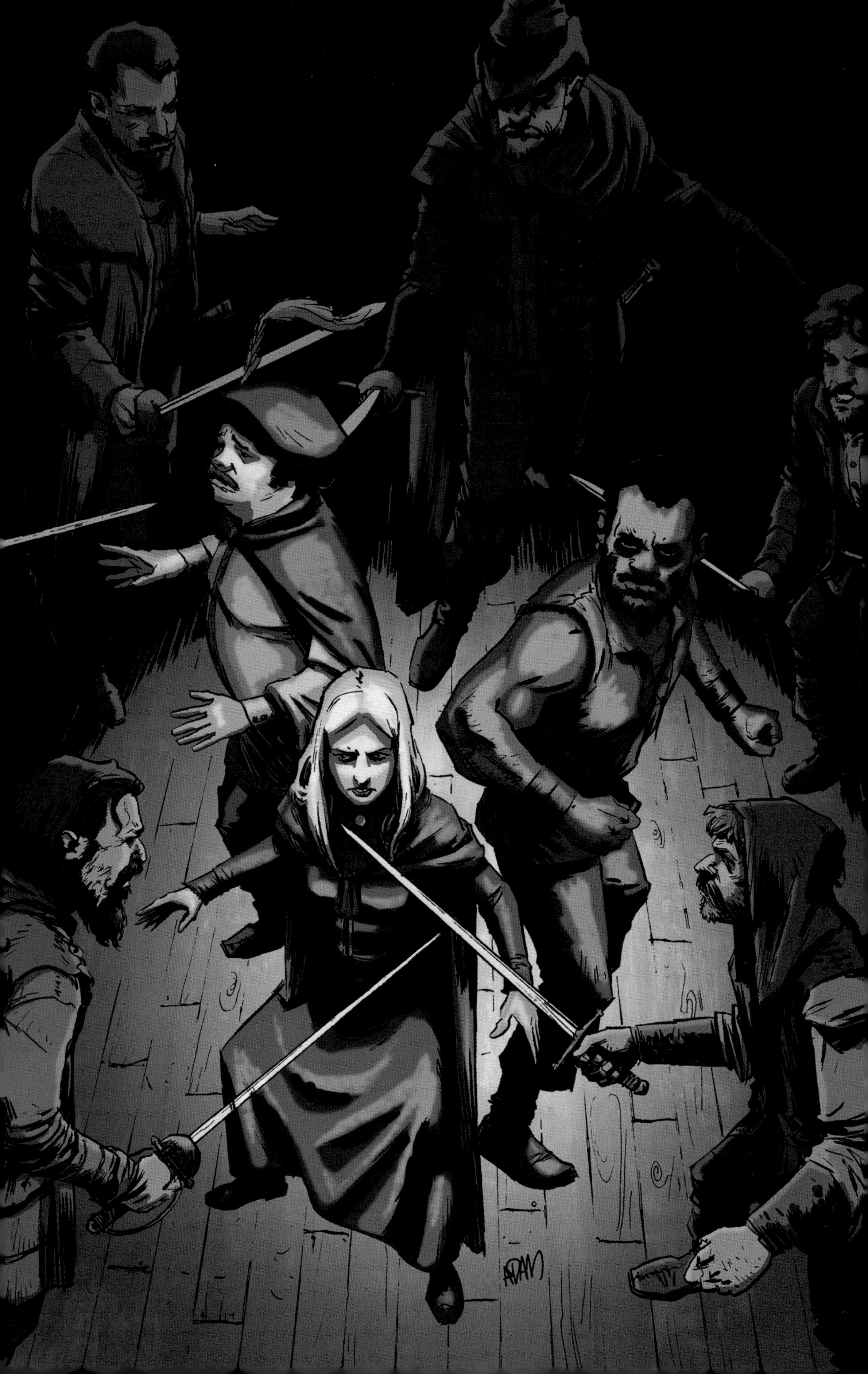
ADAM

Artwork by Adam Gorham | Colors by Dee Cunniffe – Issue #3

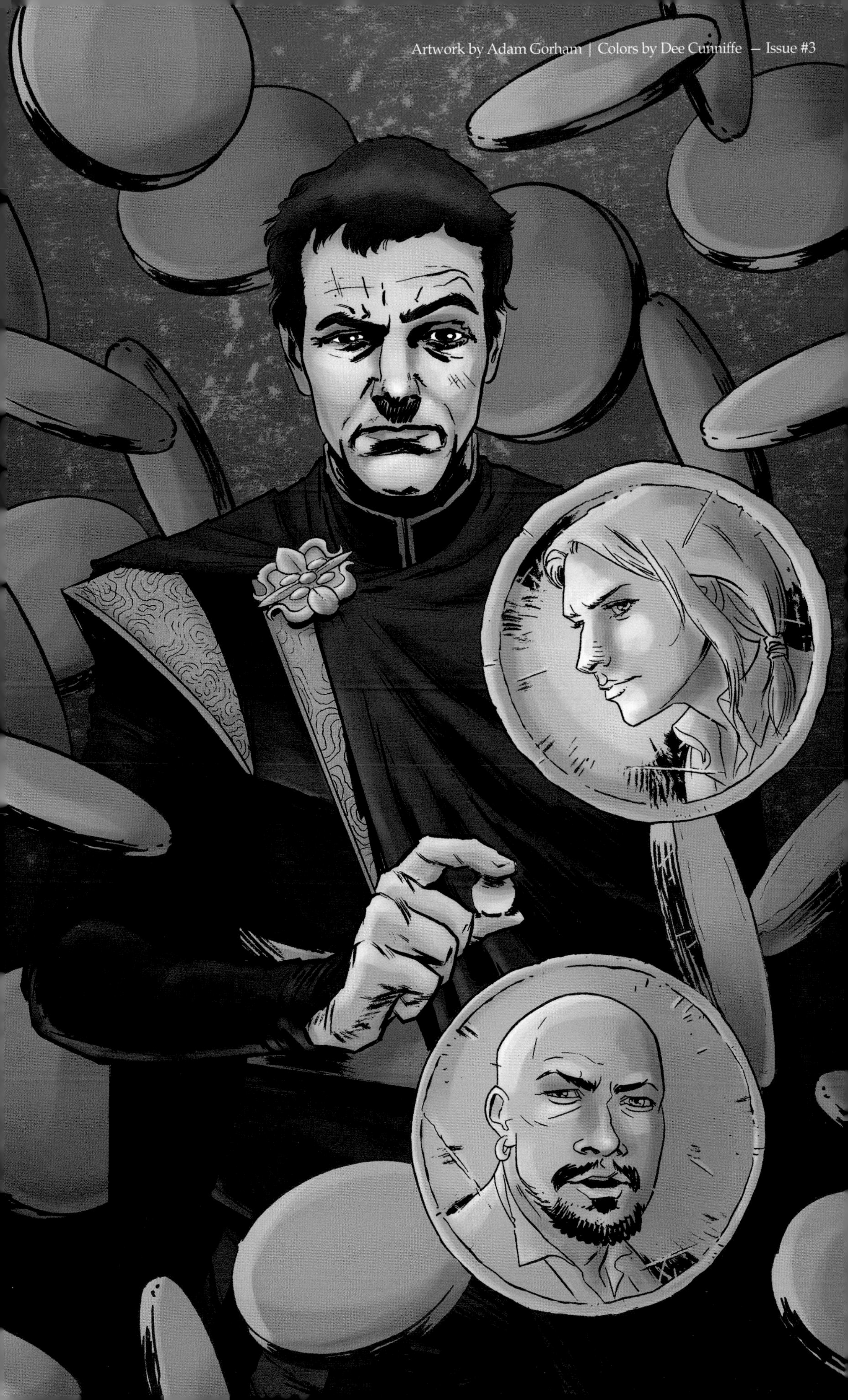

Artwork by Adam Gorham | Colors by Dee Cunniffe — Issue #4

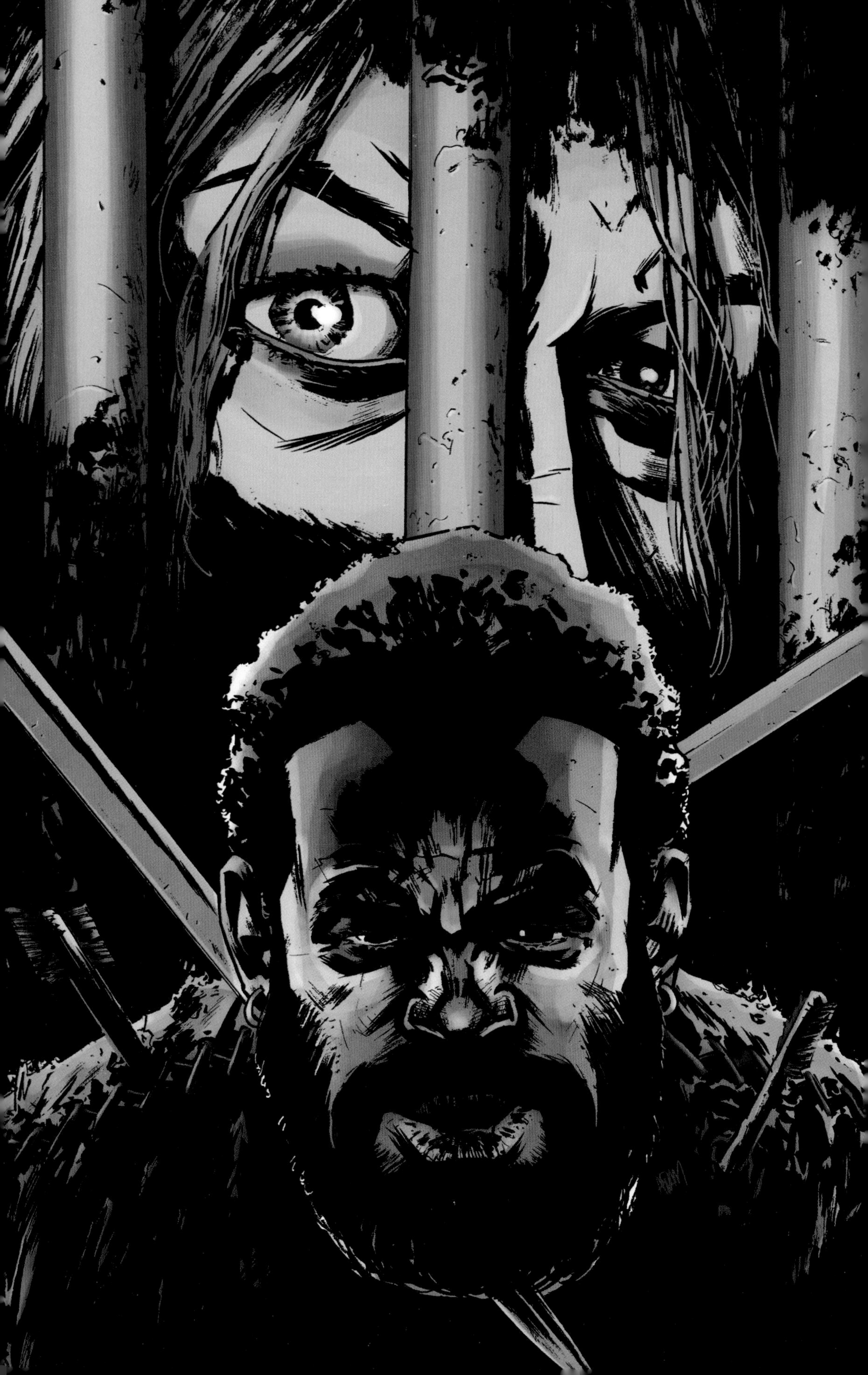